Defence
Policy
Making:
A Comparative Analysis

Defence Policy Making: A Comparative Analysis

edited by
G.M.DILLON

65795

1988
Leicester University Press

First published in 1988 by Leicester
University Press

Copyright © Leicester University Press 1988

Designed by Geoffrey Wadsley
Photoset in Linotron 101 Plantin
Printed and bound in Great Britain by
Biddles Ltd, Guildford and King's Lynn

British Library Cataloguing in Publication Data
Defence policy making: a comparative
analysis.
1. Military policies
I. Dillon, G.M.
355'.0335

ISBN 0-7185-1268-5

Contents

Notes on contributors vii

1 **Introduction** 1
G.M.DILLON

2 **Britain** 9
G.M.DILLON

3 **United States of America** 53
PHILIP WILLIAMS

4 **The Soviet Union** 83
ALAN WOOD

5 **West Germany** 119
REGINA COWEN

6 **France** 147
JOHN FENSKE

Index 171

Notes on Contributors

Michael Dillon is Lecturer in Politics, University of Lancaster, and author of *Dependence and Deterrence* (1983) and *The Falklands: Politics and War* (1988).

Philip Williams is Lecturer in Politics and International Relations, University of Southampton. He is the author of *Crisis Management* (1976) and *The Senate and US Troops in Europe* (1985).

Regina Cowen is Senior Research Fellow, Stockholm International Peace Research Institute, and co-author of *The ABM Treaty: to Defend or Not to Defend* (1987).

Alan Wood is Lecturer in Russian History, University of Lancaster, and editor of *Siberia, Problems and Prospects for Regional Development* (1987).

John Fenske is Assistant Professor in the Department of Political Science, Williams College, Williamstown, MA 01267.

1
Introduction

G. M. DILLON

Asking how defence policy is made is easy, but answering the question is far from simple. The chapters offered here provide a useful starting-point, and moreover offer a more direct answer to a second question – *where* does defence decision making take place? Defence policy is made at the interface of domestic and international politics, and at the interface of peace and war (see fig. 1.1). Its location there has basic theoretical and practical implications. Theoretically, defence policy making is both constructive and mediatory. Operating at the boundaries of the state, defence policy plays an influential role in constructing and reconstructing the political community by mediating its internal as well as its external relations through the threat and use of force. The bulk of the defence effort of the countries examined here is externally oriented, and their armed forces are largely concerned with the outside world. By and large their police and paramilitary forces deal with internal security matters. The relationship between internal and external security, however, represents a continuum rather than a disjuncture, and defence policy becomes more internally oriented the more the domestic composition of the political community is challenged through internal dissent, subversion or armed insurrection. Practically speaking, defence policy making is also subject to both domestic and international influences in a world where domestic politics are deeply penetrated, in any event, by the dynamics of international economic and political forces.

Defence policy making is also dominated by the operations of state organizations like Ministries or Departments of Defence. If we follow Max Weber's definition of the state, as that organization which claims a monopoly over the legitimate use of force in a given territory, we can also add that state structures are largely responsible for defining the threat to a territory, its peoples and its institutions including, of course, the state itself.

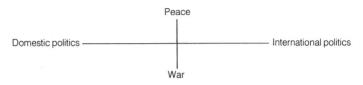

Figure 1.1 The twin interfaces of defence policy making

One cannot comprehend the interplay between states, therefore, without having a view about the nature of individual states and, in particular, about how they manage the interface between domestic and international politics. If managing defence policy confronts the decision maker with a complicated politico-military task, it also demands from students of defence decision making a knowledge of domestic politics as well as an understanding of international affairs. Even amongst the NATO allies, who comprise a large part of this study, no two states have identical defence policies or policy processes.

Yet there is much that is similar between the policy processes of these powers: first, because we are dealing with *modern* states which have quite distinct features and forms of rule; and secondly, because we are dealing with an equally distinct *modern* strategic environment. A product of many factors, not least the modern state itself, that environment is distinguished by nuclear, industrial and technological dynamics. For these reasons there are important points of comparison between our five states, despite the wealth of difference in political, economic, military and ideological terms. What is especially fascinating is that as comparable but different countries they perceive the threats and opportunities of a strategic environment (which their own historical processes were largely responsible for creating) in comparable but different ways. There are two basic reasons for this.

First, no defence policy community operates in a vacuum; each is located in its own particular historical time and national political space. Secondly, defence decision making does not operate like a voiceless mechanism and neither does international conflict. Quite the contrary, national decision making and international relations are both filled with the noise of competing voices: individuals, groups, state organizations and global ideologies. Each defence policy community, therefore, has its own voice which speaks through an inherited vocabulary. By this means it provides a particular rendition of the national values it seeks to defend, in addition to an interpretation of the international threats against which these values require defence. Thus as they translate the goals of national politics and the perceived demands of the strategic environment into national defence policy, so defence decision makers contribute to the formation of the state and of the inter-state system. Moreover, as these decision makers deal with all the changing issues on their policy agenda, so they adapt their vocabulary of policy making: handing on to their successors not eternal verities but an evolving language of national security. Responding to what they see and meet in the way of national values and international threats their successors reformulate that language also.

Though each modern state is the product of its own historical experience, each has also been shaped by more general historical processes. The most important of these for our purposes include the philosophies (political, economic, social and scientific) of Enlightenment rationalism, the rivalry of competing nationalisms, the processes of industrialization and, finally, the bureaucratization of decision making. On this count they are comparable, though not identical with each other, because modern industrial societies do not fight or prepare for war in the same way as, for example, did feudal ones. Populous and industrialized societies governed by sophisticated systems of rules which rely on complex bureaucratic decision making structures, the United States, the Soviet Union, Britain, France and West Germany are recognizably modern states each with its own changing identity. In waging war or preparing for it they reveal the character of their political, economic and social organization – in addition to the circumstance of conflict or the nature of the strategic environment.

In more specific terms, for example, their routine processes of defence decision making are both institutionalized and deeply influenced by the impact of changing industrialization. As Maurice Pearton has argued, industrialization shaped the nature of war as much as it influenced the character of peace. More to the point, it transformed the nature of the relationship between the two; and that is precisely where defence policy making takes place. During the last hundred years the state became reliant on the products of industry in order to threaten and wage war. That in turn required the state to organize itself in particular ways for defence purposes: War Ministries, mobilization plans, strategic stockpiling, an increasing association with the development of industry, science and technology including the mass mobilization required for the prosecution of total war. But armed forces no longer rely simply on the products of industrial economies. Nor do Defence Ministries currently concern themselves solely with mobilization plans or the formation of alliances. Each is concerned in peacetime now with a whole host of additional tasks: from strategic analysis and threat

3

assessment to planning, programming and budgeting of the defence effort including, in particular, the organization of weapons procurement and the recruiting, training and deployment of military forces maintained at the highest state of readiness. Each is also concerned, to a greater or lesser extent, with mobilizing political support for the defence effort and managing dissent from it.

Defence policy planning, therefore, reflects the developments taking place in industrial societies generally. Just as industrial economies rely increasingly upon the fruits of scientific research and technological change – while also being revolutionalized by these developments – so also defence planning has become increasingly involved in the organization, direction and exploration of knowledge, in the form principally of its research and development programmes. Similarly, just as corporate industrial planning in effect seeks to colonize the future, so defence planning also seeks to anticipate and shape the strategic environment. Knowledge, therefore, has also become a product of organization (from corporations to research establishments and universities). As such, it is increasingly packaged in the form of 'information' and managed through rapidly expanding information and communication technologies. These are as vital now in defence decision making for financial management and weapons acquisition purposes, as they are for battlefield management on land and in the air or for fighting ships at sea. Preparing industrial states for war through large-scale bureaucracies creates similar problems for defence decision makers and poses similar challenges to them.

For instance, defence policy communities have to decide how much to spend on defence and how best to spend it. But because there are different states they produce different answers (see table 1.1). Only in the abstract world of defence economics, or certain organization theories, is it sometimes assumed that there might be an optimal solution to these questions. In the intellectually grubbier world of defence decision making, the answers are always provided through a combination of power and persuasion, and they are always partial answers dependent upon circumstances and change.

That which separates also joins. Consequently international confrontation between East and West has created common problems to which the defence policy communities of the powers concerned have responded in similar ways. In many respects they have actually grown more like each other. A Pentagon official would not feel especially out of place at the Hardhöe in Bonn, where the *Bundesministerium der Verteidigung* is situated. One of Moscow's defence bureaucrats, at least in professional terms, would also find much that was familiar there.

Table 1.1 Comparison of Defence Spending and Armed Forces

	Gross domestic product ($bn)	Population (000s)	Defence expenditure ($bn)	Defence expenditure per capita ($)	Defence expenditure as percentage of gross domestic product	Total armed forces	Army Navy Air Force
United States	3,619.2	239,600	250.011	1,043	6.9	2,151,568	780,648 (A) 568,781 (N) 603,898 (AF)
USSR	(est.) 1,672– 1,920	276,500			12–17 (Western est.)	5,300,000	3,500,000 (A) 460,000 (N) 920,000 (AF)
France	492.270	55,170	15.859	288	3.2	476,560	300,000 (A) 67,710 (N) 96,550 (AF)
Federal Republic of Germany	613.163	61,200	19.184	313	3.1	478,000	335,600 (A) 36,200 (N) 106,000 (AF)
United Kingdom	400.038	56,020	23.072	412	5.8	327,100	163,000 (A) 70,600 (N) 93,500 (AF)

Totals may not add up owing to extra and reserve forces

Source: Military Balance, 1985/6 (London International Institute for Strategic Studies, 1986).

Indeed, defence officials of the NATO powers (military and civil) routinely talk to one another and contract their common defence business at NATO headquarters in Brussels and in NATO's various strategic commands. Because decision making is heavily institutionalized and organizations tend to operate in comparable ways, so each country's decision making community has its own form of bureaucratic politics. Each country also seems to have experienced the same recurring need to rationalize its defence organizations. Centralization of defence decision making, and periodic drives for economy and efficiency, mark bureaucratic life in Bonn, London and Paris just as they do in Moscow and Washington.

On the Western side, in particular, there is clear evidence that defence officials borrow and copy each other's ideas and practices. It was no coincidence, for example, that during and following McNamara's rationalization of defence decision making in the United States, similar drives took place in Britain and the Federal Republic of Germany. But those rationalizations were also influenced by their own local needs, and conducted in their own distinctive ways. Comparability and individuality run together throughout defence decision making. It is remarkable that defence institutions seem to be so resistant to rationalization, and that they have regularly to be shaken up and reordered. It is also odd that this pattern can be found in more than one or two national defence establishments. From a comparative perspective these repeated rationalizations look more like ritual purifications. In addition, they also seem to coincide with basic shifts in general policy and with changes in the locus of power within the policy community. Evidently they are concerned with other matters in addition to the desire to get value for money from defence spending or to improve the rationality of decision making.

Finally, if these countries are comparable but different they nevertheless share the same strategic environment, which they themselves have produced. Again, they perceive that environment in similar but different ways. Amongst the NATO powers there is a greater commonality of outlook; at least they do not regard each other as arch enemies. But even within the alliance there is considerable divergence of views over the role of nuclear weapons, for example, or arms control and military strategy. The basic fault line here is between the United States and the European powers who, on occasions, fear in particular a superpower condominium against their interests. But even this division has to be qualified, say, by Britain's special relationship with the United States or the importance which West Germany attaches to good transatlantic relations. The threat which the Soviet Union poses is perceived differently depending upon whether you are acting in London, Paris, Bonn or Washington.

Comparative analysis is probably most useful in raising questions about things we would otherwise take for granted and casting them in a different light; though we do not need to rely on a comparative perspective alone. What we do need, however, is that critical distance from the object of study which comparative analysis, amongst other devices, can help us to achieve. Distancing ourselves from the current practices of defence decision makers by placing them in historical perspective is a second means of doing so; a temporal rather than a spatial distancing. Finally, we can create critical distance by bringing different analytical and conceptual perspectives to bear upon decision making.

In one way or another the chapters in this book attempt all three, but the book is comparative in the sense that quite distinct portraits emerge. It is important to be clear, therefore, what comparative analysis is intended to achieve here. Indeed, the first comparative point to be made is that we are dealing with individual decision making communities. The danger of imposing a generalized comparative analytical scheme on such processes is clear. An abstract comparative analytical framework might be elegant and eloquently argued in academic terms, but it might be so abstracted from individual decision making processes that it would remain academic in the pejorative sense of the term – removed from and without a feel for the way things are done in what after all are human communities with specific histories and cultures. Conversely, we would lose an equal but different amount in understanding decision making by treating each country as if it were unique.

This study thus has a dual purpose. By juxtaposing the distinctive process of defence decision making in each state it draws attention to what is comparable between them while seeking to convey the very different characters of their respective policy communities.

As such the book is designed to give students an introduction to the way defence policy is made. Its chapters provide an account of the basic mechanisms at work in the United States and the Soviet Union as well as in Britain, France and West Germany. Each chapter also situates the defence decision making of those countries in its own historical and cultural setting. None seeks to provide an exhaustive or comprehensive treatment of its subject. Together they represent, instead, an invitation to take defence decision making seriously, a process sufficiently complex and important in its own right as to constitute a distinct field of study. Comparable across certain political systems, defence decision making is a process which is heavily redolent, also, of all the characteristics of contemporary policy making. Hence the study of the apparatus of the state as it engages in the management of security questions (internal as well as external) has relevance far beyond the narrowly drawn boundaries of defence. It incorporates, in addition, the character of the modern state and the operation of politics within it, together with the economic, social and technological dynamics of mass societies.

2
Britain

G. M. DILLON

With a martial record that is closely allied to its political tradition, Britain's wars (international, imperial, civil and dynastic) have always played an influential part in the evolution of its political system and the conduct of its domestic politics. Though the pretence is often maintained that Britain's international history has been determined by 'national interests' and *realpolitik*, in fact there has been a continuous and intimate connection between the play of power internally in British society and the exercise of power externally by the British state. The most recent and vivid example of this defining interplay in defence decision making between domestic and international politics was the Falklands conflict.

Janus and Policy

Forms of war and forms of political life are correlated. So, for the United Kingdom, war made the state as much as the state made war. In the twentieth century, for example, the First and Second World Wars made a significant contribution to the development of collectivism in British politics.[1] Waging total war successfully both required and produced value consensus in Britain. But it also needed government intervention to mobilize and direct society's resources for the purposes of the war effort. That, in turn, demanded effective cooperation between the state, private industry and organized labour. Victory brought an end to war, but the legacy of the 1939–45 conflict, in particular, was value consensus (especially about what sort of peace people thought they had fought for), and an experience of tripartite cooperation in the economy whose virtues as well as vices were acknowledged. State planning had become respectable. These were precisely the sorts of circumstances in which collectivism flourished. Indeed they were its prerequisites. There were many other domestic, political and social influences at work, of course, but after 1945 the legacy of war was employed to construct the Keynesian social democratic system of demand management and social welfare which became known as the age of consensus politics.[2] The outcome of the Second World War had as much impact on Britain's domestic political order as it did on the country's international position: bipolarity and decline abroad, consensus politics at home. This link has had not a little to do, also, with the current disparagement of the political achievements (both domestic and international) of the period 1945–79.

The relationship between domestic and international politics remains central even in an age when defence decision making has become dominated not by the need to mobilize for war, but by the demands of deterrent-based defence policies. Maintaining high levels of military capability and readiness in peacetime, in order to deter war, has its own special impact, therefore, on domestic politics.[3] It does so, for example, through the competition for financial resources in the government's budgetary process. There are, in addition, the effects which a large defence-related industrial base have upon the national economy, together with the political and economic interests which it serves. Moreover, deterrent defence if successful is never invoked. Short of war it can only be tested for efficiency and effectiveness through critical analysis and domestic political debate. There is, then, a constant need to legitimize the defence effort by mobilizing support for it through the vocabulary and processes of national politics. Conversely, domestic politics may feed into defence decision making. At a micro level it will have an influence, say, through lobbying on behalf of defence contractors and through the employment that the defence economy brings. At a macro level it will be felt through the values and vocabulary which constitute the political culture of the United Kingdom. A certain domestic value consensus is as integral to the maintenance of deterrent defence as it is to waging total war, and of equal concern to today's defence policy community.

Little time in this chapter will be spent defining 'policy' or distinguishing it from 'decision', nor will there be a discussion about the extent to which decision making might be called 'rational', or the ways in which it might be made more rational. As will become evident, the position adopted here is that words can be put to many different uses. I am going to use 'policy', therefore, in the way that one of the best books on policy making in British government defined it, as 'a series of ongoing understandings built up by political administrators over time, understandings left to run where practicable, repaired where necessary, and overturned where they are desperate'.[4] Heclo and Wildavsky's definition will serve admirably as a *working* definition for the purposes of this chapter; and the debate about rationality will be regarded as just one form of argument (or discourse) in the many that make up the total discourse of defence decision making in the modern state.

Understandings such as those to which these American authors refer comprise the life of any community. In defence they happen to be concerned primarily with the provision and use of armed forces to protect the state from external attack and internal subversion, as well as to advance what those in power consider to be in the country's international interests. Defence policy making is thus essentially Janus-like; simultaneously looking to both international and domestic contexts, and continuously mediating between the two. Naturally, defence is also concerned with security. But security – like health – is a subjective state of mind that depends upon a web of institutions, practices and relationships. It can be measured by all sorts of indicators such as economic, technical and military resources, the size of armed forces or the strength of alliances. These indicators – which have their counterparts with respect to health also – are surrogates for the real thing.

Security itself remains quite intangible; a result of complex and changing perceptions, standards and expectations. There is an undeniable difference between being dead or alive, of course, but that contrast does not provide much of a guide to routine defence decision making. It cannot, for example, help to answer the two basic questions which confront the defence policy community in Britain – *how much, and what, is enough to deter?* Neither can it help with answering what these questions amount to in practice – *how much 'security' can we afford?* – not only in financial terms but also in relation to all the other things we value, like freedom, which an obsession with security alone would debase. That is why defence questions are basically political ones concerned with the authoritative allocation of the things we value. In the final analysis, answering them comes largely through the power play of political argument in and out of the policy community (see fig. 2.1).

Thus the politics of defence decision making is concerned not only with negotiating resources for defence and deciding how they should be allocated, but also with the political construction of the boundaries and character of the political community itself.[5] This includes what it teaches its members to fear as well as value, together with its twinned sense of security/insecurity. This bifurcation is exemplified by nuclear weapons, which those both for and against simultaneously fear and value, though in quite different ways.

Because defence decision making is Janus-like, 'security' is threatened

11

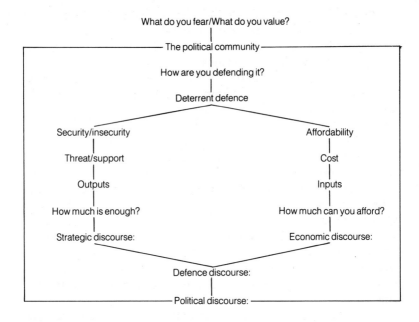

What do you fear/What do you value?

The political community

How are you defending it?

Deterrent defence

Security/insecurity

Threat/support

Outputs

How much is enough?

Strategic discourse:

Affordability

Cost

Inputs

How much can you afford?

Economic discourse:

Defence discourse:

Political discourse:

Note: The flow of influence is up as well as down this chain; back and forth within the debate about defence and security between politics, values and fears.

Figure 2.1 The discourse of defence in the discourse of a political community

by a continuum of challenges from internal to external threats. For most of the time Britain's defence policy community devotes the bulk of its attention to the external end of that continuum; but not always and exclusively so, as the long-running counter-guerrilla operation in Northern Ireland illustrates, or the work of the security services demonstrates.[6] Sometimes internal and external threats may be connected, as with certain forms of terrorism and subversion, and sometimes not. Sometimes, also, a link may be claimed for political purposes in the conduct of defence debate; such as when the suggestion is made that the Campaign for Nuclear Disarmament, intentionally or unintentionally (ambiguity is a great resource in political argument), assists the Eastern bloc in advancing its designs against the West. However, internal security and external defence are usually dealt with by separate institutional arrangements, though there is a point at which the institutional division of responsibilities and the questions they deal with merge and interpenetrate.

There are, none the less, other ways of identifying challenges to security from both internal as well as external sources. In Britain, especially, the authority of the state and its agents in these matters is generally accepted. From an entirely different perspective, however, the power of the state itself might be regarded as a threat to the security of its citizens, in terms, say, of denying them rights or interfering with their freedom. States may even wage war covertly or overtly against their peoples. What is, or is not, a security question is largely determined by the state, but that does not mean that its claim to a monopoly of the legitimate definition of threat (to adapt Max Weber) always goes uncontested in domestic politics.

The twin coordinates which fix all decisions are time and space. Any choice is located both in history (time) and circumstances (the political space or constellation of forces and interests that happen to exist when a choice is made). But, as Einstein has taught us, space and time are neither independent nor constant. Both are relative and related one with the other. Each develops in ways which necessarily change the relevance and significance of what we do. That said, a political choice is also an intervention in time and space. It consequently affects the course of history and the inter-relationships of political power. For these reasons we both construct our political worlds and are in turn constructed by them. Every choice is then both positive, because it helps to construct one form of life, and negative, because it forgoes other alternatives. Its wisdom can only be judged on the basis, therefore, of argument and the contest which exists between all the competing values which infuse different conceptions of the world; those only imagined and desired as well as those which are lived. And argument is constituted and conducted through language.

Language and Policy

Language is our basic social skill, but because policy makers are people who live and work in communities it is their basic professional skill also. To know a community, and to be influential within it, is to speak its language to powerful effect with style and invention. Not everybody can do this, of course, but these criteria provide some of the means by which professional success in policy making is judged and personal advancement gained. Thus policy making is an argumentative activity in which many forms of discourse are involved. A full-scale and detailed analysis of policy making would specify the different types of discourse employed – as well as the different sorts of texts used. It would also consider what new forms of argument have entered the discourse of the defence community since 1945 and why, as well as examining their impact on the distribution and operation of power within it. We would nevertheless be mistaken if we thought that because policy making is conducted through argument it is a gentlemanly affair, or that all the talk involved is so much hot air – though it might be. Modern students of language have taught us two vital things which are absolutely central to an understanding of policy making and which dispel any ideas of this sort. The first is that language is constructive. It makes rather than reflects life. Remembering that we construct our political worlds, therefore, language is the means by which we do so. In all its many forms and technologies (from symbol and myth to speeches and texts, computers and informatics) it is at the very heart of the policy process – it *is* the policy process.[7]

Secondly, power is immanent in language and cannot be divorced from its use. To speak is to act, and to act is to exercise power. Power and persuasion is the name of the language game of policy making; and that includes the persuasiveness of power itself. We can all speak but we are not equally powerful and persuasive, and we cannot all speak at once if we are to be listened to and understood. Some voices are also more powerful than others, for all sorts of reasons, and the rules of argument – who is allowed to speak and when, who speaks to whom about what, and how matters are to be discussed – are all designed to structure power through structuring language in action. Thus an organization chart of the Ministry of Defence might best be regarded as a formal and rudimentary statement about the rules of conversation within the defence policy community. Formal, because it tells us nothing about the tone, style and texture of all the conversations involved. Rudimentary, because it tells us nothing about what makes a particular voice powerful in practice; what makes one sort of argument more persuasive than another; or how and why a topic is classified in a particular sort of way, amenable only to certain sorts of discussion. And neither feature tells us about the gossip and whispering (informal insider, deeply layered and knowledgeable) private talk of defence decision makers. Skill in the use of this talk is also a powerful asset in the art of transacting the community's business and getting things done.

An illustration of all these and other points which I shall make later, indeed a microcosm of the defence decision making process itself, is the drafting of what used to be called the *Defence White Paper*, but is now officially referred to as the Statement on the Defence Estimates (which is actually blue!). For familiarity and convenience the old title is preferable. A public document, it is drafted in private. A statement about Britain's international status and commitments, it equally relies upon assumptions about domestic politics and is designed to have an impact upon domestic debate. Some of its contents may even become domestic political issues; though the bipartisan political consensus which has characterized much of post-war British defence policy has had a restraining effect in this regard. A political text, it is drafted by bureaucrats. A major reference for determining British defence policy, it is none the less produced largely by redrafting earlier statements. A detailed account of Britain's current defence capabilities and commitments as well as their costs, it hides at least as much as it reveals. Drafted with mandarin care, its publication is orchestrated by the defence policy community with the finest attention to detail and protocol. But its debate in Parliament (*pace* the House of Commons Defence Committee) is for the most part ritualistic and ill-informed. Despite criticism of it, the Defence White Paper is none the less a bulky and sophisticated text, a summary of all the news of the defence community's discourse that is fit to print; though it is the government that defines what is 'fit'.

The first *centralized* statement on defence was produced in 1935. Such statements were usually short and produced only on special occasions until 1964, when the services were centralized under one Ministry of Defence. Thereafter the papers grew larger but still provided a relatively limited amount of information in a standardized form. From 1979 onwards, as defence became a major political issue and the bipartisan consensus, on nuclear affairs especially, broke down, the annual statements became big and glossy affairs accompanied by a detailed statistical appendix. The final document is now between 40,000 and 50,000 words long, plus illustrations and graphics.

Work on a new White Paper begins around September shortly after the preceding year's exercise has ended, with the House of Commons debate on the previous White Paper which takes place sometime in June or July. Hence the drafters begin where they left off, for at least half of the White Paper consists of an 'end-of-term report' on equipment developments, organizational changes, the activities of the services through the year and so on. These have to be updated and new developments incorporated into the forthcoming statement. The rest of the White Paper is concerned with more political issues: those matters that reflect the political direction and priorities of the immediate political supervisors of defence policy, the Secretary of State for Defence and his Junior Ministers of State, together with any directives and known preferences from Downing Street. How and with what effect such political influence works is one of the more obscure and mysterious aspects of defence policy making, because we do not yet

have a sound theoretical – allied to a detailed operational – understanding of the work of ministers in British government, beyond the
traditional mantras of political control. These formal assertions of
political authority and responsibility obscure more than they reveal
about ministerial politics and policy making. Some would argue that in
recent years even formal subscription to ministerial accountability has
been subtantially eroded; and that there is little in the way even of a
doctrine with respect to prime ministerial accountability. Consequently
it is as easy to underestimate as exaggerate the role of ministers. Often
the drafters of the White Paper may have as little to go on as the
unhelpful order to 'make it better than last year's'.

A sketch White Paper is produced and circulated for comment
throughout the Ministry of Defence in the autumn, so that a working
manuscript can be produced by Christmas. Around 150 copies of
this first substantial draft are then circulated, with requests for
further contributions where necessary. That is where the political in-
fighting begins in earnest because it provides people with their first
opportunity to scrutinize everybody else's contributions. Though the
Naval Secretariat, say, will have cleared its initial papers with the Naval
Staff, these will not have been shown to the Army or Air staffs. Once
they become available through this first draft, however, the issue of
service balance raises its ugly head. Replies to this draft consequently
always contain whole new sections designed by partisan groups to
rectify what they see as offending 'imbalances'.

Once these sorts of responses are in, a second draft is prepared and
circulated again (this time including a copy to the Secretary of State's
office) for departmental comment. A third draft is then submitted for
the Secretary of State's approval. When that has been given, the paper
is sent up to the Defence and Overseas Policy Committee of the
Cabinet. Finally, the document goes to the full Cabinet. Little in the
way of material contribution from ministers is expected during these
last two stages because the ground would have been prepared by
officials through interdepartmental discussions. Once the Cabinet
approves it, the draft White Paper is prepared for publication, which
usually occurs in March. Publication, however, is accompanied by
press briefings, press summaries, covering letters for copies that are
sent to allies, defence attachés, senior officers and academics. Briefings
for the House of Commons Defence Committee hearings on the White
Paper are then prepared, and ministers furnished with speeches and
further background information to see them through the Commons and
House of Lords debates on the White Paper in June or July.

Much defence policy making is determined by who speaks to whom about what, and with what authority. The social conventions and bureaucratic routines of the defence community can be regarded as dealing directly with these questions. Indeed the whole process of defence decision making should be regarded as a vast, non-stop and highly variegated conversation. Much of the most relevant talk goes on within the Ministry of Defence (MOD). But, of course, the MOD has to talk to other Departments of State, like the Foreign and Commonwealth Office (FCO), the Treasury, the Department of Trade and Industry and the Cabinet Office. In addition it has to talk to its allies: it does this collectively through NATO's institutions, and bilaterally (especially with the United States) through a huge web of personal, bureaucratic and service connections. Finally, it talks to Parliament and the British public, again via a whole host of channels.

If policy making is done through talk, that talk is always based upon texts. Composition and interpretation of texts, then, comprises much of the routine of defence decision makers. There are all sorts of different texts: paper rather than money is what makes the Ministry of Defence go round. Defence officials in fact are the most adept of literary critics. Their genre is the defence text. They are skilled in all the arts of its composition and criticism. Moreover, they can also turn their hands to deconstruction when they wish. Post-modernism, they would be surprised to learn, is not all that far removed from the analysis and some of the practices of defence decision making.[8]

Turn-taking in conversation is also a highly ritualized process, and so it is in the MOD. By convention, therefore, Her Majesty's Senior Service must always come first. See, for confirmation, the *1987 Statement on the Defence Estimates*, Chapter 4, 'The Armed Forces'.[9] Habitually the Royal Navy is also the most sensitive of the three services, believing that it is very difficult for other people to appreciate the subtleties of sea power in a nuclear age. No trick is willingly lost in the formulation of this most visible of defence documents. A table designed to show the *unit* cost of defence equipment, for example, was seriously contested by the Navy in the discussions over the 1985 White Paper because a Type 23 Frigate looked too expensive when compared with an RAF Tornado or a Challenger main battle tank. Instead the Navy wanted to substitute a Tornado *squadron* and a Challenger *regiment*.

This rivalry is easily and sometimes justifiably parodied, but it is no mere comedy. The White Paper is the most public of the defence community's texts and so locks the defence programme into place in political terms. A powerful statement about defence plans, it also reflects publicly upon the reputation of the services and their place in the scheme of things. Policy making is not about 'where do we go?', but about 'where do we go from here?' The Defence White Paper is an annual statement about where we are at! Little surprise, therefore, that different groups in the MOD should want it to define their current position as accurately or favourably as possible.

A model of the continuity and change (constraint and choice) characterizing the entire activity of defence policy making, the Defence White Paper is also an exercise that describes the politically acceptable limits which circumscribe defence decision making, together with a summary of the most important choices made within them. Contrary to many analytical and ideological perspectives, structure and agency (the capacity to choose) are not opposed but complementary. Without limits there is no effective freedom of choice. Amongst the most important questions which defence analysts should ask, therefore, are: What is the nature of these limits? Who or what sets them and how do they change? How do policy makers interpret and respond to them, and why? For particular structures interpreted in particular ways offer a particular form of choice, and the result might be one which many will reject because they do not like the options which it presents, or they do not accept the validity of the limits which define it.

Much of the public defence debate in Britain in recent years, especially that concerning nuclear weapons for instance, becomes more intelligible when considered in this way. Fundamentally it is a political, rather than a technical, debate about defence choices. Such choices are a product of structures which themselves are often a function of other choices made through the discourses of the policy community. Later in the chapter I shall talk about the ways in which crises structure decision making. For the moment, however, we can draw a parallel between crisis and structure which illuminates the point being made here. Crises pose severe threats not only to the policies of policy communities but also to their reputation and survival. But a crisis is not merely a threat, it is also an opportunity – to validate, for example, the values and beliefs of policy makers, as the Falklands crisis did for many political decision makers in Britain. Structure similarly and simultaneously limits and enables decision. Moreover, structures themselves though in a sense given are also a matter for choice, because the central issue is not so much what they are but what we make of them. As we construct our political worlds, therefore, so we are also responsible for them. Thus structure, which is often used as an escape from accountability, legitimately falls under the remit of public criticism and debate also.[10]

Perhaps the most basic structural feature of defence policy making, to which Britain's defence decision makers had to respond after 1945, has been the changing nature of the strategic environment. The disposition and distribution of military, economic and political forces in the world has undergone many transformations since the end of the Second World War. But none has equalled the introduction of that bipolar and eventually global nuclear system which replaced the old Eurocentric international order of great powers, with industrialized but pre-nuclear military capabilities. That profound shift in international relations, together with all its attendant changes – the decline of empires, the growth of American and Soviet power, ideological confrontation between East and West, defeat and division of Germany, the division of Europe, and finally the invention and use of nuclear weapons – provided the two strategic determinants of post-war British defence policy: *strategic vulnerability* and *strategic dependence*.

Strategic Determinants of Policy

Victory in 1945 was the beginning of the end of Britain's status as a maritime empire and global power. The United Kingdom's naval supremacy had been under threat long before the defeat of Germany, and the British Empire was becoming increasingly difficult to police and defend even before Japan exposed its frailty. Similarly, the growth of American and Soviet power was driven by independent impulses long before the war against Hitler launched them on to the international stage. In industrial and technological terms, also, Britain's economic superiority had long gone by the time German forces in Europe surrendered in May 1945. Finally, the strategic bombardment of Britain's cities by the Luftwaffe, followed by the devastation of those of the Third Reich by the British and United States Air Forces, was powerful evidence of the new strategic vulnerabilities of modern warfare. Thus the United Kingdom, together with its overseas possessions, was becoming increasingly vulnerable, even in conventional terms, throughout the first decades of the twentieth century. The introduction of nuclear weapons and ballistic missiles allied to the conventional military might of the Soviet Union, however, introduced a novel strategic danger of an extreme and undeniable sort that was to determine much of post-war British defence policy (see fig. 2.2).

Taking account of its historical origins and conventional features, therefore, it is still reasonable to argue that British decision makers had to contend with a unique and comprehensive form of strategic vulnerability after 1945. For our purposes the significance of this development was the impact it had upon the two dimensions of British

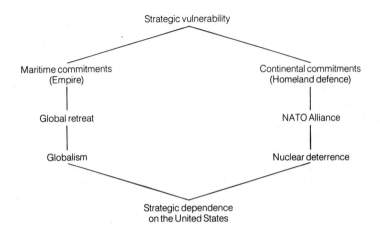

Figure 2.2 Strategic determinants of British defence policy making post-1945

defence policy making: the United Kingdom's maritime and continental commitments. Each was open to the formative influences of that strategic vulnerability and each was to be shaped by them. In the process maritime and continental demands competed even more strongly than in the past for Britain's defence resources, because their needs were so different not only in military but also in political terms.[11]

So, for example, the military requirements of the central front in Germany, in terms of equipment, training and logistics, were quite different from the forces required for imperial holding actions in the Far East, Africa or, as it turned out later, the South Atlantic. Similarly the politics of imperial retreat in South-East Asia or East Africa were different from the alliance politics that had to be conducted in Brussels or Washington.

This strategic vulnerability had an equally important corollary: strategic dependence upon the United States not only to deter the Soviet Union in Europe but also to sustain Britain's international position globally.

In Europe, strategic vulnerability meant, in the first instance, a continental alliance against the Soviet threat. That alliance required, in addition, the commitment and leadership of the United States. Only the United States had the resources and indeed the political status to underwrite the military security and economic revival of Western Europe. In this regard Britain shared its strategic vulnerability and dependence with that of its European neighbours.

In short, NATO is a military alliance premised upon the indispens-
ability of United States power for the defence of Western Europe, with
whose security and prosperity Britain's fate is also inextricably involved. NATO has a continental strategy of Flexible Response and
Forward Defence based upon nuclear deterrence. Britain is fully
committed to that strategy, and the demands which this makes on
Britain's military capabilities now preoccupy defence decision makers
in London. As the United Kingdom became more involved with
meeting these demands, however, so it contracted its maritime commitments. In much reduced circumstances its defence resources would not
stretch to cover both. Hence we have the familiar story of the mismatch
between commitments and capabilities, together with repeated attempts
to balance them, which has characterized post-war British defence
policy.

As Philip Darby and Paul Kennedy have explained, Britain's global
retreat was driven by the strategic factors we have briefly considered
but conducted at a pace and in a manner dictated by local and regional
circumstances, rather than by any form of strategic planning.[12] None
the less, where Britain's desire to retain its global status conflicted with
United States interests or preferences, in the Middle East for example,
and most explicitly at the time of Suez, London had to give way.
Conversely, where the United States welcomed the presence of its
European ally, in South-East Asia in the 1960s for instance, Britain's
global preferences were encouraged a little longer.

Of the two, Britain's continental commitment became dominant
because it was the one most directly concerned with the physical
protection of the British Isles against a novel strategic danger. The
continental commitment also prevailed for all sorts of other domestic as
well as international political and economic reasons. For instance,
imperialism fell into political disrepute not least because it was difficult
to reconcile with the values of liberal democracy. But these points need
not concern us here because despite its global retreat, and as a legacy of
its maritime traditions and imperial past, Britain still continues to
maintain certain global aspirations and horizons in addition to
its NATO responsibilities. A member of the Security Council of
the United Nations, and a leading member of a Commonwealth of
Nations, its policy makers continue to pronounce on global issues and
play a prominent part in the game of global politics. The United
Kingdom also retains some extra-European military commitments and
capabilities in, for example, the Gulf, the Indian Ocean, Hong Kong,
the South Atlantic and Central America (Belize). Indeed, those who
draft the British government's annual Defence White Paper insist that

21

these involvements 'can represent some of the most economical and cost-effective ways of protecting and advancing the United Kingdom's interests outside the NATO area'.[13]

This global dimension to British power continues to be valued, therefore, as an important symbolic contribution to the United Kingdom's international status, as well as a substantive contribution to its material interests. Although there are many critics who regard this globalism as pretentious and misconceived, the evidence suggests that it remains a popular stance with the general public and that it is valued by both left and right in British politics, though each would bring a different value system to it.[14] In short, British policy makers not only believe that they continue to have a stake in global affairs, they also think that they can do good in the world. This, too, has important consequences for current policy making. First, it provides part of the cultural context within which contemporary defence decision making takes place. Secondly, it ensures institutionally that British decision making has a global reach.

Structure and Constraint

Other more fixed elements of national and international life also help to provide the context of defence policy making. British decision makers have to deal with a global as well as a regional international system that is composed of factors like geography, economics, technology, ideology and military power which are in many respects structural. That is to say they have to be treated more or less as givens – most of the time.

1. Geographic and Geostrategic Considerations
The United Kingdom is a highly industrialized and densely populated offshore European island, with a long-standing but less than uniform attachment to capitalism and liberal democracy. Its European hinterland is also composed of industrialized and populous states. Historically these have been by turns both friends and allies as well as enemies. Communications and international trade, however, link Britain into an international system which is global in scale. For the past 40 years two of the most important features of this international environment have been the growing interdependence (military and economic, so also political) between states, especially in Western Europe, together with bipolar confrontation between East and West. Each of these developments has also shaped British defence policy making in its own special ways. Interdependence, for instance, has encouraged and facilitated British collaboration with the United States as well as with its European

partners in weapons research, development and production. Bipolarity, of course, has had a pervasive influence on all aspects of defence decision making: from military preparedness in an armed alliance, to arms control discussions designed to reduce the levels of military capability involved in NATO's confrontation with the Warsaw Pact.

There are limits also to the United Kingdom's economic resources, to its technological base, to its existing and potential military capabilities and to what its political culture will stand ideologically; though none of these is unchanging. There is also the threat of nuclear destruction against which there is no certain defence in principle, and currently no effective defence in practice.

None of these structural factors, however, *automatically* determines Britain's security interests or the specific policies through which they are pursued and explored. Just as there is no simple way of satisfying the demand for security, so there is no simple explanation of defence decision making or the course of defence policy. Rather, it is the complex and dynamic interplay between the internal and external contexts of British politics, as perceived and mediated through decision makers in the defence policy community, which is decisive. Even then we have to make considerable allowance also for chance, accident and coincidence. It is because of the character of this interplay, amongst other reasons more usually cited, like the inertia and self-interest of bureaucracies, that defence policy making is conservative and change continuous though incremental. For the world in which defence decision makers live and act is a hybrid one of continuity and change. Choice is always limited and constrained, but ever present.[15]

2. Planning, Procurement and Budgets

Through planning on the basis of five-, ten- and even fifteen-year programmes for financial management and weapons procurement purposes much defence policy making is also locked into long-term programmes. These naturally acquire a momentum and a combination of vested economic, political and military interests all of their own. Sometimes this combination of forces encompasses only domestic agents. In collaborative weapons procurement projects with two or more nations involved, like the MRCA (Multi-Role Combat Aircraft) Tornado Project, the combination is multinational. The momentum is that much greater, therefore, because cross-national understandings, once formed, are even more difficult to break or redirect than domestic ones. Defence budgets and other resources are ordinarily committed very many years in advance and the scope for change is consequently limited.

The defence budget is controlled through long-term costings on the basis of ten-year projections. Financial competition consequently takes place in defence of existing programmes and their needs, at the margins where extra or uncommitted resources might be found, and in staking out claims for resources in the future. Each year is not begun anew, but with the legacy of all the previous agreements, commitments, outstanding claims or unresolved conflicts of previous battles. Management of the defence budget in this sense is little different, in principle, from the experiences and routines of household management. There, too, long-term and regular commitments of income to staple items like mortgage/rent, heating, rates, food, clothing, travel and so on leave little in the way of *disposable* income at the end of the week or month. And it is around that disposable income, made available one way or another through careful management, cutbacks or growth in resources – such as that which occurred in the defence budget during the first two Thatcher administrations – that the fiercest conflict takes place. That also is where practical choice routinely lies.

3. Political Commitments
Basic political commitments further constrain the freedom of choice of defence decision makers. Once commanding a global empire, the United Kingdom is now a middle-ranking European power, and a fully committed member of NATO to which the vast bulk of its armed forces are currently dedicated. Membership of NATO and its integrated military command structures is thus one of the most generally determining features of British defence policy. According to the 1987 Defence White Paper, 'Our contribution to NATO accounts, directly or indirectly, for more than 95% of our defence budget.'[16]

The two most important commands to which British forces are assigned are the Supreme Allied Command Atlantic (SACLANT) and the Supreme Allied Command Europe (SACEUR). Each is headed by a senior American military commander. SACEUR is responsible for ground and air forces in Europe, with headquarters near Mons in Belgium. SACLANT is responsible for naval and naval air forces in the North Atlantic, with headquarters at the American naval base at Norfolk, Virginia. The Royal Navy provides nearly 70 per cent of NATO maritime forces deployed in the Eastern Atlantic and Channel areas, while the 'centrepiece' of the British Army's contribution to NATO is its role on SACEUR's central front for the forward defence of Germany. There 55,000 men and women of the British Army of the Rhine provide 1(BR) Corps and its logistic support, which, together with corps from Belgium, the Netherlands and the Federal Republic of Germany, forms NATO's Northern Army Group (NORTHAG), currently commanded by a German general. Outside the central front there are, in addition, commitments of mobile forces to NATO's Northern and Southern flanks. The Royal Air Force, finally, makes significant contributions to SACEUR's theatre nuclear forces, provides for the air defence of the UK, maintains a tactical air force in Germany, contributes units for the early reinforcement of the Northern Flank and has important maritime tasks in the Eastern Atlantic and Channel.

4. Conclusion

Together with the interplay of bureaucratic politics through which the armed services, amongst other groups, fight their corners to maintain their share of defence resources, these structural features ensure a large measure of continuity in British defence policy. Most defence debate takes place within their confines. Thus at the level of alliance politics, British defence decision makers do not so much argue about whether they should support NATO's strategy of Flexible Response and Forward Defence, as about how they should contribute to operationalizing it in terms of weapons, military forces and logistics. Similarly, in national decision making, at least within the defence policy community, the nuclear debate has revolved less around whether Britain should deploy a strategic nuclear force, and more around what nuclear systems it should acquire in order to remain a strategic nuclear power. Hence the progression from V-Bomber force, through the aborted Blue Streak and cancelled Skybolt programmes to Polaris, Chevaline and the new Trident project.

Just as the services struggle to ensure their fair share of space within the Defence White Paper, so they fight for their share of the defence budget. But the availability of space in both is largely determined by what has gone before and, in each instance, the scope for change is limited. Once again language as well as money (and language is the way money is acquired, through the bidding process for financial support) emerges as a critical resource in defence decision making. Like all resources language too is a scarce commodity, not only in terms of the space or time allotted to talk or to texts, but also in the sense that there is a high premium on the linguistic inventiveness required to play all the language games of policy making (of which the budget process is only one) successfully.

Choice and Change

Structure itself is a matter of choice and a product of discourse. Commitment to Flexible Response, for example, was not inevitable or automatic. Instead it was the product of protracted military and political debate within NATO, in which British defence decision makers played a central part. Much less was the strategy a product of rational analysis of the threat posed by the Soviet Union and the Warsaw Pact, or a product of the ineluctable logic of nuclear deterrence. Deterrence theorists provided the vocabulary of debate and some of its arguments, of course, but they constituted only one voice, one set of considerations, in the discourse of national and alliance decision making which fashioned Flexible Response. Rather, the strategy should be regarded as a delicate but resilient political formula, drafted after much agonized argument, which satisfied a whole range of political as well as military considerations by the time it was adopted in 1967. Precisely because it proved to be so politically accommodating, it became one of the most important parameters within which British and alliance policy making was to be conducted from that time onwards. And it has lasted much longer than its drafters ever anticipated.

Many of the 'givens' of defence policy making are often politically constituted, therefore, within and by the defence policy community. Produced and reproduced through the complex national, international and alliance processes of defence decision making, such fixed features take on a permanence which belies their problematic and contingent origins. Much of the rhetoric of defence decision making disguises, sometimes consciously sometimes not, their fabricated nature. Mythologizing or obscuring the history of some of these structural features, like deterrence itself, is part of the process by which they become accepted as the framework within which all the other myriad defence decisions can be taken. This then is an important feature of the whole process of defence decision making. Though it is seldom acknowledged or analysed, it is an integral part of that endless making and remaking of policy which is designed to create and maintain some manageable order in the flux of defence affairs.

This flux, however, is more evident the closer one gets to the routine management of defence issues, and the more one concentrates upon the day-to-day, or year-to-year, preoccupations of the policy community. From the point of view of defence decision makers, the interplay of domestic (including their own bureaucratic) and international politics which determines defence decisions often presents a radically uncertain vista of intractable difficulties, unreliable actors and changing technologies. It is what some early systems analysts would have called a turbulent task environment.[17] The policy maker's job is to impose order on this environment through all the political and bureaucratic processes by which defence goals and programmes are formulated.

Creating and recreating what is in effect a form of life (a way of doing things which embodies what those involved value), which in addition makes an important contribution to the life of national politics, defence decision makers also defend that order against the counter-challenges of those whose interests it frustrates, or whose values it denies. Alternatively, they may adapt it in response to political directives or because they are forced to do so by circumstances.[18]

From this perspective defence decision makers confront a world of scarce resources (time as well as money, political priority as well as military capabilities), full especially of other international actors whom they cannot readily influence or control. Moreover, it is a world composed of social, economic, political and religious forces which they sometimes barely comprehend, much less manipulate.

Change, therefore, takes place at all levels and throughout all aspects of the policy process. In some areas it might be barely detectable; though even the management rituals of bureaucratic life, which are often the most resistant to change, have been repeatedly reformed in Britain over the post-war decades. Other times change has been both public and pronounced; such as that announced by Duncan Sandys in the 1957 Defence White Paper which ended conscription, enunciated the policy of nuclear deterrence, cut back the Royal Air Force's planned airplane projects and redefined the Royal Navy's role that of an anti-submarine force. Or Denis Healey's 1967 Defence White Paper which, amongst other things, announced the planned withdrawal of British forces from their remaining commitments east of Suez. Though such shifts in policy are often self-consciously portrayed as watersheds it should not be forgotten that they are usually the outcome of much earlier choices, some large others small, which pointed in the direction which the White Papers publicly embraced. Broadly speaking we can also identify three other decision points (opportunities for choice and change) to which defence decision making is subject.

The first are THE *annual rituals* of the defence policy community. One of these is the drafting of the Defence White Paper. Another is the annual preparation of the Defence Estimates. Like the painting of the Forth Bridge (or any large structure for that matter) these are repetitive processes. Thus the Defence White Paper annually records the yearly incremental decisions and developments in the life of the defence policy community. Updating the previous year's statement it can none the less be used to announce new departures and signal obvious as well as subtle shifts in priorities. In particular it may be the means of announcing or producing new detailed information about a second category of change in defence policy: *life-cycle* decisions. These refer

27

primarily to weapon system developments. *Crisis* is a third source of change, one that has its own quite distinctive impact on the process of defence decision making.[19]

Procurement of major new weapon systems proceeds largely on the basis of the follow-on or replacement imperative (but see also *Procurement Talk* below). As old equipment becomes increasingly obsolescent and reaches the end of its useful life, so it is replaced by more modern systems. For major procurement decisions, like those covering strategic nuclear weapons, a separate and full-scale publicity exercise may be required to reveal and explain the choice of the next generation. That is not to suggest that everything is managed smoothly or, indeed, that the taking of the decision corresponds to the public announcement of it. Quite the contrary. These public announcements are more or less successful and more or less carefully orchestrated exercises in public policy management. They are the public tip of an otherwise private (often very private) iceberg of bureaucratic decision making. They should not be discounted for that reason, but their political and promotional function should be properly understood.

Sometimes, as in the past when Britain decided to manufacture nuclear weapons and later when it decided to modernize the re-entry vehicle of the Polaris missile (the Chevaline project), no public announcement is made at all; and news of a major development only leaks into the public domain perhaps years later.[20] If defence decision making is Janus-like it is also shot through with secrecy and confidentiality. Who should speak to whom might be part of the process of regulating policy making within the defence community, but whether or not, how and when to speak to the public about defence matters are equally important questions which occupy defence decision makers.

Life-cycle decisions also do not happen overnight. Like the annual round of consultations about the composition of the Defence White Paper and the defence budget, they usually arise naturally out of the rhythms – in this case weapons procurement rhythms – of policy making. Those rhythms may be natural in as much, say, as a decision had to be made at some point about whether or not to replace Britain's ageing Polaris nuclear system. But there is considerable scope for manipulating such processes, especially by extending the life of a piece of equipment or simply delaying a choice. Timing is thus another essential ingredient in the management of policy. Judging when to make a decision, as well as choosing how and when to announce it, is vitally important; though, again, defence decision makers do not have complete freedom here either.

For instance, on 15 July 1980 Francis Pym, then Secretary of State for Defence, told the House of Commons that the British government was going to replace its Polaris force with a new squadron of nuclear submarines equipped with the Trident C-4 missile, which was to be bought from the United States. Secret negotiations between teams from the Ministry of Defence and the Pentagon had been going on for quite some time and speculation had been rife, in Parliament and in the press, that some decision was about to be announced. Indeed, letters of agreement had been signed in great secrecy between the negotiators on 13 June. It was first planned to make an official announcement on 4 July, but this was postponed to 17 July because West Germany's Chancellor, Helmut Schmidt, was about to undertake a visit to Moscow and US–Soviet negotiations on nuclear weapons were going through a delicate phase. Congressional leaders were confidentially briefed by President Carter on 14 July but Senator Howard Baker immediately leaked the news to the *New York Times*, which prepared to publish the story in its next edition. Late on the 14th British ministers learned of the impending leak. The British Cabinet, however, had not yet authorized the deal and there had, of course, been no official announcement from London. Cabinet members were quickly contacted, mainly by telephone, to avoid the worst of the embarrassment and Pym's parliamentary statement was rapidly brought forward to the following day. According to one authoritative account no formal full Cabinet approval was, therefore, ever given to Trident, earlier decisions having been made by a Cabinet Committee (Misc. 7). In the event the newspaper decided not to publish the story anyway![21]

Timing can be finely judged or bungled on matters such as this. But the deep rhythms of weapon procurement cycles are the structuring factors in equipment decisions. Just as the preparation of the Defence White Paper begins where the last one left off, so consideration of what was going to replace Polaris began very soon after the Royal Navy took over the deterrent function from the Royal Air Force's V-Bombers in 1969. As early as 1973 the House of Commons Expenditure Committee reported that 'Important decisions relating to the future of the deterrent will have to be taken by about 1977 or even earlier.'[22]

It was then assumed that the hull-life of the submarines was about twenty years, and a new force would have to be phased in during the early 1990s. As all weapon programmes have long lead times – that is, their research, development, production and testing takes many years before a new system becomes operationally available – a decision could not wait until the Polaris force itself became unfit to go to sea. Throughout the 1970s, however, it suited Heath's Conservative government to keep Britain's nuclear deterrent off the political agenda, because the defence policy community was wrestling with a costly and secret Polaris improvement programme (Chevaline), and because it was not clear whether Britain wanted Poseidon, or whether the United States was willing to make it available. In the second half of the decade the Labour administrations of Wilson and Callaghan were equally happy with secrecy, because the whole question of nuclear weapons divided the Labour Party from top to bottom. None the less, a decision could not responsibly be postponed for ever, and Callaghan admitted in 1979 that the future of the deterrent had to be decided within two years. Much in fact was done by way of investigating, researching and preparing that decision long before it had finally to be made – as it was by the incoming Thatcher government in 1979 – and then announced.

Pym's parliamentary statement was quickly followed by an informative Open Government Document (DOGD 80/23) in which the choice of Trident was explained and defended in unusual detail. That was not the end of the matter because the Trident programme was in effect a form of international collaboration. Its progress and success accordingly depended as much upon events in the United States as those in Britain. Consequently when President Reagan announced, in October 1981, that the C-4 missile was going to be replaced by a new and more powerful Trident D-5 missile, Britain was forced to accede to the procurement rhythms of its nuclear partner.[23]

On 11 March 1982 John Nott, Pym's replacement, received Cabinet endorsement for a move to the D-5 and the House of Commons was informed that same day. Similarly, the D-5 decision was backed by a new Open Government Document (DOGD 82/1) in which the virtues of maintaining commonality between the British and United States submarine missile forces were extolled as the reasons for the decision. Three weeks later Argentina invaded the Falkland Islands and the future of the British deterrent quickly receded from the centre of public attention.

Choice of the Trident missiles, of course, did not determine every aspect of the new deterrent force. A submarine design had to be authorized and nuclear propulsion units for the submarines chosen. Design and manufacture of new warheads for the new missiles had also to be undertaken, and new manufacturing plants at Burghfield and Cardiff developed. Neither was the decision one which left Britain's nuclear capabilities unchanged or its special nuclear relationship with the United States unaffected. Britain's new Trident force will be a much more powerful and accurate one than Polaris, with about a fourfold increase in the number of deployable warheads. Equally, Britain's nuclear dependence upon the United States has not only been confirmed but also increased in certain areas: for example, with respect to the servicing of the missiles and reliance upon the United States for targeting of Trident's warheads.

Nuclear decision making in the past made Britain reliant upon the United States for the provision of a nuclear delivery system. That dependence had its costs as well as its benefits, champions as well as opponents. If the benefits of dependence were to be secured, however, Britain's missile system had to be the same as that in operation with the United States submarine force. Otherwise, for example, it would be difficult and costly for Britain to buy spares for a device which had already gone out of production. There were other issues involved as well, but the central point is that the choice of Trident was not only structured by Britain's historical nuclear relationship with the United States, it also opened up a new chapter in that relationship. Further binding London to Washington, the Trident decision necessarily closed other options, nuclear as well as conventional, political as well as strategic. Hence Britain's strategic nuclear dependence upon the United States is to persist, but in new forms and, no doubt, with new political and strategic implications as we move from the world of the 1960s and 1970s to that of the 1990s and beyond. Thus life-cycle changes also embody the continuity and change which characterizes defence policy making.[24]

In contrast to life-cycle decisions *crises* are by definition unexpected and unplanned. They are often a product either of bureaucratic failure, political incompetence and miscalculation, or the sheer coincidence of a large number of factors which independently cause few difficulties but combine to provoke a major disruption to the work and plans of defence decision making. Usually they result from a combination of all these features. Quite outside the annual routines and long-term procurement cycles of the defence policy community they none the less also vividly expose the way of life lived there.

Argentina's invasion of the Falkland Islands on 2 April 1982 caught Mrs Thatcher and her government totally unprepared. A consequence of political failure rather than bureaucratic incompetence, the crisis which followed precipitated important changes in British defence policy, reversing in particular John Nott's plans for scrapping the selfsame amphibious forces which the Royal Navy was to use in recapturing the Falkland Islands.[25] Accident played its part here more than ever. Britain's response to Argentina's attack also demonstrated in the most explicit way the relevance of the point about language and policy making. As the Prime Minister and other members of her War Cabinet mobilized the country for war, they did so by revising much of the vocabulary of the long-running Falklands dispute. Turning the Falklands issue into a drama of national credibility, Britain's political leaders struggled for their political survival, and what they saw as the international reputation of their country, by giving voice to public responses, and leading, amplifying and focusing these opinions in the process.[26] Before 2 April 1982, however, hardly anybody in Britain knew where the Falkland Islands were. But by 8 April the Prime Minister was telling the House of Commons, to widespread acclaim, that in response to the invasion 'I took a decision immediately and said that the future of freedom and the reputation of Britain were at stake. We cannot therefore look at it on the basis of precisely how much it will cost.'[27] The Falklands crisis was thus a 'critical discourse moment'.[28]

There are times when our modes of understanding (our policies, to refer back to Heclo and Wildavsky) face a profound challenge and the regular pattern which they bring to the life of a policy community (in this instance also a political community) is radically interrupted. That is when we have to reassert our existing understandings and defend the order which they create, or refashion them so as to create a new order (or policy) and keep chaos at bay. Then, also, agreement and conflict over the underlying values of the political system emerge in stark relief. These are the moments, too, when the constructive and deconstructive roles which language plays in social and political affairs are no longer disguised by usage (*common* sense). As a result we see history literally in the making, through the interplay of all the argument, mythologizing and accident which comprises it. The Falklands episode was a classic in this regard, but it also serves to illustrate some other general features of policy making: those concerning the character of defence policy issues and the pace of life in the defence community.

An 'issue' is what defence decision makers make of it through the processes of analysis and deliberation by which they conduct the business of the policy community. Hence all policy issues, like that of the Falklands, are mobile and malleable. And they can also be turned to one use or another in national politics just as much as in the politics of the policy community.

Wittgenstein (a language specialist rather than a defence analyst) said that we should not ask for the definition of a word but consider how it is used. That should also be a basic rule in defence policy analysis. We could apply it with great effect to what is currently the 'biggest' word in the vocabulary of the defence policy community – deterrence. 'Big' words are those which are open to a multitude of meanings and interpretations. Those, in short, which can be used in many different ways for many different purposes. 'Deterrence', for instance, seems to play the same role in the nuclear age as 'balance of power' played in the preceding world of Eurocentric international relations. The general point, however, is that just as the vocabulary of defence has no fixed meaning – its words are what the discourse and conventions of defence say they are, which is why power infuses the whole process – so no defence issue is fixed either. Moreover, individual reputations may be won and lost in the handling of them, as the different careers of Mrs Thatcher and Lord Carrington illustrate.

Sovereignty was the big word of the Falklands dispute. But in practice, possession of the Islands was one of those small post-imperial anomalies which caused British decision makers so much trouble, once the tide of Britain's imperial power receded leaving them stranded and exposed in a changed and hostile world. Prior to 1982 the fate of the Islands was a politically underprivileged issue trapped in a cycle of political deprivation which displayed all the political arts of how *not* to make a decision. This reminds us that much decision making is also non-decision making; decision avoidance is the other face of policy making.[29] The Falklands moved up and down the hierarchy of the policy process (principally within the Foreign and Commonwealth Office) passing from bureaucrat to junior minister, to Foreign Secretary. From there it moved to the Defence and Overseas Policy Committee of the Cabinet and to the Prime Minister. Then it returned down again into the bowels of the policy community. Similarly, the issue was debated back and forth between Departments of State; as, for instance, when the FCO and the MOD periodically considered the future of Britain's naval presence in the South Atlantic, the ice-patrol ship HMS *Endurance*.

Routinely officials worked out the details of policy at the bureaucratic level, but options were regularly put to government ministers. Proposed courses of action were similarly reviewed at ministerial and Cabinet level, and sanctioned by the Cabinet before being implemented. Detailed advice about the military situation was also regularly available from the government's Joint Intelligence Committee (JIC) which furnished the Cabinet with intelligence briefings.

The outcome of the issue, however, was to provide a particularly explicit example of how defence officials manage policy in a way that is materially influenced by a climate of opinion set by ministers. It also showed that without the investment of adequate political resources, in the form of political control and direction, manageable international disputes can degenerate rapidly into military confrontation. In illuminating the relationship between domestic and international politics, the Falklands dispute also revealed as much about the post-imperial character of the United Kingdom and its policy making processes as it did about the nature of international crisis and conflict.

Mobile in the sense indicated, the Falklands issue was also malleable. For the FCO it represented a diplomatic problem with a human face. A constant irritant in Anglo-Argentine relations, the colony on the Islands also became an economic problem during the 1970s, as its mono-crop economy and fragile social structure began to disintegrate. From the perspective of the MOD the Islands were a military liability, a commitment so far outside the mainstream of defence responsibilities that no good argument could be made for devoting anything but the most token of forces to their defence. In 1981 it was decided that even this token would be removed; a decision which the Prime Minister Mrs Thatcher defended in the House of Commons against parliamentarians, like former Prime Minister James Callaghan, who appreciated the impact it would have on the course of the Falkland's dispute. Amongst members of the Falklands lobby, as well as amongst many MPs, the fate of the Islands was bound up with the symbolism of sovereignty and nostalgia for the global age of British power, in addition to some genuine sympathy for the predicament of the individuals who actually lived there. Island opinion was divided, though no Islander welcomed the prospect of Argentine sovereignty, but it none the less united in a form of loyalist politics.

The work and processes of defence decision making create the biorhythms of the policy community, providing the Ministry of Defence with what might be called its institutional metabolism. The pace of life of the community, however, is transformed by crisis and that is when its responses also quicken. Everything speeds up and certain characteristic patterns of behaviour emerge most of which were in evidence at one time or another during the Falklands conflict. First, decision making becomes centralized as it was in the War Cabinet. Secondly, the volume of information that decision makers have to process increases exponentially, making it more difficult for them to decide which messages and signals are really important. Thirdly, the options which they consider narrow automatically because during a crisis people have neither the time nor the resources to consider a wide range of alternatives effectively. In the process military and political leaders quickly come to depend upon basic images of their situation and of their opponents, often acting on worst case assumptions as Britain's Task Force commanders evidently did in tracking and attacking the Argentine cruiser the *General Belgrano*. Paradoxically, while crises create their own characteristic problems, and the price of failure in defence may be death for many people (millions in a nuclear crisis like that of Cuba in 1962), they are also a spur to action and are relished for that reason. Things get done which otherwise would never have been attempted or contemplated, and at a speed which astounds those familiar with all the delays and difficulties which afflict routine decision making. So, Britain went to war in 1982, mobilizing the bulk of its Navy and all of its amphibious capabilities, refitting naval vessels and modifying commercial ships faster than most decision makers thought possible. As the British Task Force approached the Falkland Islands and counter-attacked Argentine forces on them, so the logic of conflict took hold, culminating in the sinking of the *Belgrano* by the British nuclear attack submarine HMS *Conqueror*, with great loss of life.[30]

The Defence Policy Community and Its Habitat

Finally we come directly to the policy community itself. It is large and pluralistic. Byzantine in its complexity it is also subject to frequent changes. All discussions of the central organization of defence in Britain begin by documenting its size and that is sensible for at least one important reason. Britain is committed to deterrence and that itself demands a large defence and defence economy related defence establishment. Much that distinguishes the discourse of defence decision making, therefore, is directly influenced by these two further and basic features of security in the modern age: the *institutionalization* and the *industrialization* of defence.

By any standards managing the defence of the United Kingdom is big business. Even in this respect defence is distinguished from other Departments of State because its policy making is not so much dependent upon legislation as concerned with resource allocation and management. The MOD's military and civilian workforce exceeds 550,000 people. Its civilian workforce alone is close to one-third of the British Civil Service, and MOD's budget for 1986/7 exceeded £18 billion.[31] Over £8 billion of that was earmarked for equipment, the bulk of this from domestic suppliers. It has been calculated that 225,000 jobs are directly supported and 180,000 indirectly supported by defence equipment spending.[32] The significance of these figures is enhanced because so much of this expenditure is directed to high technology industries. Thus Britain spends more of its military budget on Research and Development than its competitors, and in the past has spent more on military R&D as a proportion of GDP than either the United States, France, West Germany or Japan.[33]

Centralization and rationalization have been persistent themes in the post-war development of the MOD.[34] To these, in more recent years, have been added efficiency and value for money. As the MOD has gone so in many respects has the Civil Service. All post-war governments have looked to make the British Civil Service more efficient and cost-effective. In general terms, and this holds especially for MOD, the shift has been towards instilling a management ethos and borrowing management practices from commercial life. Currently these trends are best exhibited in the Financial Management Initiative (known rudely and cynically in some quarters as the Financial Management Illusion) and in the MINIS reforms (both introduced by Michael Heseltine, John Nott's successor as Secretary of State for Defence).[35] They are also in evidence in the trend towards privatization or commercialization of, for example, the Royal Ordnance Factories and the Royal Dockyards.

Similarly, though the whole process of centralizing defence decision making by reducing inter-service pluralism and rivalry began in 1946 (with the first post-war reappraisal of policy and the establishment of a small Ministry of Defence led by a Minister for Defence with the power to allocate resources), centralization has featured prominently in MOD life since 1945 and is still an issue there. It continued through the 1950s with changes introduced by Anthony Eden and Duncan Sandys. In 1958 the position of First Chief of Defence Staff was created and under its first incumbent, Lord Mountbatten, further reforms were initiated during the early 1960s. These moves led to the Thorneycroft proposals of 1963 which introduced more centralization, though less than Mountbatten had lobbied for, and provided the basic structure of the MOD until the 1980s. Between 1963 and 1983 there was a succession of additional piecemeal changes, but in 1984 there was a further full-scale reorganization. On the Defence Staff side alone this required 600 office moves involving 1,200 staff, and it further reduced the independent power and authority of the individual service chiefs.[36] Henceforth they were required to submit their views on policy to the Secretary of State through the Chief of Defence Staff whose position was substantially reinforced.[37]

All accounts of these processes of centralization and rationalization approve of the direction in which the MOD has gone, merely lamenting the fact that it is so incorrigible that it needs such regular appraisal. Behind the arguments and descriptions is the assumption that progress towards some (implicitly suggested but unspecified) final ideal of a centralized, harmonious and efficient machine is being made but not yet complete, and there is often a further unstated assumption that one day it will be. There are good grounds not so much to be cynical about all this, but to be more analytically and critically circumspect. Critical not in the sense of carping, but in the sense of asking what is going on besides and beyond the declared aims and ambitions of the reformers. One recent study, for example, acknowledges that the early post-war reforms had as much to do with general policy needs as with some notional ideal of efficiency and effectiveness.

> The position and power of the United Kingdom was declining and there were signs that the power of the Commonwealth as a unified and effective world force was diminishing. Our defence commitments were changing rapidly and the nation was in no mood to sustain costly and elaborate forces; consequently defence decisions became more difficult and the cost factor more significant.[38]

In short, beyond the rhetoric of managerialism, simply having to reduce the rich variety and size of an imperial defence establishment and adapt defence policy to Britain's regional power status were just as influential in the process of organizational change as any ideal of rational management. As policy changed so resistance had to be overcome and obstacles removed through the process of reorganization, and this was often achieved under the banner of rational decision making. Circumstantially, therefore, there are good grounds for hypothesizing that management rhetoric cloaks decision making reforms that have been made for all sorts of additional political, economic and bureaucratic reasons.[39] Organizational change in MOD, therefore, is not a simple history of how a poorly managed operation has become much better through the work of reformers themselves equipped with a more enlightened view of how it should be run; though that is sometimes how it is portrayed. Figure 2.3 provides an organization chart of the Higher Organization of the Ministry of Defence which came into effect after the 1984 reforms. As we argued at the beginning of the chapter, the best way to make sense of this – and it is a highly simplified version of what goes on – is to regard it as a formal version of who speaks to whom about what. In broad terms the ministry is divided between the military and civilian staffs. Each is headed respectively by the Chief of Defence Staff (CDS) and the Permanent Under-Secretary of State (PUS). They talk to each other regularly as, also, according to need and routine, do other branches of the organization.

Within the MOD, therefore, and roughly speaking, there is: Service Talk; Money and Management Talk; Intelligence Talk; Science and Technology Talk; and Procurement Talk. Regularly, in each of these very broad discursive forums, people are talking about the same thing – such as an item of equipment – but they are doing so from their own departmental perspectives. Through various devices like committees and the circulation of papers at one level, or through *ad hoc* meetings,

G. M. DILLON

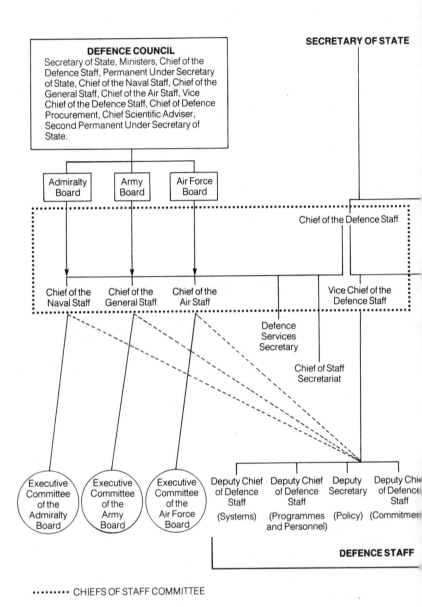

Figure 2.3 Higher organization of the Ministry of Defence (source: S.A.A. Firth and M.S. Heath, 'The Higher management of defence; Annex A', pp. 60–1: *Seaford House Papers*, 1986).

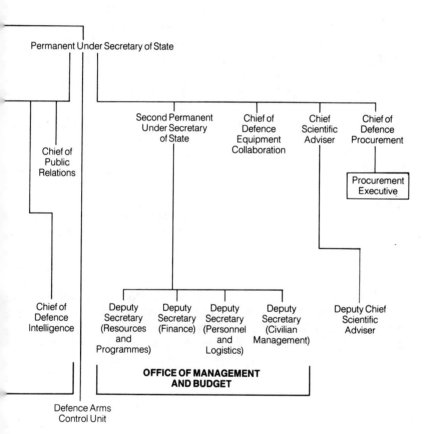

Permanent Under Secretary of State

Chief of Public Relations

Chief of Defence Intelligence

Second Permanent Under Secretary of State

Chief of Defence Equipment Collaboration

Chief Scientific Adviser

Chief of Defence Procurement

Procurement Executive

Deputy Secretary (Resources and Programmes)

Deputy Secretary (Finance)

Deputy Secretary (Personnel and Logistics)

Deputy Secretary (Civilian Management)

Deputy Chief Scientific Adviser

OFFICE OF MANAGEMENT AND BUDGET

Defence Arms Control Unit

conferences, lunches and dinners at another, officials also constantly talk to each other. The system is hardly perfect and often those who should be talking together are not, or they are not doing so as soon and as frequently as they should be. That is not to say, either, that everybody should be talking to everybody else all the time. Such a process would be ridiculous and unworkable. There is not enough time in the day for it, and nor does everyone need to know what everyone else is doing. That much is self-evident, but there is a more important and revealing reason which explains why information flow through interdepartmental talk is restricted and patterned.

The MOD is not a debating club. Instead it is concerned with language in action, with getting things done. Winning the argument, or more to the point dictating its outcome, is concerned with determining the course of events. It is not enough for an actor to be 'right', he or she must be adept at all the language games of the ministry, bearing in mind the skill of the other players and the interests of the various audiences involved. Talk, in short, is concerned with knowledge and knowledge is power.

There is, in addition, one other general point to be made about these forms of talk before we consider the general character of just three of them. Each section of MOD comprises its own subculture, so that each form of talk, though intelligible in varying degrees to the others, is none the less distinct.[40] Sometimes the military men understand the scientists (sometimes they *are* scientists). Sometimes financial planners make themselves understood to project managers (who are increasingly obliged to become financial planners themselves). But each, while talking across the ministry to colleagues in other departments, is also talking in their own idiom. Britain's defence culture provides them with a common vocabulary, a vernacular, but by definition this is too broad and general to provide for all the specific tasks of defence decision making. MOD is not (quite) a Tower of Babel, but it *is* a richly diversified language community speaking many subtly different dialects.[41] The following account, therefore, only provides a very brief sketch of three of the major sub-groups within that community.

1. Service Talk

In the past, 'service talk' was more prominent and directly influential because it used to be organized in separate service ministries and addressed directly to the Secretary of State. All that has been changed by successive reforms until now the service chiefs, organized in the Chiefs of Staff Committee and sitting on the Defence Council, report through the Chief of the Defence Staff (CDS). The Defence Council

and its Service Boards is a civil-military institution comprising the
Secretary of State (who is its chairman), his four junior ministers, the
Chiefs of Staff, the Chief of Defence Staff and his Vice Chief of Defence
Staff, together with the senior civil servants of the Ministry. The
Council meets according to the wish of the Secretary of State.[42]

Even before the 1984 reforms strengthened the office, Admiral
Lewin described his operational task as CDS to be 'responsible for
seeking the advice of my colleagues, taking their views into account,
then presenting my own view as the view of the Department'.[43]
Although the individual service chiefs still retain most of their operational staffs, a newly created Defence Staff organization reporting to the
Chief of Defence Staff, who is supported by a powerful Vice Chief of
Defence Staff, encompasses most of the other functions of the central
Military Staffs. These are organized into four sub-groupings each itself
comprising a very substantial discursive forum. They include a Deputy
Chief of Defence Staff for Systems, Programmes and Personnel, Policy
(including long-range strategic and nuclear questions), and Commitments. In short, operational matters aside, formulation of policy and
advice in all the areas associated with the management of the services
has become centralized in one unified Defence Staff speaking through
the CDS to the Secretary of State.

Interestingly, the means by which this reorganization came about
also illustrates the way policy making has been characterized in this
chapter. Further reduction of service autonomy was a contentious
issue, especially as it was originally planned to deprive the service
Chiefs of Staff of their independent operational staffs. Heseltine
debated and planned his reforms, therefore, through a series of private
discussions with selected officials and advisers, specifically excluding
the current Chief of Defence Staff (Field Marshal Sir Edwin Bramall)
and the Chiefs of Staff of the other three services. When the plans for
the reform were complete, the CDS and the Chiefs of Staff were given
four days' notice (two of which were a Saturday and Sunday) that
the MOD was to be reorganized and the details made public in an
Open Government Document. Therefore top-level discussions were
described as 'vigorous' while the military men registered their objections and achieved some concessions with respect to their operational
responsibilities before the reforms were implemented.[44]

Part of Heseltine's scheme had been to create a dynamic tension
between the service side of the MOD and the civilian side, where
management and budgetary issues were to be similarly centralized in an
Office of Management and Budget (OMB). Led by a Second Permanent
Under-Secretary, policy advice here was to be channelled to the
Secretary of State through the PUS (see fig. 2.3).

2. Money and Management Talk in OMB

Money and management go together because much of the MOD's work is concerned with bargaining for resources with the Treasury, allocating resources between conflicting claimants within the ministry and projecting the cost of what it wants to do as well as what it is currently committed to doing.[45] Take the management of a complex equipment programme. Money operates there not simply as a means to ensure that a weapon system can be researched, developed, tested and produced to a price specified. It is also a device for managing the work well (or badly), imposing discipline on the management of the programme and providing early warning of trouble (when costs rise, something for some reason is wrong and may well get worse). Money talk is pervasive and money talks in many different ways. Indeed to the extent that defence decision making has become 'how much can you afford to defend', defence economics has become its science.[46] Much defence policy debate, both in public and in the privacy of the defence community, therefore, is conducted in the language of the defence budget, weapon costs and financial management.[47]

Throughout the post-war period money management has been one of the central preoccupations of the MOD. Moreover, it is through the repetitive complex procedures of drawing up the annual Defence Estimates and revising the long-term costings of the defence programme, which now takes place centrally in the new OMB, that the MOD speaks with other ministries in Whitehall, especially the Treasury. In that way its money talk becomes integrated into the entire public expenditure round through the Public Expenditure Survey process. Throughout the 1980s that process has itself been subjected to greater financial control and the operation of cash limits in order to meet the government's desire to reduce expenditure and simultaneously gain greater value for money from it. To some extent the MOD suffered less than other public expenditure programmes because between 1979–80 and 1985–6 defence spending was allowed to grow in real terms by 3 per cent per annum in line with the NATO agreement to strengthen the alliance by devoting more resources to defence.[48]

Under the OMB money talk is divided into four basic areas: Resources and Programmes, concerned with the long-term costings and coordination of programmes; Finance, responsible for cost control, new financial management procedures and parliamentary accountability; Personnel and Logistics; and Civilian Management, concerned largely with training and industrial relations. Hence, it is now able to operate not only as a coordinator of financial planning but also as an auditor of cost control and management efficiency through supervising the specification and operation of new Executive Responsibility Budgets within the ministry.[49]

Standard service tactics in the language game of money talk, in addition to the general strategies mentioned earlier, include: bidding high for resources on the basis that if all the services have to take cuts, the higher the base line from which any individual service has to take its own cut the better; offering up cuts on, or claiming an inability to fund, the most desirable equipment; tolerating high costs in certain sensitive areas to 'emphasise and demonstrate the urgent needs of increased funds'; asking for more than is needed on the basis of the argument that battlefield success is essentially a matter of statistical probability in which 'more' always improves the odds.[50]

3. Procurement Talk

Acquisition of weapon systems and other defence equipment is a mammoth task in its own right. Consequently ever since 1971 it has been organized through a large sub-department within the MOD known as the Procurement Executive (see fig. 2.3). Though the follow-on imperative is a dominant one in weapons procurement, requirements for new military equipment can arise from three other sources in addition to the obsolescence of the old material. A new assessment of the military threat, the development of a new capability or a change in the concept of military operations may each be influential in the debate about procurement. And arguments based on these positions may enter the discourse in any number of ways. Scientists in one of the defence research establishments may come up with a bright idea, or an industrial contractor may offer a new capability. University scientists may make a new discovery or the military staffs rethink how they might have to fight their battles. As one recent study concluded:

> Indeed to refer to the 'source' of a new project may be to commit a category mistake. It implies the injection of a new factor into an otherwise static picture. In reality, however, the Ministry of Defence runs on a complex set of interconnections between its parts ... Thus there is constant interplay between the services, the civilian secretariat and scientific staffs, and the staff of the Procurement Executive.[51]

Within the constantly changing discourse of procurement, however, certain recurring themes stand out. First is the rising cost of defence equipment together with the economic, bureaucratic and political challenges this poses to weapon system managers. Second is the difficulty in a market dominated by a monopsonist purchaser (the MOD) and often a series of monopoly suppliers of ensuring competitiveness and efficiency. Defence procurement does not take place in a perfect market, and there are valid reasons for this beyond the self-interest of the groups concerned. None the less, the absence of free market disciplines means that the negotiated environment of customer–contractor relationships is open to all sorts of inefficiencies and occasional abuse. By making more MOD contracting subject to competitive tendering and by privatizing or commercializing defence industries (the list includes British Aerospace and Vickers as well as the Royal Ordnance Factories and Dockyards), the current government has tried to get better value for money. Despite all the organizational and managerial reforms over previous decades, however, the MOD and the defence industries still make enormous and very costly mistakes in weapons procurement, as the recent Nimrod case has again demonstrated.[52]

A third theme in defence procurement, and one related in large part though not exclusively to cost, is international collaboration. Because defence equipment is so expensive involving huge investment of resources over many years in high technology/high risk developments, Britain has been priced out of certain areas (like ballistic missile technology) and is in danger of being priced out of many others. All advanced industrial societies seek to maintain extensive and sophisticated defence economies for economic as well as defence purposes. But only the richest, like the United States, can afford to maintain a comprehensive defence industrial base. And even the United States, for commercial as well as technological and political reasons, has found itself forced to pursue certain forms of collaborative and cooperative ventures with its allies. In aerospace, especially, Britain's plans for defence procurement start from the premise of collaboration (witness, for example, the Jaguar and MRCA programmes and discussions about a new European Fighter project). In weapons acquisition the centrality of NATO to British defence decision making is also strongly exhibited.

There are many forms of collaboration and much disappointment (mainly serious, sometimes mock) that it has not proceeded further and more systematically. It is assumed that, though more expensive to set up than an individual national programme, its cost advantages are twofold. First, Britain's resources no longer stretch to national projects. So no collaboration might mean no project. Secondly, a multinational project means sharing the R&D costs between several countries and having a larger production run, which should reduce the unit cost of equipment. There are in addition, however, many political and military considerations involved in the whole process of weapons collaboration as well. Procuring the same equipment, for instance, contributes to rationalizing NATO's weapons inventories, thus helping to rationalize and standardize NATO forces, making more efficient use of the alliance's resources and creating more effective inter-operability between its various national army, navy and air forces.[53]

Finally there is public accountability. This is an issue central to defence policy making in general but in procurement it is especially important because of the huge sums of money involved, the economic resources given over to military work and the intimate relationship between the MOD and the defence industries involving also the movement of people from the public service into private industry. There are many specific and detailed issues involved here, but what procurement talk above all illustrates is not only the Janus-like quality of defence decision making but also the crisis of accountability in the modern institutionalized and industrialized state.[54]

All the work done in the Procurement Executive, as elsewhere in the MOD, is subject to the political supervision of ministers and to public scrutiny by Parliament. Parliamentary procedures include the traditional debate and questioning but public accountability also involves, more effectively, the House of Commons Defence Committee, the Public Accounts Committee and the National Audit Office. These are complex areas of discourse and decision in their own right. But all the evidence points to how difficult effective accountability is to achieve at ministerial and parliamentary level because of the sheer complexity of the procurement process. There is no denying, either, that there is a confluence of interest between MOD and the defence economy which has its own dynamics resistant to the counter-claims and interests of the civil sector of the economy and society. Beside the MOD's preoccupation with efficiency and internal managerial effectiveness, therefore (and these constitute public values also), are public concerns with detailed political control and public scrutiny of the whole defence effort. Moreover, public accountability and managerial effectiveness are not necessarily compatible. The former requires openness and wider debate, the latter (precisely because power is knowledge and the object of the game is to get things done) may well require secrecy, speed and decisiveness. Reconciling these values entails cost, and that cost might be paid in less public control on the one hand or less effectiveness on the other. It is only in an ideal and abstract world that the potentially conflicting values of accountability and effective performance are reconciled without somebody (in terms of a set of interests and values) having to pay a price.

Conclusion

This conclusion is designed less to summarize what has gone before than to identify some of the most important things left out. These include not only all the other aspects of the MOD's work from intelligence gathering through to science and technology research, but also the web of inter-ministry discussions with the FCO (where the discussions are most dense and detailed), with the Treasury (on finance) and the Department of Trade and Industry (on industrial and procurement questions). Two of the most critical areas of discourse not considered in any detail, however, have been the political oversight of defence decision making and, secondly, the way in which the MOD links into the NATO forum of defence debate. I shall end with these, though the special relationship with the United States, which is a quite distinct subset of the alliance-based discourses about defence policy, and upon which there is an extensive and detailed literature, will not be examined.[55]

1. Political Talk

There are all kinds of political talk about defence issues. They include that which takes place in Whitehall, where the executive branch of government is situated, and that which takes place in Westminster where Parliament is located. Broadly this defines the private and public dimensions of defence discourse. But there is also the wider public debate which revolves around the defence community via the media and through a series of university departments and other research institutions in which an interested and more or less expert public of defence specialists (some, so to speak, accredited, some not) confer and write about defence questions.

Within the executive branch, one Secretary of State and four junior ministers supervise the Ministry of Defence on what might be called short-term contracts of between two and three years (military and civilian staffs are the tenured members of the defence community – though they change their individual jobs frequently – with all the consequent advantages that that entails in the detailed conduct of policy). Beyond the Secretary of State are the Cabinet and Prime Minister.

The arts of political supervision, however, are equally important aspects of defence decision making. Though they also derive from the interplay of power and persuasion, they are exercised in their own distinctive ways, for different types of audience and with different sorts of purposes in mind. Ministers are marginal men. Supervising the defence community they mediate between the public and private faces of defence discourse – literally moving back and forth between Whitehall and Westminster (between office desk and television studio).

Neither individual ministers nor the Prime Minister can be expected to acquire an intimate technical knowledge of all aspects of a ministry's business. Each is concerned, instead, with supervision, intervention and general direction. Such leadership requires timing, political judgement, style and resolution – political skills rather than the forensic ones of a scientist or financial analyst. Ministers have access to the many texts (papers, reports, and so on) through which professional advice is made available, but they also have to draw upon their own political expertise and wider political interests in dealing with this material. Just as ministers have to range widely within their departments to provide this political impetus and direction so they are also engaged in arbitration of disputes and coordination of policy. Similarly the Prime Minister does the same for the government as a whole, exercising the authority as well as the power that comes from holding office. The Cabinet and the MOD, therefore, are intimately related centres of debate about defence questions.[56]

In practice the relationship between the two is conducted through the Cabinet Office linking the top echelons of MOD to the Defence and Overseas Policy Sub-Committee of the Cabinet, composed of the Prime Minister, Foreign Minister, Chancellor of the Exchequer, Secretary of State for Defence and one or two other senior ministers in the government. This sub-committee manages most of the business for the government on defence questions, with the whole Cabinet ratifying its decisions or being employed as a final court of appeal in the case of an unreconciled dispute between ministers. In this regard the 'Westland Affair', concerning the future of a small British helicopter manufacturing company, is instructive.

Michael Heseltine, in accordance with a general defence commitment to European collaboration and cooperation, wanted to see Westland taken over by a European consortium to save it from liquidation. His Cabinet colleague at the Department of Trade and Industry, Leon Brittan, favoured a takeover by the US firm Sikorsky for different reasons. This interdepartmental dispute went to full Cabinet level and the way it was handled there (power, information and persuasion in clear evidence again) precipitated Heseltine's resignation in protest against the Prime Minister's deliberate management of the debate in favour of the Sikorsky deal. In the process Downing Street also engaged in the public manipulation of the dispute by arranging for the leaking of papers damaging to Heseltine's position.[57]

2. NATO Talk

NATO members routinely consult on defence issues through the formal consultative mechanisms of the alliance. Just as each forum within the domestic policy process has its own idiom, so alliance politics also has its distinctive vocabulary and values. Similarly there is both a military and a civilian side to NATO.

Britain, like each member of the alliance, has a Permanent Representative who heads the United Kingdom's National Delegation at NATO's headquarters in Brussels. The Permanent Representative is an ambassador and the National Delegation his embassy. Members of these Delegations represent their countries on the various committees established by the North Atlantic Council which is the highest political forum of the alliance, meeting twice a year at Foreign Minister level and occasionally at heads of government level. In permanent session at the level of Permanent Representative the Council meets at least once a week (see fig. 2.4). The Council's Defence Planning Committee (DPC), dealing with matters directly related to defence, meets both in permanent session at the Permanent Representative level and twice yearly at Defence Minister level. Nuclear issues are discussed in the Nuclear Planning Group (NPG) in which fourteen countries are now represented, and in the more exclusive High Level Group (HLG).

On the military side NATO's Military Committee is the highest military authority in the alliance. It functions on a continuous basis through the operation of Permanent Military Representatives (with the exception of France, which withdrew from NATO's integrated military command structure in 1966, and Iceland, which has no military forces), but convenes twice yearly at the Chiefs of Staff level. The Military Committee is supported by an International Military Staff. Below this level are NATO's strategic commands – SACEUR, SACLANT and Commander-in-Chief Channel (CINCHAN).[58]

Through these mechanisms NATO seeks to coordinate national defence planning and political cooperation in the light of commonly agreed NATO defence requirements. If the domestic politics of defence decision making is marked by partisan competition within the Ministry of Defence and between MOD and the rest of government, NATO discourse naturally is plagued by national rivalry. Given that as a basis, it none the less has induced and sustained a remarkable degree of defence cooperation between its members in the past 38 years. If the reality is 16 formally sovereign nations constantly seeking by partisan negotiation to identify where their collective interest lies, how its specific terms and conditions should be defined and how, in turn, these should be translated into coordinated military forces and policies, then

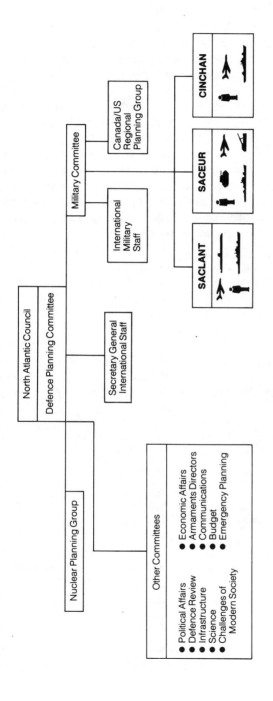

Figure 2.4 The civil and military structure of NATO (source: *Statement on the Defence Estimates 1986* (HMSO, 1986, Cmnd 9763–I, p.22)

its collective values none the less are solidarity and cooperation. These may be more honoured in the breach, but they are still an important aspect of the language games played within NATO itself.

And so the Janus-like nature of defence policy exhibits itself, finally, in the operation of an alliance whose politics and commitments, negotiated at an international level, feed back into national debate. Thus conflict about the stationing of United States' cruise missiles at air bases in Britain is conducted in terms both of Britain's obligations to NATO and its domestic sovereignty. Similarly Britain's own strategic nuclear status is debated in terms of national potency as well as membership of an alliance whose strategy is also based upon nuclear deterrence. In such an interdependent world there is no way of effacing either face of Janus. Defence decision making, therefore, is concerned with the endless interplay between the two, and with how each manifests itself in the formulation of policy.

Notes

Note Throughout the volume, places of publication are given only for those works published outside the United Kingdom.

1 K. Middlemas, *Politics in Industrial Society* (1979). W. H. Greenleaf, *The British Political Tradition*, vol. I: *The Role of Collectivism* (1983).

2 S. Beer, *Modern British Politics* (1965). D. Heald, *Public Expenditure* (1983).

3 M. Pearton, *The Knowledgeable State* (1982).

4 H. Heclo and A. Wildavsky, *The Private Government of Public Money* (1974), 346.

5 W. J. M. MacKenzie, *Political Identity* (1978). A. P. Cohen, *The Symbolic Construction of Community* (1985).

6 Sometimes improperly. See P. Wright, *Spy Catcher. The Candid Autobiography of a Senior Intelligence Officer* (New York, 1987).

7 M. Shapiro, *Language and Political Understanding* (1981). J. W. Danford, *Wittgenstein and Political Philosophy. A Re-Examination of the Foundation of Social Science* (1976). A. Sheridan, *Michel Foucault. The Will to Truth* (1980).

8 For an introduction to post-modern theory see V. Descombes, *Modern French Philosophy* (1980); and J. F. Lyotard, *The Post-Modern Condition: A Report on Knowledge* (1986).

9 *Statement on the Defence Estimates 1987*, Cmnd 101–I (1987), CM 101–I, 25, para. 403. See also Erving Goffman, *Forms of Talk* (1981).

10 P. L. Berger and R. Luckman, *The Social Construction of Reality* (1966).

11 M. Howard, *The Continental Commitment. The Dilemma of British Defence Policy in the Era of Two World Wars* (1972).

12 P. Kennedy, *The Realities behind Diplomacy* (1981). P. Darby, *British Defence Policy East of Suez 1947–68* (1973).

13 *Statement on the Defence Estimates 1983*, Cmnd 8951–I (1983), para. 114.

14 D. Greenwood, 'The defense policy of the United Kingdom', in D. J. Murray and P. R. Viotti (eds), *The Defense Policies of Nations* (Baltimore, Md, 1982).

15 See also W. Wallace, *The Foreign Policy Process in Britain* (1975).

16 CM 101–I, 15.
17 F. E. Emery (ed.), *Systems Thinking* (1969).
18 According to Wittgenstein, in sharing a language a language community constitutes a form of life. D. Bloor, *Wittgenstein: A Social Theory of Knowledge* (1983).
19 P. Williams, *Crisis Management* (1976).
20 L. Freedman, *Britain and Nuclear Weapons* (1980).
21 C. McInnes, *TRIDENT: the Only Option?* (1986), 12–26.
22 *Ibid.*, 11.
23 G. M. Dillon, *Dependence and Deterrence. Success and Civility in the Anglo-American Special Nuclear Relationship 1962–82* (1982).
24 *Ibid.*
25 Nott's plan had been announced in *The United Kingdom Defence Programme: The Way Forward*, Cmnd 8299 (1981).
26 G. M. Dillon, *The Falklands, Politics and War* (1988).
27 *The Falklands Campaign, A Digest of Debates in the House of Commons 2 April to 15 June 1982* (1982), 70.
28 This phrase belongs to Paul Chilton.
29 Adapted from P. Bachrach and M. S. Baratz, 'The two faces of power', *American Political Science Review*, 56 (1962). See also S. Lukes (ed.), *Power* (1986).
30 This account is based on Dillon, *The Falklands, Politics and War*. But see also M. Hastings and S. Jenkins, *The Battle for the Falklands* (1983).
31 S. Mclean (ed.), *How Nuclear Weapons Decisions Are Made* (1986), 99.
32 *Ibid.* See also, G. Kennedy, *The Defence Business in the United Kingdom. Part 1: The Ministry of Defence. Part 2: The Defence Suppliers*, Heriot-Watt University, Edinburgh: Defence Finance Reports nos. 2 and 3 (March and April 1985).
33 *UK Military R&D. Report of a Working Party Council for Science and Society* (1986), 7–15.
34 M. Edmonds (ed.), *Central Organizations of Defence* (1985), ch. 5. F. H. Johnson, *Defence by Ministry* (1980).
35 *MINIS and the Development of the Organisation for Defence*, Open Government Document (OGD) 84/03 and OGD 1/84.
36 S. D. A. Firth and M. S. Heath, 'The higher management of defence', *Seaford House Papers*, 1986.
37 *The Central Organization of Defence*, Cmnd 9315 (July 1984).
38 Firth and Heath, 'The higher management of defence', 43.
39 This and other points are borne out in the following studies of organizational and managerial reform of public administration in general in Britain: G. Fry, *The Changing Civil Service* (1985), and C. Pollitt, *Manipulating the Machine* (1984).
40 Culture like all useful terms is a vexed one. The view taken here is based upon anthropology and particularly the work of Clifford Geertz, *The Interpretation of Cultures* (1975). In brief, knowing a culture is knowing how to behave like a native.
41 See in general G. Steiner, *After Babel* (1975).
42 This account is based on Firth and Heath, 'The higher management of defence' and Edmonds, *Central Organizations of Defence.*
43 Lewin to the House of Commons Foreign Affairs Committee in *Third Report from the Foreign Affairs Committee. Session 1984–85 Events Surrounding the Weekend of 1–2 May 1982*, HC 11-iv (22 July 1985), para. 439.
44 Firth and Heath, 'The higher management of defence', 45.
45 M. D. Hobkirk, *The Politics of Defence Budgeting: A Study of Organisation and Resource Allocation in the United Kingdom and the United States* (1983).
46 As McNamara's systems analysts and econometricians concluded. See, for example, the classic study by C. J. Hitch and R. N. Mclean, *The Economics of Defence in the Nuclear Age* (Cambridge, Mass., 1960); and also C. J. Hitch, *Decision Making for Defense* (Berkeley, Calif., 1965). For a similar but simpler British rendition see G. Kennedy, *The Economics of Defence* (1975); and Kennedy, *The Privatisation of Defence Supplies*, Hume Paper no. 5 (1986).
47 With particular effect especially by David Greenwood. See, for example, D. Greenwood and D. Hazel, *The*

Evolution of Britain's Defence Priorities, 1957–76, Aberdeen ASIDES no. 9 (1977–8).

48 L. Pliatzky, *Getting and Spending* (1982, rev. edn 1984).

49 *Progress in Financial Management in Government Departments*, Cmnd 9297 (1984).

50 Firth and Heath, 'The higher management of defence', 49–50.

51 *UK Military R&D*, 16. See also G. Kennedy, *Management of Research Work in UK Industry*, Heriot-Watt University, Edinburgh: Defence Finance Report no. 5 (December 1986).

52 'British Defence Committee begins to evaluate proposals for new AEW Aircraft', *Aviation Week and Space Technology*, 15 September 1986; 'Britain makes final decision on the AEW aircraft', *Aviation Week and Space Technology*, 15 December 1986.

53 See M. Edmonds (ed.), *International Arms Procurement* (New York, 1981).

54 Dan Smith is one of the few defence specialists specifically to note that any theory of defence decision making equally entails a theory of the state. See his introduction to *The Defence of the Realm in the 1980s* (1980).

55 See J. Baylis, *Anglo-American Defence Relations, 1939–84: The Special Relationship* (1984).

56 For an excellent, though theoretical, account of political judgment see R. Beiner, *Political Judgement* (1983).

57 *House of Commons Third Report From the Defence Committee, Session 1985–86. The Defence Implication of the Future of Westland plc.*, HC 518 (1986). Also, M. Linklater and D. Leigh, *Not without Honour. The Inside Story of the Westland Scandal* (1986); and 'The Westland affair', *Aviation Week and Space Technology*, 24 February 1986.

58 *Statement on the Defence Estimates 1986*, Cmnd 9763–I (1986), 22. See also the *NATO Handbook* (Brussels), produced annually.

3
United States of America

PHILIP WILLIAMS

The terms defence policy and defence policy making suffer from
familiarity. Everyone knows what they mean; consequently they are
rarely defined. Part of the reason for this is the scale and extent of the
activities that they encompass. Defence policy is in some respects an
amalgam of foreign policy, fiscal policy and industrial policy. It ranges
from routine decisions about acquisition of spare parts and ammunition
stocks to major decisions about the development and deployment of
costly weapons systems, and is perhaps best regarded as encompassing
the provision, organization, deployment and use of military capabilities.
Defence policy is essentially instrumental and is directed towards the
negation of external threats and the fulfilment of national objectives by
military means. It involves broad political questions such as 'how much
is enough to deter adversaries from mounting threats to one's national
security?', and narrower technical issues such as determining the most
effective and efficient weapons systems to carry out key roles and
missions.

Of all areas of public policy, defence is perhaps the most important.
Yet it is also one of the most tangled and arcane. The choices that are
made by the defence policy making community are not simply rational
responses to perceived threats; they also reflect domestic political and
economic considerations of all kinds. Furthermore, different elements
in defence policy making operate in very different ways. Many decisions
are made at low levels of the bureaucracy as a matter of routine, others
have to be made at the highest political level; some are the subject of
intense private and public pressure, others are made relatively free from
external political considerations. Another complication is the dynamic
nature of both the external and technological environments to which
planners and policy makers have to respond. Changes in the international system and developments in technology require changes in
national defence policy. Although the necessary adjustments are

sometimes slow in coming because of the power of established procedures and practices, and the persistence of old mind-sets, this is not
invariably the case. At times the United States has responded to change
with considerable alacrity. This is not entirely surprising as one of the
most remarkable aspects of the American defence policy making
community is the rapidity and extent of its growth.

The rise of the defence policy making establishment in the United
States is something which, for the most part, has occurred since the
Second World War. Although the United States has a tradition of
military intervention in Latin America and Asia, historically its interventions tended to be rapid and decisive, had little impact on the
normal functioning of American society and were carried out by
expeditionary forces. They were generally regarded as part of the
American 'civilizing mission', and reinforced rather than challenged the
American sense of uniqueness. The United States regarded itself as
very different from the Machiavellian European powers whose quarrels
it attempted to ignore. When Washington used force it was a necessary
last resort for the highest of moral purposes. Accordingly, the United
States did not have a large standing army, and

> with the major exception of naval expenditures preceding the First World
> War, defence spending was crisis oriented. During years of European
> peace the armed services were allocated only a small fraction of the
> resources they would require in the event of war. Even with the outbreak
> of general war abroad, the threat to American security was not immediate.
> In both world wars the distribution of power among the belligerents was
> such as to make total victory neither immediate nor certain.[1]

Consequently, the United States was able to rely on its massive
mobilization capabilities. After decisive American intervention on the
side of right, there was to be a reversion to normality. Mobilization and
victory were to be followed by demobilization and relaxation.

This pattern was interrupted after 1945: with the onset of the Cold
War, and the development of atomic weapons, threats to American
security became not a temporary aberration but a permanent feature of
international relations. Consequently, the United States was compelled
to abandon its traditional approach to defence policy making. The
result has been the growth of a massive military industrial bureaucratic
complex which intrudes into many aspects of American society and
economy. The Department of Defense employs over two million active
service personnel, one million reserve personnel and one million
civilians. In addition, another million private employees are under
contract to DOD. Goods and services are bought from 300,000

suppliers and 52,000 contract actions are signed every working day.[2] The defence budget is so large that it has a major influence on American industry, although there are continuing disagreements about whether investment in defence is a burden or a prop to the economy. If this issue remains a matter of considerable debate amongst economists, however, America's West European allies need little convincing. They have expressed considerable concern that the research programme stemming from President Reagan's Strategic Defense Initiative will provide a major boost to the American economy especially in high technology areas, and that Europe will become little more than a technological backwater. Whether or not these fears are justified they illustrate the extent to which defence-related research and development has become a major factor in the American economy.

This chapter sets out initially to highlight the policy context within which this growth has taken place. It looks at the American perception of the Soviet threat and shows how defence policy has been related to the implementation of the basic objective of containing Soviet power. The chapter then examines the defence policy making apparatus – the organizations and procedures which were established in the late 1940s to meet the threat to American security. Although there have been subsequent modifications to this apparatus, the policy making structure has remained decentralized and fragmented. Inter-service rivalry, in particular, has had a pervasive impact on American procurement practices. As well as examining the causes and consequences of this rivalry, the chapter describes the budgetary process in both the executive and legislative branches and shows how every stage of this process is highly politicized. Defence policy, however, is not simply about the acquisition and maintenance of military force: it is also about its use. Consequently, the chapter looks at the American use of force in the post-war period, with particular attention being paid to the role of the President in decision making. The final section of the chapter considers initiatives taken in 1986 to reform the policy making process.

The Foreign Policy Framework

The United States after 1945 had to come to terms with a new sense of vulnerability. There was no longer an indigenous balance of power in Europe to act as a first line of security. After two years of uncertainty in Soviet–American relations, the Truman Doctrine in 1947 effectively established the containment of Soviet power as the central aim of American foreign policy. There remained significant differences amongst key policy makers about the nature of the threat to American security and, in particular, about the extent to which this threat was essentially political or military in character. In June 1948 the State Department advised the Secretary of Defense that in view of the Soviet threat a defence policy 'based on the permanent state of adequate military preparation' rather than an effort 'pointed toward a given peak of danger' was necessary.[3] This directive, however, did not succeed in establishing a consensus about the threat, nor did it lead to agreement about what had to be done to protect America's security. This was evident in the continuing controversy over the size of the defence budget – and President Truman's decision to maintain fairly low ceilings on defence spending. In the period from 1947 to 1950 the United States accepted obligations to underwrite the security of Western Europe without developing the capabilities necessary to fulfil those obligations in the event they were challenged. The 'fall' of China and the Soviet explosion of an atomic bomb, however, created considerable consternation in Washington, as did intelligence reports of Soviet military plans. Consequently, a major reassessment of the threat and the appropriate American response was initiated in a joint State and Defense Department study under the chairmanship of Paul Nitze who had just become head of the State Department's Policy Planning Staff. The subsequent report known as NSC-68 was important for several reasons.

In the first place, NSC-68 established a new assessment of Soviet–American relations. The Soviet Union, it was contended, posed a permanent military threat to the security of the United States and its allies. Not only did this confirm the State Department directive of 1948 referred to above, but it provided what has been the dominant framework for American policy ever since. The arguments of the previous head of the Policy Planning Staff, George Kennan, that the Soviet threat was political rather than military were effectively overruled – partly because of more alarming intelligence estimates – while Kennan's attempts to differentiate between vital and peripheral interests were superseded by an indiscriminate globalism in which commitments were regarded as interdependent. Secondly, NSC-68 provided a rationale for a continued build-up of both nuclear and conventional forces. In what was an early statement of the logic which underlay the Kennedy-McNamara Flexible Response strategy of the 1960s, NSC-68 contended that the United States had to deploy comprehensive military forces and could not simply rely on its temporary advantages in atomic weaponry: it should 'increase as rapidly as possible our general air, ground and sea strength and that of our allies to a point where we are militarily not so heavily dependent on atomic weapons'.[4] This did not mean that the

United States could afford to neglect its atomic arsenal; in view of Soviet progress this would be a mistake. It was simply that atomic weapons had to be supplemented by large-scale conventional forces in an effort to achieve comprehensive deterrence.

If NSC-68 was important in defining the Soviet American relationship predominantly in military terms, it was also significant because of its basic assumptions about America's relations with its allies. The report started from the premise that the North Atlantic Treaty in 1949 had marked an end to American avoidance of entangling alliances and that American obligations to its European allies would continue indefinitely. Indeed, all its recommendations were based on the premise that the Soviet–American competition was a long-term one and that therefore the United States would play a continuing and indeed expanding role in international politics.

Although NSC-68 laid out the threat in very stark terms and highlighted what had to be done to meet, Nitze's recommendations encountered considerable resistance from President Truman who was determined that, for the sake of the economy, defence spending should be kept under control. The outbreak of war in Korea, however, led to a much greater sense of alarm and provoked a major rearmament programme similar to that envisaged by Nitze's report. Indeed, it was the Korean War which not only encouraged the extension of containment to Asia, but also led to the militarization of containment in Europe. Four divisions of American troops were deployed to Europe on a more or less permanent basis, and the process of German rearmament was set in motion.

The architects of this build-up remained concerned that the United States would not be able to sustain the degree of sacrifice necessary to compete effectively with Moscow. Although these anxieties were exaggerated they were not wholly without foundation. American defence spending, in particular, has been rather uneven and has gone through a series of peaks and troughs. Yet the conceptions of security that were established in the late 1940s and the early 1950s have proved both compelling and resilient. Furthermore, many of the issues that became controversial in this period – the extension of the American security guarantee to Western Europe, the precise balance between conventional and nuclear weapons, and the difficulty of reconciling commitments and capabilities – have become permanent features of the American defence debate. Arguments about extended deterrence, burden sharing and priorities within defence are, if anything, even more salient in the late 1980s than they were in the late 1940s and early 1950s. There is even greater continuity in terms of institutions and procedures. Indeed, many of the problems that bedevil the American defence establishment in the late 1980s can be traced back to the late 1940s.

The Making of Defence Policy

To understand the way in which United States defence policy is made, at least in the executive branch, it is necessary to consider the National Security Act of 1947 which was designed to integrate domestic, foreign and military considerations into a coherent design. This was to be done primarily through the National Security Council, which included as statutory members the President, Vice-President, the Secretaries of State and Defense, and the Director of the Office of Civil and Defense Mobilization. Initially intended as a forum for ensuring that the President took advice, the NSC became a means of ensuring that the President maintained some control over policy in the White House itself. This trend was apparent in the rise of the NSC staff, especially the national security adviser, and the decline of the NSC as a formal advisory body. The post of special assistant to the President for national security affairs – a position which later became known as National Security Adviser – was created by President Eisenhower. Although this office was not particularly important in the 1950s, its significance increased during the 1960s, and in the early 1970s Henry Kissinger used the position to dominate many aspects of US foreign and defence policy making. The post retained considerable significance in the Carter Administration when Zbigniew Brzezinski effectively challenged the primacy of Secretary of State Cyrus Vance as Carter's chief adviser on foreign and security policy.

President Reagan had a series of NSC advisers, none of whom firmly established his imprint on the policy making process to anything like the same extent as did Kissinger and Brzezinski. Nevertheless, as the 'contragate' scandal revealed, the NSC staff seem to have had considerable discretion in devising a policy which used the illegal sale of arms to Iran to finance the operations of the contras in Nicaragua. Indeed, the activities of Colonel Oliver North revealed just how different the role of the NSC was from that envisaged in the late 1940s. Set up to restrain the President, it had become a means of avoiding restraint.

As well as creating the NSC, the National Security Act of 1947 established military departments for the Army, the Air Force and the Navy (including the Marine Corps and naval aviation). It also created the position of Secretary of Defense to provide authoritative co-ordination and unified direction of the services under civilian control and established a statutory basis for the Joint Chiefs of Staff.[5] The implications of this legislation were far-reaching. In a sense, the emphasis on coordination rather than merger was simply a reflection of the organizational realities. Yet such an approach perpetuated the divisions between the services, divisions which the creation of an executive department – the Department of Defense – did nothing to overcome. The Secretary of Defense was given 'direction, authority and control' over DOD, but the three departments – army, navy and air force – were to be 'separately administered' by their respective secretaries. Furthermore, provision was made to allow the service secretaries and members of the Joint Chiefs of Staff to make their own recommendations to Congress. The result was that DOD was created as an umbrella organization which sat on top of what were at the very least semi-independent fiefdoms. At best, therefore, it was a partial and flawed attempt at centralization. As one analyst has observed,

> The National Security Act of 1947 was a compromise between those who favored a centralized unified military force and those who wanted to continue the previous decentralized structure, and between those who wanted a single chief of staff system and those who did not. The services were not really unified, but the principle of unification was established.[6]

Such a system could hardly fail to encourage inter-service rivalry and inevitably hindered the efficient formulation and implementation of coherent policies.

The weaknesses were compounded by the system created for military advice. The principal military advisers to the President and the Secretary of Defense were the members of the Joint Chiefs of Staff (JCS). The JCS include the Chiefs of Staff of the Army and Air Force, and the Chief of Naval Operations. In 1952 the Commandant of the Marine Corps was allowed to participate on matters affecting the marines. In practice this meant involvement on most issues and in 1978 the position was regularized and the Commandant was made a full member of the JCS. The other member of the JCS is the Chairman. The post of chairman was created in 1949, but the role of the incumbent was carefully circumscribed: 'although he was given precedence over all other officers of the armed services, he was prohibited from exercising military command over the JCS or any of the military services.'[7]

Inevitably problems developed with a system in which the powers of both the Secretary of Defense and the Chairman of the JCS were limited. The Secretary faced a formidable task in attempting to integrate the separate services, and the first incumbent, James Forrestal – who had helped draw up the specifications for the post – bemoaned the fact that his job 'combined too much coordination and too little control, and too much responsibility with too little power'.[8] Forrestal committed suicide soon after his resignation. Subsequently there was some tampering with the system, but little was done to augment the power of the Secretary of Defense until the late 1950s. The DOD Reorganization Act of 1958 strengthened the position of the Secretary of Defense and enabled him to take measures to bring about 'more effective, efficient and economical administration and operation and to eliminate duplication'.[9]

If the 1958 legislation strengthened the position of the Secretary of Defense, it did little to enhance the position of either the Chairman of the Joint Chiefs of Staff or the JCS as a body. Although the Joint Chiefs were permitted to have up to 400 people working for them, they were effectively removed from the operational chain of command. A new structure was established which created unified commands for specific geographical areas such as the Pacific under the control of four star commanders or CINCs (e.g. CINPAC). In addition, the Act acknowledged the continued importance of specified commands, such as Strategic Air Command, which were functionally rather than geographically based. Although a directive from Secretary of Defense McElroy in 1958 made clear that orders to the CINCs would be transmitted through the JCS, the JCS had no power to originate orders of its own and consequently acted as no more than an agent for the civilian leadership. At best, therefore, the JCS role has been one of coordination and supervision. Furthermore, the members and the chairman have not only lacked real power but have had to fulfil a dual function in that they have been expected, on the one hand, to act as neutral arbiters and, on the other, as service chiefs.

Inevitably this system has been deemed unsatisfactory and provoked many demands for reform of the system. Critics have argued convincingly that the fundamental problem with the DOD structure is that organizationally powerful services are responsible for designing, training and equipping the forces, while weak joint institutions are responsible for setting overall defence budget priorities (OSD), planning their use (the JCS) and actually commanding them (the CINCs of the combat commands).[10]

The implication of all this is that although there has been a trend towards centralization within the Defense Department – a trend which has been most evident in the growth of the Office of Secretary of Defense (OSD) – the defence policy making system has remained fragmented and highly competitive. Yet this is not entirely surprising, as it accords with a broader political structure based on separate institutions sharing powers. The President is Commander-in-Chief but Congress retains the power to declare war. Congress also has the authority 'to raise and support armies' and 'to make rules for the regulation of the forces'. Furthermore, the presidential appointments of key officials are subject to the advice and consent of the Senate. Consequently, the congressional role in defence policy making is both significant and intrusive.

The defence policy making community in the United States, however, goes well beyond the Pentagon and Congress. It encompasses a large and diverse intelligence establishment. The Central Intelligence Agency was established in 1947 as an independent source of information for the President. Nevertheless, the military services continued to engage in information gathering and assessments of their own. In 1961 Robert McNamara attempted to end this by establishing the Defense Intelligence Agency which he hoped would provide intelligence appraisals which were relatively free of service bias. The performance of the DIA, however, like that of the CIA, has been mixed to say the least. Indeed, the American intelligence establishment has often underestimated or overestimated the Soviet threat. During the early years of the Cold War the tendency was towards underestimation and the United States was caught by surprise by several developments, including the Soviet explosion of an atomic bomb in 1949 and the launch of Sputnik in 1957. Following Sputnik, American intelligence overestimated the threat, creating fears about a 'missile gap' which never materialized. During the 1970s the CIA produced some judicious analyses of Soviet capabilities but was challenged by critics who claimed that the Agency had become overly complacent. This led in 1976 to the Team B episode when a group of outside analysts were given access to the information used by the agency and arrived at much more pessimistic conclusions than those of the professional analysts. In retrospect, it is clear that the Team B analysis exaggerated the Soviet threat. Although the exercise politicized the intelligence evaluation process, however, it had considerable impact on the public debate and contributed to the decline of US–Soviet détente. Even in the absence of outside intervention of this kind, of course, the intelligence process is not immune to distortions and mistakes. Nevertheless, it plays a key role in the threat assessments which are a crucial dimension of defence policy making.

Not all the assessment and analysis comes from within the intelligence community. Since the late 1940s there has been an enormous growth of what in Britain would be called quangos – research institutes set up to provide information and advice to the Defense Department or some of its constituent units. One of the earliest – and still one of the most important – of these institutes was the RAND Corporation which was established initially to undertake studies for the Air Force and which inculcated a systematic and rigorous approach to strategic analysis. Over the years RAND has had considerable influence. During the 1950s, for example, a RAND study by Albert Wohlstetter helped to establish the requirement that American strategic retaliatory capabilities have a high degree of invulnerability. The other services also have their think-tanks. The Center for Naval Analyses, for example, plays a large part in assessing the Soviet maritime threat as well as in developing American naval doctrine. In addition to these dedicated and semi-official 'think-tanks' there are research institutes which have a far wider scope than defence issues but nevertheless do important work on defence. Perhaps the most important of these is the Brookings Institution which, among other things, produces an annual assessment of the Administration's defence budget proposals with suggestions as to how the money might be spent more efficiently and effectively.[11] Brookings also produces other options studies which contribute significantly to the policy debate in Washington.

There has also been a vast growth in what are sometimes rather disparagingly referred to as beltway bandits. These are consultancy firms which undertake contracts for analyses of particular security problems. At worst these firms provide rationalizations for what one or other of the services want to do anyway. On occasions, however, these companies or particular individuals within them can have a considerable impact on the defence debate. The writings of Colin Gray, President of the National Institute for Public Policy, for example, have helped to shape the evolution of American nuclear strategy. Indeed, Gray provided part of the rationale for the increased emphasis on nuclear war-fighting that was evident in the strategic doctrine of both the Carter and the Reagan Administrations. Even where they are less obviously influential, the analyses that are done at the research institutes and consultancy firms are usually highly analytical and professional. Yet they become part of a defence debate in which parochial considerations often dominate. This is largely because of the policy making structure outlined above. A structure which is highly decentralized and fragmented encourages inter-service rivalry and a parochial rather than analytical approach to defence issues.

Inter-Service Rivalry

The way in which the United States defence establishment is structured not only makes coordination difficult, but encourages inter-service rivalry. In fact, such rivalry is a feature of most military establishments and may well be inescapable. There are several reasons for this. In the first place, the different responsibilities of individual services lead almost inexorably to differing views of what is important in military planning. There is nothing contrived about this. On the contrary, it may be inherent in the existence of specialized organizations, each of which almost invariably develops its own values, its own view of the world and its own assessment of its place in this world. The members of the organization have a conformity of outlook which stems partly from shared experience. It is not surprising, therefore, that organizations often develop goals other than those for which they were originally established. Set up to serve society they become concerned with survival as an autonomous entity. The health of the organization is deemed to be synonymous with the good of the society. Competing organizations tend to be regarded as potential threats to well-being and resources, while technological innovation is considered not on its merits but in terms of its impact on the organization. This is not surprising. 'Military organizations are societies built around and upon the prevailing weapons systems.'[12] Changes in weapons, therefore, not only portend internal changes in these societies, but may also affect their status vis-à-vis the rival services.

A second factor encouraging inter-service rivalry is the inherent uncertainty of military planning. Threat assessment is far from being an exact science, and involves not only assessments of the adversary's capabilities but also estimates of intention – at both the strategic and tactical levels. It is natural and inevitable, therefore, that military organizations engaged in threat assessment focus on those capabilities of an adversary which are most relevant to their own roles and missions. Similarly, when attempting to predict the shape of future warfare each of the services tends to emphasize those aspects which help to magnify its own contribution.

This tendency is exacerbated by the fact that the military services are in competition for resources which are, more or less, scarce. The fewer the resources available the more intense is the rivalry likely to be, as each of the military services attempts to obtain its share of the pie. In periods of budgetary stringency the opportunity costs within defence become more obvious and there is a temptation, therefore, for each service not simply to extol its own virtues but also to denigrate the efficiency and effectiveness of its rivals.

This competition is not just about organizational survival but also about professionalism and career patterns. Careers are tied to the success of organizations: if the organization flourishes then many of those within it will also flourish. More important, however, the military services demand a degree of professionalism, loyalty and commitment which are rarely matched in civilian organizations. The judgments that are made may have to be put to the test in the most brutal way possible. Consequently, organizational loyalty and esprit de corps are essential. Those who demand more resources for their organization, therefore, are not simply concerned with self-promotion or bent on organizational imperialism. They are public servants who believe that the organization they serve is vital to national security – and that it should be funded at an appropriate level. Since judgments about what is or is not an appropriate level are inherently subjective, and each of the services believes that its own contribution to national security is decisive, competition over resources is unavoidable.

These considerations do much to explain inter-service rivalry in almost any nation. In the United States, however, this rivalry takes on a particular intensity because of the failure in the 1940s to establish a more centralized decision making structure. The peculiarities of the American political system also give inter-service rivalry a very distinctive flavour. Congress acts as what might be described as a court of appeal, so that if one of the services loses out in the competition within the executive branch it can always attempt to mobilize support within the legislature.

If inter-service rivalry is a natural and inevitable feature of defence decision making in the United States, this does not mean that it is without serious drawbacks. It encourages a disaggregated approach to military planning in which each of the services prepares to fight its own war with little reference to its rivals. This was perhaps most evident in the late 1940s, when the services were operating under severe financial constraints. Forrestal had to preside over a military establishment in which the Air Force was responding to the introduction of atomic weapons with an attempt to establish its total pre-eminence over the Army and Navy. By claiming that the next war would be won by strategic bombing alone, in effect the Air Force was attempting to relegate the Army and Navy to minor roles. Both the other services reacted strongly to this challenge, but the Air Force had succeeded in setting the terms of the debate. The cause of the Army was championed by Secretary of State George Marshall who contended that although a future war might start in the air it would 'end up in the mud and on the ground'. The strongest opposition to the Air Force, however, came from the United States Navy which recognized the importance of nuclear weapons. The Navy emphasized the utility of naval air power in interdicting enemy forces and attempted to establish a nuclear niche for itself through the development of the 'super-carrier'. The cancellation of the 'super-carrier' led to the 'revolt of the admirals' and an attempt by the Navy to cast doubt on the effectiveness of the new Air Force bomber, the B-36. Although the Navy presented its case in a series of congressional hearings, it was unable to halt the trend towards increased reliance on strategic air power. With the outbreak of the Korean War in June 1950, however, the budgetary constraints were loosened and both the Army and the Navy were able to go some way towards re-establishing their positions.

Inter-service rivalry has continued to bedevil the making of American defence policy. One of its consequences is that it encourages a parochial and highly selective attitude towards technology and new weapons developments. The development and deployment of new weapons systems invariably involves complex inter-relationships between 'technology, strategy, organization and politics'.[13] Nevertheless, it is possible to discern certain patterns. Perhaps most important, if new technologies offer to enhance existing roles and missions they will be exploited to the full and their effects exaggerated; if they jeopardize those roles and missions, they will either be neglected or encounter active opposition.

One of the best examples of organizational parochialism adversely affecting the introduction of new weapons systems concerns the Intercontinental Ballistic Missile (ICBM). One analyst has argued very persuasively that the United States could have developed an ICBM considerably earlier than it did had it not been for the Air Force emphasis on manned bombers and a 'cultural resistance' to the very idea of long range ballistic missiles.[14] Up until 1954 the Air Force stance towards ballistic missiles was one of 'neglect and indifference' – an attitude which resulted in insufficient funds for research and development.[15] The meagre results from what limited research took place were then used to claim that ballistic missile technology was simply not feasible. At the same time, the Air Force was extremely resistant to the development of ballistic missiles by any of the other services. As Beard has pointed out, 'the Air Force approach to long range guided missiles had a dual nature – missiles were downplayed within the Air Force, while they were urged over competing projects of other services.'[16] Indeed, one of the great victories for the Air Force was achieved in March 1950 when it was given exclusive responsibility for long range guided missiles and responsibility for tactical missiles.

If the other services had been effectively excluded from the long range missile business, they were determined to remain involved with tactical missiles. This highlights another consequence of inter-service rivalry – it encourages duplication. Each of the services attempts to obtain the funding to develop its own version of new weapons systems. This was apparent during the 1950s as the Air Force on the one side and the Army and Navy on the other developed Intermediate Range Ballistic Missiles. This particular battle led to the Thor–Jupiter Controversy and was once again won by the Air Force.

If the Air Force was successful in establishing itself in a dominant position during the late 1940s and the 1950s the other services were not totally out-manoeuvred. Both engaged in defensive responses designed to ensure that the political, bureaucratic and budgetary superiority of the Air Force did not become overwhelming. Naval concerns about the dominance of the Air Force in the period after the Second World War were a major factor both encouraging and facilitating the demands of middle ranking officers that the Navy develop a capacity for airborne nuclear strikes, and it was able to do this despite losing the early battles over the 'super-carrier'.[17] In some ways the Army was even more innovative. After it has lost the battles over Intermediate Range Ballistic Missiles in the later 1950s it placed an increasing emphasis on the development of anti-ballistic missiles. Not only did it establish close links with Bell Laboratories, but it mobilized sufficient support in Congress to place the ABM issue on the agenda and elicit a deployment decision from Secretary of Defense Robert McNamara in 1967 which ran counter to McNamara's own judgment about the desirability of the system.[18]

Even though McNamara was a strong Secretary of Defense committed to a more rational allocation of resources within the defence budget, he was not impervious to the effects of inter-service rivalry. The promulgation of McNamara in the early 1960s of a counter-force strategy and doctrine not only reflected the influence of the Air Force but enabled Strategic Air Command to demand ever-increasing resources for implementation of the strategy, thereby offsetting the Army's augmentation of its limited war capabilities as part of flexible response. As McNamara consolidated his position, however, he was able to take steps to rein in the Air Force. The growing emphasis on 'assured destruction', at least at the declaratory level, represented an attempt to establish a handle for planning which would keep the Air Force under control. If McNamara was able to impose a ceiling on missile deployments in the late 1960s, however, he did not succeed completely in bridling the Air Force. Nor did he succeed in moving American strategy away from counter-force. Despite the shift to assured destruction at the declaratory level, there has been a continuing emphasis on counter-force at the level of operational targeting. Moreover, during the

1970s and 1980s American nuclear strategy was increasingly refined in directions that the Air Force desired. The Schlesinger Doctrine based on 'essential equivalence' and 'selective nuclear options', the Carter Administration's commitment to a countervailing strategy and the Reagan Administration's attachment to 'prevailing' in a protracted nuclear war, were all much more favourable to the Air Force than an emphasis on 'assured destruction'.

The importance of inter-service rivalry, therefore, is difficult to exaggerate. Although much of the defence debate is cast in terms of meeting the threat from the Soviet Union, in fact the military services are often more concerned with the threats they pose to each other. Although there has been some tempering of the competition throughout the post-war period, things have not changed a great deal since the 1940s. The selective and discriminating approach to technology mentioned above has not disappeared. During the 1970s, for example, there was no great enthusiasm by the Air Force for the cruise missile because it was not central to Air Force roles and missions. In so far as cruise was a possible substitute for a new manned bomber it was in fact seen as a threat. The Navy was somewhat more enthusiastic about the cruise missile as it offered opportunities to extend naval activities. In the event, of course, both services ended up deploying large numbers of cruise missiles, although this was of far less significance to the Air Force than the fact that under the Reagan Administration it obtained the new manned bomber, the B-1, it so desperately wanted.

Somewhat paradoxically, alongside this highly selective approach to new weapon systems at the nuclear level there has developed what one critic has termed 'a culture of procurement' in which technological sophistication is deemed to be of paramount importance at the conventional level.[19] Military planners have opted for increasingly costly weapons systems in which sophistication has almost become an end in itself. Furthermore, the sophistication option is self-perpetuating. As one commentator has noted, 'In conventional weapons, American planners keep pushing at the frontiers of technological complexity – and then complain that since we are falling further and further behind the Soviet Union in numbers, we must push the frontier further still.'[20] Indeed, there is an interesting discrepancy between American weapons acquisition practices and American threat assessments. When it comes to acquisition the emphasis is on quality; when it comes to assessing the military balance the emphasis is on quantity. The problem is that while the Soviet numerical advantage is used to justify increasing technological sophistication in the United States arsenal, the resulting weapons often fail to perform to the standard required in combat.

The American Navy has its own variant of the procurement culture. This is evident in the goal of a 600-ship Navy and the emphasis on large surface ships, in particular the Carrier Battle Groups. Although a loose coalition of analysts, Congressmen and military officers has developed arguments in favour of military reform, including the procurement of smaller carriers, the Navy remains wedded to its traditional emphasis. Indeed, with a vigorous Navy Secretary, John Lehman, and an equally vigorous Chief of Naval Operations, Admiral Watkins, the Navy in the early and mid 1980s developed the 'forward strategy'. In the event of conventional hostilities with the Soviet Union in Europe, SSBNs would be regarded as a legitimate target for anti-submarine warfare operations. In addition, the Navy would mount offensive operations against the Kola Peninsula. One critic has argued very persuasively that, to be effective and to enable the Navy to fulfil other assignments, such a strategy would require not the projected 15 to 20 carrier battle groups which would cost 90 billion dollars over and above the funds already provided for naval procurement.[21] Despite such arguments and the general criticism that has been levelled at the maritime strategy the Navy has retained its commitment to offensive operations, seeing this as the best way to compete with the other services for funds.

Service parochialism and inter-service rivalry may be inevitable but has far-reaching operational consequences. Under most circumstances, inter-service cooperation is difficult to impose. Part of the problem with the American attempt to rescue the hostages in Iran in 1980 was that there was insufficient cooperation and coordination among the services involved. All the services wanted to participate to ensure a share of the credit if it was successful and to allow a distribution of the blame in the event that it was not. This ensured that the implementation of what was an inherently difficult operation was fundamentally flawed. Similar problems have been evident in other military operations including those such as Grenada where the opposition was relatively weak. Some critics contend that the Rapid Deployment Force created by the Carter Administration also suffers from these handicaps, not least because the Marines and the Army approach the issue of rapid deployment in fundamentally different ways. In the event that the force or, as it has become known, Central Command has to be used on a large scale these differences could prove extremely debilitating.

The other consequence of inter-service rivalry is that it leads to an overall posture which reflects the priorities of the individual services rather than an overall strategic design.

While strategies and weapons compete in the policy-making arena, the clash tends to be resolved through military bargains that produce mixes of military forces and hardware which are compatible with the basic views of all three military services but may represent contradictory elements in the overall strategic picture.[22]

Much of this bargaining process occurs during the annual budgetary cycle and it is this to which attention must now be given.

The Budgetary Process

The process whereby the American defence budget is formulated is enormously complex and protracted. It is drawn up within the executive branch and then sent to Congress for review and approval. The executive stage, which generally starts about 16 months before it is submitted to Congress, involves a relatively formalized process known as the Planning, Programming and Budgeting System which was introduced by Secretary of Defense Robert McNamara in 1961. The planning stage focuses on the Defense Guidance which comes from the OSD in close consultation with the JCS who produce an analysis known as the Joint Strategic Planning Document. This planning document is integrated both with the Presidential Directives and with the budgetary targets received from the Office of Management and Budget, in order to produce the Defense Guidance. As one commentary put it,

> The Defense Guidance is perhaps the most important document in the DOD budget process for it provides the basic rationale and justification for DOD's programs and budgets. It includes an assessment of the military threat to US interests; a statement of US defence policy and strategy; a general assessment of the military requirements for defending national interests; and an assessment of the material and financial resources available for defense programs in the future.[23]

The planning phase of the process usually lasts from August to January. The process then moves into the programming phase which generally takes another six months, during which the military services calculate the number and type of forces necessary to meet the requirements established within the Defense Guidance. Proposed programmes (Program Objective Memoranda) are reviewed by the Defense Resources Board which formalizes its decisions in Program Decision Memoranda which are organized by Major Force Program into a Five-Year Defense Plan.

The third phase generally begins in July and lasts until the following January when the budget is submitted to Congress. During this stage the financial requirements are worked out using assumptions about inflation provided by the Office of Management and Budget (OMB). The final element in this budgeting phase occurs when the proposals are sent from the DOD to be reviewed by the President and his advisers on fiscal policy. It is at this stage 'that broader political considerations become particularly important. During the early 1980s, for example, the defence budget was regarded in the White House as something which had considerable political importance. It was hoped that increased spending would symbolize the resurgence of American power and mark the end of what the Reagan Administration terms the 'decade of neglect'.

It is also at this stage that issues related to fiscal management enter the reckoning. This can generate considerable controversy over the size of the budget request to Congress. During the first Reagan Administration, for example, there were several disputes between Director of OMB David Stockman who, concerned about the overall federal deficit, wanted to scale down the budget request, and Secretary of Defense Weinberger who was reluctant to accept any cuts prior to the congressional budgetary process. President Reagan generally, but not invariably, supported his Secretary of Defense.

During the period the defence budget is being drawn up within the executive branch there are ample opportunities for the President to establish his own imprint and philosophy and make clear where defence comes in the hierarchy of national priorities. Jimmy Carter, for example, became deeply involved in the minutiae of military programmes, scrutinizing them in great detail in an attempt to find areas where savings could be made. Ronald Reagan's style has been very different. The President set the general tone of the Administration with statements about the need to restore American military strength and make the United States walk tall, but intruded very little into the detailed planning. This is not to downgrade the importance of the White House, however. The extent to which a President can intervene decisively was revealed by the Strategic Defense Initiative of 23 March 1983 in which President Reagan called upon the scientific community to develop the means of making nuclear weapons impotent and obsolete. This was essentially a top-down initiative, which took many of the President's leading advisers by surprise. With his 23 March and subsequent speeches and directives which led to the creation of a five-year research programme to assess the feasibility of defence against ICBMs the President changed the terms of reference of the strategic debate.

If the Strategic Defense Initiative highlights the power of the President in defence policy making, however, it also reveals the limits of his power. The President emphasized his desire for a leak-proof defence system which would defend the American people – a goal which was vigorously endorsed by Secretary of Defense Weinberger – but other members of the Administration have suggested that more modest defensive deployments which deny the Soviet Union its strategic objectives are the most that can reasonably be achieved. Yet others claim that SDI will be useful only in the protection of retaliatory capabilities. Defending missile silos is, of course, far less ambitious than the astrodome defence originally envisaged by President Reagan. The final shape of SDI, however, will not be decided by the Reagan Administration. Even though there has been pressure from within the Administration to opt for an early deployment, the key decisions will almost certainly be taken by Reagan's successors. Furthermore, Congress will play a crucial role and has already cut back significantly on President Reagan's budget requests for SDI funding. This reflects the fact that on defence as on so many other issues, although the executive branch proposes, Congress disposes. Once the annual defence budget has been dealt with by the White House the request goes from the executive branch to Congress where the process becomes, if anything, even more labyrinthine.

The congressional review of the defence budget goes through four major stages and typically involves a minimum of 22 points at which there are votes on the defence budget. The timetable was established by the Congressional Budget and Impoundment Control Act of 1974. This Act was designed in part to provide greater coherence in the budgetary process and enable Congress to have an overview of the federal budget rather than simply vote separately on the various components. It was an attempt to establish a degree of economic management at the macro level to complement congressional scrutiny of government programmes at the micro level. In order to achieve this, the first stage is to establish a target or ceiling for funding on all defence programmes. This is done through the First Concurrent Budget resolution which sets targets for both budget authority and outlays.

The next stage is the authorization process which provides 'the legislative authority to establish or maintain a Government program or agency'.[24] Authorization bills 'define the scope of programs and authorize funding levels', but do not create budget authority.[25] The authorization bills are reported out by the Committees on Armed Services in both the House of Representatives and the Senate. These committees authorize the Pentagon's spending for research development and procurement, construction of facilities and personnel levels, and are therefore, of immense importance. If the Armed Services

Committees give their support to a particular programme then it is likely to go ahead; conversely, if the committees do not like something then it is far less likely to proceed. In spite of their considerable power, however, the members of the Armed Services Committee are sometimes more concerned with 'real estate' than with national security. Primarily oriented towards their constituencies, they 'are less interested in questions of global strategy, than they are about ... force levels, military installations, and the distribution of defence contracts. Thus military policy is in many respects an extension of constituency politics.'[26] This is not to suggest that the committee members are completely parochial in their outlook. Democratic Senator Sam Nunn who became chairman of the Senate Committee on Armed Services in January 1987 had been a member of the committee since the early 1970s and established himself as a considerable authority on defence issues. Nunn had clear-cut views on many strategic issues and could well succeed in giving the committee a broader perspective. Indeed, in the early months of 1987 Nunn's support for the narrow interpretation of the ABM Treaty was an important constraint on the Reagan Administration which wanted to move towards a more permissive interpretation in order to facilitate SDI. As well as dealing with major strategic issues such as SDI and other new weapons programmes, however, the members of the committee also have to deal with more mundane matters which have considerable implications for their constituencies.

The Armed Services Committees, while they scrutinize and authorize programmes do not provide budget authority. That comes from bills reported by the Appropriations Committees and in particular their Defense and Military Construction Subcommittees. There are five regular appropriation bills related to defence, the most important of which is the annual DOD Appropriation Bill which covers about 96 per cent of the total budget of the Defense Department. In recent years, however, the Congress has not always decided on appropriations before the next fiscal year and stop-gap budget authority has been provided through a continuing resolution.

An additional complication is that the House and Senate clear different versions of the authorizations and appropriations legislation. Consequently, there is a need for Conference Committees to reconcile the differences. During the first Reagan Administration and the first two years of the second term this process took on very considerable importance as the Republican-controlled Senate was generally more sympathetic than the Democratic-controlled House towards the President's requests. Consequently, the work of the Conference

Committees involved a difficult process of compromise and trade-offs before final agreement could be reached.

In theory, the annual budgetary process is completed before the end of the fiscal year by a second concurrent budget resolution which establishes a binding ceiling on total federal budget authority and outlays. In practice, Congress has tended to use the budget levels in the first concurrent budget resolution and simply mandated that they become binding at the beginning of the fiscal year. The importance of budgetary ceilings has been enhanced by the passage of the Gramm-Rudman-Hollings Amendment which mandates a balanced budget and demands automatic reductions unless certain interim targets are reached.

Few descriptions of the budgetary process can avoid seeming somewhat dry and sterile. Yet the budgetary process is at the vortex of political pressure. It is often suggested that politics is about who gets what, when and how. The budgetary cycle provides the institutionalized procedures for determining this. Indeed, the planning, programming budgetary system is highly politicized at every stage. The executive branch stages are dominated by the politics of inter-service rivalry and by White House politics. In the legislative stage political considerations are even more wide-ranging. The concerns of many Congressmen with obtaining contracts which will benefit their constituency has already been mentioned. Yet defence issues go beyond 'pork barrel' politics and involve ideological or coalition politics. Defence debates within Congress can be understood in large part in terms of ideological divisions between liberal members of both parties who are generally more critical of defence spending, and conservatives who tend to be more supportive of military programmes. The task for the President and Secretary of Defense is to mobilize a winning coalition in support of the programmes they value more highly. During its first term, for example, the Reagan Administration spent considerable time and energy in an attempt to obtain congressional funding for the deployment of a hundred MX missiles. Because of concerns over the vulnerability and the basing mode of the MX, however, Congress appropriated the funding for far fewer than the President desired. This congressional willingness to challenge the executive branch on major procurement items can be traced back to the late 1960s when there was a bitter struggle over the deployment of the anti-ballistic missile. Until then Congress had been extremely deferential in its treatment of executive branch budget requests.

If the MX debate in the first half of the 1980s highlighted the continuing reassertiveness of Congress on defence issues, it is somewhat atypical. Most of the items in the defence budget are approved with little or no argument, and the general role of Congress is to make changes at the margin. More often than not this means trimming back the defence budget, although in fiscal years 1980 and 1981 Congress actually voted more money than the President had requested. Since then the tendency has been to cut back on the President's request. In view of the scale of the defence budget this obviously involves large amounts of money and may have particular significance for specific programmes. Nevertheless, it should not be exaggerated. For the ten fiscal years from 1976 to 1985 Congress did not change the President's budget request in either direction by more than 8 per cent.[27]

For all this, the budgetary process is not without serious deficiencies. Perhaps most important of all,

> the defence budget is an inexact reflection of national security policy because the budget process does not guarantee a direct relationship between avowed defence policy and military spending. The elements that help shape the annual defence budget do not exert an equal measure of influence, nor is their influence felt in consistent proportions from year to year. Judgments made by the President about defence policy, military strategy, and other more global political issues must be reconciled with the domestic political, economic and bureaucratic context in which the budget is ultimately formulated.[28]

Particularly troublesome is the lack of synchronization between the budgetary process and the weapons acquisition process. Because of the long lead time between conception and deployment of weapons systems there is considerable inflexibility in the system. Furthermore, the nature of the procurement process encourages the growth of vested interests which in turn makes reassessment or cancellation extremely difficult. Indeed, many critics have condemned what has been described as the 'iron triangle' of the armed services, defence contractors and Congressmen concerned primarily with constituency interests. In the mid 1980s as Congress became more concerned with reducing the budget deficit, there were constant calls for cuts in defence spending. Members of Congress who were strongly in favour of this, however, become less enthusiastic when the cuts mean cancelled contracts or closure of military installations in their states or districts. One commentator has suggested that something like 300 unnecessary bases are kept open because they are located in areas represented by influential members of Congress.[29] Even liberal Senators who are generally very critical of the defence budget have voted in favour of the B-1 bomber because it brought lucrative contracts to their state. In other words, the power of vested interests makes it difficult to introduce greater rationality into defence policy making.

The other problem with the system is that it is difficult to provide a consistent approach. Defence spending in the United States tends to go through periods of plenty and periods of scarcity. There have been major increases in defence spending on several occasions – following the Korean War, the early 1960s under Kennedy, the last years of the Carter Administration and Reagan's first term – but these have been followed by cutbacks – the Eisenhower emphasis on massive retaliation and the 'peace dividend' of the early 1970s as the United States disengaged from Vietnam. In the late 1980s it appeared that the pattern was repeating itself once again, as concerns over the budget deficit became increasingly insistent. A more consistent policy of steady growth would be far more beneficial than a peaks and troughs approach. The problem with the troughs is that they make it enormously difficult for the United States to maintain its security commitments; the problem with the peaks is that they encourage the military to engage in forward planning on assumptions about continued growth in defence expenditure which are far too optimistic. They also help to create a bloated defence establishment in which considerable resources are wasted. Despite the Reagan Administration's increases in defence expenditure some critics contend that there have not been commensurate improvements in combat capabilities which are decisive when it comes to the actual use of American military power in crises. Indeed, it is to decisions about the use of force that attention must now be given.

The Use of Force

Defence policy making involves not just the development of military power but also its use. Decisions about the use of force by the United States tend to be made at the highest level, and by a relatively small number of policy makers and advisers. Despite differences of decision making style from one Administration to the next the key decision maker on questions involving the possible use of force is almost invariably the President. In June 1950, for example, Truman's belief that the North Korean attack on South Korea was analogous to the totalitarian aggressions of the 1930s helped to determine the American response.[30] Although Truman met with his advisers and discussed the various options, the key to the decision was the President's belief that it was essential to stand up to aggression. Eisenhower was a far less activist President than Truman, but when it came to decisions which might involve the United States in hostilities, he too played a decisive role and acted as a powerful constraint on his Secretary of State, John Foster Dulles, who was less cautious. In 1954, for example, Eisenhower's reluctance to get involved directly in Indochina over-rode Dulles's concern with containing the communist threat. This is not to suggest that Eisenhower was totally averse to the use of force. Indeed, the Administration engaged in a sharp decisive intervention in Lebanon in 1958 and also began the planning for what proved to be the abortive Bay of Pigs operation which took place under Kennedy in 1961.

The quality of advice in the Kennedy Administration's decision to use Cuban *émigrés* in an attempt to overthrow Castro left a great deal to be desired. In large part the operation was based on wishful thinking about the likelihood of a popular uprising against the Cuban leader. Yet the optimistic assumptions that underlay the invasion were not seriously challenged by any of the President's advisers, partly because of the impact of 'groupthink'.[31] All the members of the advisory group surrounding the President valued their membership to such a degree that they felt it better to suppress doubts and conform to the dominant optimism rather than raise objections. The result was disastrous. The Bay of Pigs experience, however, proved a useful one for Kennedy and made him more aware of the need for greater care in thinking through proposals regarding the use of force. He also became sceptical about military advice. Both consequences were apparent in the Cuban missile crisis in 1962 when the President opted for a blockade of Cuba rather than an air-strike which would have killed Russians and might have provoked an impetuous response from Khrushchev.

If Kennedy had learned certain lessons about decision making in relation to the use of force, these were not heeded by his successor, Lyndon Johnson. Whereas Kennedy, during the missile crisis, actively sought advice and encouraged disagreements among his staff, Lyndon Johnson, in a series of decisions escalating the American involvement in Vietnam, did the opposite. Apart from the protests of George Ball, who was sometimes described as the President's tame dove, Johnson would not tolerate dissent and the decision making systems became very closed. Nor was it very different under Nixon, when decision making was dominated by the President and by his National Security Adviser, Henry Kissinger. Although Nixon and Kissinger were the major architects of Soviet–American détente they still tended to see develop-ments within the Third World within the framework of superpower rivalry and were obsessed with the need to maintain American credibility, in the face of the withdrawal from Vietnam. This concern sometimes led to an over-zealous approach which threatened to transform local and regional problems into East–West crises.

The use of force by Johnson and Nixon in Vietnam aroused enormous controversy and brought to the fore once again fundamental constitutional issues. Constitutionally, the power to declare war resides with Congress. The period since 1945, however, has been one in which the United States has fought large-scale wars in Korea and Vietnam as a result of decisions made exclusively within the executive branch. Although there was some protest over the failure to consult Congress over the intervention in Korea in 1950, it was the Vietnam War which provoked the most serious confrontation between the President and Congress, and led to a major effort to reassert congressional prerogatives. The most important manifestation of this was the War Powers Act of 1973 which set a 60-day limit to an American use of force unless Congress formally votes to extend it or to declare war. The legislation also made consultation with Congress mandatory whenever it was possible, and established certain reporting requirements. The congressional desire to avoid becoming entangled in local conflicts through a process of incremental decision making was also evident in 1975 when Congress cut off funds to help the anti-Soviet factions in the war in Angola.

Similar concerns were prevalent in the Carter Administration and the only use of force was the ill-fated attempt to rescue the American hostages in Iran. If Carter was philosophically opposed to the employment of American military capabilities, however, Ronald Reagan has been less inhibited. Although the Reagan Administration has used force successfully in Grenada and in a retaliatory strike against Libya, military involvement in the Lebanon was far less successful. The intervention in Lebanon also brought the President into conflict with Congress over the scope and applicability of the War Powers Act, with the President accepting the consultation and reporting requirements but reluctant to acknowledge congressional power to terminate the deployment of troops. Direct confrontation was avoided when, in the aftermath of the attack on the Marine base in Beirut, the Administration itself decided to withdraw.

Differences over the use of force are not confined to congressional–executive relations. During the 1980s the most important debate over military force has been within the Reagan Administration with Secretary of State George Shultz and Secretary of Defense Caspar Weinberger as the key figures. Shultz has demanded maximum flexibility in resorting to force in order to enhance the effectiveness of American diplomacy. Weinberger, in contrast, has argued that force should be employed only if certain conditions are met. In particular it should be used only if victory can be achieved and there is a strong probability that public and congressional opinion will be supportive.

In presenting what has been dubbed the Weinberger Doctrine, the Secretary of Defense has been influenced very clearly by the thinking of senior military officers concerned about a repetition of the Vietnam experience. The extent to which previous military advice has also been cautious is a matter of debate. On the one side, a major study of military advice in Cold War crises concluded that – with the exception of the Chief of Naval Operations who tended to be more belligerent in his approach than other members of the Joint Chiefs of Staff – it was not markedly different from that offered by civilian advisers to the President.[32] On the other side, however, is the argument that during critical episodes such as the Cuban missile crisis the military advisers to the President displayed little sensitivity to the demands of crisis management. Furthermore, once the United States was involved in hostilities, as in Vietnam, there were powerful demands from the military for the commitment of increasing resources and a loosening of political constraints on military operations.

The issue of military advice has become bound up with broader questions relating to the role of the military in politics. There has been a general acknowledgment that during the Cold War the apolitical officer paradigm which dominated prior to the Second World War has given way to the soldier-statesman concept based on an irreversible fusion between political and military affairs.[33] The extent to which the soldier-statesman model has become accepted can be seen in the fact that two of President Reagan's National Security Advisers (Bud McFarlane and Admiral Poindexter) were retired or serving officers, as well as in the prominent role played by other military officers on the NSC staff. Yet this trend towards 'fusionism' is not something which everyone finds comfortable. It has aroused criticism from those concerned about the impact on military institutions and from those worried about the effect on civilian policies.

> Military critics fear that a military policy-making role will politicize and divide the armed forces and directly involve them in partisan controversy; that the emphasis on non-military operational programs will undermine military expertise and preparedness; and that the close integration of the professional military with civilian society implicit in the soldier-statesman model will make it more difficult to sustain the military values, cohesion and morale thought to be essential to military effectiveness.[34]

On the other side are those concerned that the 'increased weight within the policy process of the military as an institution is likely to increase the weight of military considerations in high national policies'.[35] Although these concerns are understandable, the nature and intrusiveness of Soviet–American military competition make it difficult to maintain a clear demarcation line between political and military considerations. Furthermore, although there are dangers in the soldier-statesman model, it has the long-term virtue of making military officers more sensitive to the broader political and diplomatic requirements necessary for tasks such as crisis management. Ultimately the issue is one of organizational philosophy and training in which the aim must be to increase the sensitivities of the military establishment to the needs of civilian policy makers in the nuclear age, while still allowing military officers an opportunity to provide undiluted military advice whenever necessary. These questions about the appropriate role of the soldier are of continuing relevance. In the mid 1980s, however, the issue of organizational reform was of more immediate concern.

Reforming the Process

The defence policy making process established in 1947 has long been deemed unsatisfactory. In the mid 1980s, however, demands for reform became rather more insistent. There were several reasons for this, ranging from the conceptual and operational flaws revealed by American military actions in Lebanon and Grenada, through to the revelations about waste and duplication in the defence establishment. The result was that in 1986 serious, if still modest, attempts were made to reform the weapons acquisition and policy making process.

In response to widespread publicity given to revelations about the flagrant corruption and waste in procurement, the Reagan Administration set up a blue ribbon panel to investigate the problems of defence management and make recommendations as to how best they could be dealt with. In April 1986 the commission, under the chairmanship of David Packard, issued its final report which called for several reforms of both weapons acquisition and of the policy and planning process. One of the most important of these was a proposal to establish a new position of Under-Secretary of Defense for Acquisition. The Administration accepted this idea and subsequent legislation established the position of what was sometimes described as an 'acquisitions czar', who would exercise precedence over the service secretaries on weapons acquisition issues.

The other major reform of 1986 was the Goldwater–Nichols Department of Defense Reorganization Act which dealt with many aspects of Pentagon reorganization along the lines laid down by the

Packard Commission. Debate over this legislation focused on the issue of how much initiative and independence the individual military services should be given, with particular attention being paid to the role of the Joint Chiefs of Staff, and especially its Chairman. As the Packard Commission, and indeed several other reports had advocated, the Act increased the authority and responsibility of the Chairman to provide military advice to the President, the National Security Council and the Secretary of Defense. Although the Act recognized that the other JCS members had a continuing role in military assessment, planning and advice, certain duties were transferred from the JCS as a corporate body to the Chairman. The Chairman's position was further strengthened by allowing him a third two-year term and by the creation of the position of Vice-Chairman. An attempt was also made to clarify the chain of command between the President and the Commanders-in-Chief of the various commands, the CINCs. Under the new law the Chairman has responsibility to oversee the activities of the unified and specified commands while the CINCs themselves were given authority for those administration and support functions necessary to accomplish their missions. An attempt was also made to clarify the responsibility and the authority of the CINCs over their commands. In addition, the legislation included a scheme to promote joint training and joint duties, thereby, it was hoped, ensuring that high-ranking officers have at least some experience of the requirements of joint planning and operations.

How effective these reforms will be remains to be seen. The narrowness and parochialism of the individual services will not be easily overcome. Nevertheless, the legislation of 1986 goes at least some way towards tackling problems which can be traced back to the late 1940s but which have nevertheless become increasingly debilitating. The strengthening of the Chairman of the JCS in particular was a long overdue step and one which could prove extremely advantageous. The problems of the late 1980s and the 1990s, however, remain formidable. Furthermore, some of these problems are inherent not in the military organization but in the American political system. A system which encourages peaks and troughs in defence spending does not provide a particularly propitious environment for military planning. Furthermore, the congressional role is not always conducive to rational force planning. Not all the problems result from a fragmented political structure, however. Tasks such as the integration of force planning and arms control are intellectually as well as organizationally intractable. Indeed, it is hardly surprising that over 40 years after the national security apparatus was formed the problem of policy coordination remains immense. The reforms of the mid 1980s, however, seem likely to strengthen the prospects for efficient and effective management. In view of the structure established in 1947 as well as the idiosyncrasies of the American political system, this may be the most that can be achieved.

Notes

1 W. Schilling, P. Hammond and G. Snyder, *Strategy, Politics, and Defense Budgets* (New York, 1962), 7.
2 Caspar Weinberger, Secretary of Defense, *Annual Report to the Congress, Fiscal Year 1987*, 21.
3 Quoted in Schilling *et al.*, *Strategy, Politics, and Defense Budgets*, 9.
4 Quoted in S. L. Rearden, *The Evolution of American Strategic Doctrine*, SAIS Papers no. 4 (Boulder, CO, 1984).
5 See J. Buck, 'The establishment: an overview', in S. Sarkesian (ed.), *Presidential Leadership and National Security* (Boulder, CO, 1984), esp. 42–3.
6 *Ibid.*, 58.
7 *Ibid.*, 48.
8 Quoted in G. Hoxie, *Command Decision and the Presidency* (New York, 1977), 149.
9 Quoted in Buck, 'The establishment', 49.
10 R. Goldich, *Department of Defense Organization: Current Legislative Issues*, Congressional Research Service Issue Brief (16 January 1987), 4. Goldich provides an excellent summary of the arguments for and against reform.
11 See, for example, J. Epstein, *The 1987 Defense Budget* (Washington, DC, 1986).
12 E. Morison, quoted in E. Beard, *Developing the ICBM* (New York, 1976), 233.
13 Morison, *ibid.*, 4.
14 Morison, *ibid.*, 219.
15 Morison, *ibid.*, 8.
16 Morison, *ibid.*, 100.
17 V. Davis, 'The development of a capability to deliver nuclear weapons by carrier-based aircraft', in M. Halperin and A. Kanter (eds), *Readings in American Foreign Policy* (Boston, Mass., 1973), 261–74.
18 See M. Halperin, *Foreign Policy and Bureaucratic Politics* (Washington, DC, 1974).
19 J. Fallows, *National Defense* (New York, 1981), 57.
20 *Ibid.*, 60.
21 Epstein, *The 1987 Defense Budget*, 42.
22 D. Tarr, quoted in Beard, *Developing the ICBM*, 226–7.
23 R. Foelber, *A Defense Budget Primer*, Congressional Research Service Report no. 85–85 (2 April 1985), 30.
24 *Ibid.*, 39.
25 *Ibid.*
26 S. Patterson, R. Davidson and R. Ripley, quoted in D. Kozak, 'Defense decisionmaking in Congress: what every President needs to know', in Sarkesian, *Presidential Leadership*, 151.
27 See E. Collier, *The Power of the Purse in Foreign Policy*, Congressional Research Service Report no. 85–182 F (4 September 1985), 32–3.
28 A. Maroni, 'The defense budget', in Sarkesian, *Presidential Leadership*, 194.
29 L. Korb, 'The process and problems of linking policy and force structure through the defense budget process', in R. Harkavy and E. Kolodziej (eds), *American Security Policy and Policy-Making* (Lexington, Mass., 1980), 189.
30 See G. Paige, *The Korean Decision* (New York, 1968).
31 See I. Janis, *Victims of Groupthink* (Boston, Mass., 1973).
32 See R. Betts, *Soldiers, Statesmen and Cold War Crises* (Cambridge, Mass., 1977).

33 See J. Slater, 'Military officers and politics I', and J. Garrison, 'Military officers and politics II', in J. Reichart and S. Sturm (eds), *American Defense Policy*, 5th edn (Baltimore, Md, 1982), 749–67.

34 Slater, 'Military officers and politics I', 751–2.

35 *Ibid.*, 752.

4

The Soviet Union

ALAN WOOD

Each of the other countries treated in this volume is a member or supporter of the North Atlantic Treaty Organization. That organization was established in April 1949 specifically to counter what was seen to be a potential military threat to the West posed by the Soviet Union in the aftermath of the Second World War. In the cases of Britain, France, West Germany and the United States, therefore, we are dealing with military and political allies. In the case of the Soviet Union we are dealing not only with a state which is perceived to be a potential foe, but one whose entire historical, cultural, political and ideological background is to most people in the West alien, unfamiliar and to some extent inscrutable. In a much-quoted phrase Winston Churchill once described Russia as 'a riddle wrapped in a mystery inside an enigma'. Despite the well-publicized spirit of frankness or 'openness' (*glasnost*) in the public discussion and reporting of major issues in the USSR since Mikhail Gorbachev became General Secretary of the Soviet Communist Party in March 1985, there is still a great deal about the machinery of government and of policy making in the Soviet Union which remains obscure and arcane. Although this applies to other areas of the Soviet system, it is particularly true in the highly sensitive and secretive field of military and defence policy making. Despite highly sophisticated intelligence gathering operations using the most advanced technology and information gleaned from Russian *émigrés* or even once highly placed defectors to the West, it is nevertheless the case that large areas of ignorance remain about what goes on in the corridors of Soviet power. Even the very existence of the Defence Council – the most senior organ of state to be directly and exclusively involved in defence matters – was not officially acknowledged until the late 1970s, though it had been in operation since at least 1964, and even now Western analysts remain unclear as to its precise functions, composition and institutional relationship to other state and party organs.

With this caveat in mind it is possible, by taking known institutional, military, ideological and historical factors into consideration, to reach an informed understanding of how policies concerning the defence of the Soviet Union are formulated and implemented. Since the end of the Second World War the course of international relations has been dominated by the superpower rivalry between the Soviet Union and the United States, and their respective allies or clients organized into antagonistic military alliances. The origins of the East–West confrontation, however, go back much further into history even beyond the Russian Revolution of 1917 and are rooted in the ambiguity which has marked the relationship between Russia and Europe since the early eighteenth century. Any real understanding of current Soviet attitudes, policies and behaviour can only be attained by setting recent and contemporary structures, processes and objectives against the complex legacy of the past.

It is also vitally important to bear in mind the geographical context in which the Soviet Union operates. Eurocentric and Atlantic-oriented attitudes often cause Westerners to forget or overlook the Central Asian, Oriental and Pacific interests of the Soviet Union. Dramatic events such as the Soviet military intervention in Afghanistan in 1979, the shooting down of the Korean KAL007 airliner in the Far East in 1983 and sporadic clashes between Soviet and Chinese troops along their 4,000-mile-long frontier periodically, though fleetingly, capture the headlines of the Western press. But the multiplicity of the diplomatic, strategic and security interests of the Soviet Union from the Baltic and Black Seas to the Pacific and Arctic Oceans is of course a *permanent* preoccupation of the Soviet policy makers.

In analysing defence policy making in the USSR, therefore, it is essential not only to describe the institutional mechanisms involved, both political and military, but also to take account of the historical, ideological and 'geo-cultural' determinants at work.

Historical Background

It is axiomatic that military security has been a paramount concern of the highly centralized and authoritarian Russian state since the time of the Muscovite Tsardom in the sixteenth and seventeenth centuries. Although it may seem strange, even illogical, to modern Europeans, nevertheless it is true that the experience of the Mongol invasion and occupation of Russia from the thirteenth through to the fifteenth century, combined with simultaneous aggression on her territory from the West, has left a lasting scar on the Russian mind. It has led to the development of what has been described as a 'siege mentality', with images of Genghis Khan and the medieval Teutonic Knights becoming blurred with the recent reality of three major wars with Germany and/or Japan, and the possibility of further 'two-front' military confrontation in Europe and the Far East where Soviet forces are deployed in roughly equal proportions against such an eventuality.

Having shaken off the 'Mongol yoke' in the late fifteenth century Moscow swiftly consolidated her newly acquired sovereignty in European Russia and, despite continuing internal disorders, managed by superior military prowess and for largely commercial objectives to expand right across Siberia to the Pacific littoral and bring the vast continent of Northern Asia under her sway. The only power capable of halting Russia's *Drang nach Osten* was the well-organized Chinese Manchu Empire. The defence of these enormous Asian territories which were, in a sense, 'inherited' from the Mongols was a prime consideration for the authorities in Moscow and led to a vigorous programme of both voluntary and enforced migration and settlement in the region, in which military service personnel played a major role. Meanwhile, on her southern and western flanks Muscovy continued to be engaged in a series of military confrontations with the Ottoman Empire and Poland–Lithuania. Peter the Great's victory over Sweden in the Great Northern War (1700–21) for the first time established the Russian Empire as the major military power in northern and eastern Europe. The results of the Battle of Poltava (1709) and the Treaty of Nystadt (1721) secured for Russia a place in the forefront of European military, diplomatic and political history which she has occupied to the present day. The establishment, too, of a strong Russian naval presence in the Baltic also introduced a new factor into the configuration of international relations and provided the Empire with an extra military capacity. Further maritime gains were made by Catherine the Great (r. 1762–96), this time on the northern coast of the Black Sea and at the expense of the Turkish Porte, though the simultaneous incorporation of Poland into the Russian Empire did nothing to enhance the internal security or defence capabilities of Catherine's realm. However, Russia's continuing military strength was shown to best effect by her participation in the defeat of Napoleon in the wars of 1812–15. Bonaparte's retreat from Moscow, Alexander I's leading role in the formation of the Holy Alliance and Nicholas I's awesome reputation as the 'Gendarme' of post-Napoleonic Europe perpetuated the impression of the Empire's sustained military superiority and invincibility in central Europe. That myth was shattered in the Crimea (1853–6). The clay feet of the Russian Colossus crumbled at Sevastopol, and the country was to remain a second-rate military power for almost a century, that is, until the latter stages of the Second World War.

Before examining the consequences of her contribution to the Allies' victory in 1945, it is important to remember that the wartime alliance between the Soviet Union and the Western powers was in a sense an aberration, a deviation from the traditional pattern of their relationships since the 1917 Revolution and the Civil War. The military intervention from 1918 to 1921 of British, French, American and Japanese troops in support of counter-revolutionary forces intent on destroying the infant Soviet government made a deep psychological impression concerning the West's aggressive intentions vis-à-vis the Soviet Union, which subsequent attitudes and events have done nothing to dispel. Although the purely military input of the Allied intervention was rather limited, nevertheless the very fact that the armed forces of the capitalist powers had physically interfered in the internal affairs of the country (with which they were not technically at war) and that determined attempts had been made to thwart the policies of the new socialist government and (to quote Churchill once more) 'strangle Bolshevism in its cradle' was to leave a bitter legacy of suspicion and hostility towards the West from the earliest days of Soviet power.

The vulnerability of the Soviet Union in the face of the hostile 'capitalist encirclement' in the 1920s meant that early Bolshevik ideas about dismantling the imperialist armies and replacing them with a people's militia rapidly evaporated, and circumstances dictated that the victorious Red Army inherited the traditional military role of defending the country against internal and external enemies. Despite the prospect of having to take on single-handed the armed might of the capitalist powers, Lenin's New Economic Policy (1921–8) did very little to develop the country's military strength and resources. Only after Stalin defeated his political rivals and introduced the first five-year plan for the rapid industrialization of the economy in 1929 was a new sense of purpose and a determination to develop the military power necessary to defend 'socialism in one country' injected into official thinking. Military, as well as economic, considerations were very much in Stalin's mind when he declared in a famous statement, 'We are fifty to a hundred years behind the advanced countries. We must make good this distance in ten. Either we do it, or they will crush us.'[1]

Throughout the 1930s the building up of the country's industrial base went hand-in-hand with the strengthening of its military defences. The emphasis on heavy industry was seen to be a prerequisite for both economic and military power, and by the end of the decade what can be described as a powerful military-industrial complex had been successfully established. However, the military effectiveness of the Soviet Union's armed forces had been fatally undermined by Stalin's purge of the Red Army in 1937. Ever since the introduction of the system of 'dual command' in the Red Army during the Civil War under which each military officer was 'shadowed' by a political commissar, relations between the party and the professional military had been at least ambiguous. During the 1930s, however, there developed a growing identity of purpose between the Army and the party leadership which was shattered by the bloodletting of 1937 – this at a time when Stalin was faced with the possibility of a war on two fronts.[2] Armed clashes with Japan at the battles of Lake Khasan (1938) and Khalkhin-Gol (1939) in the Far East proved inconclusive, but the decapitation of the High Command and the near total destruction of the officer corps contributed to the ineffectual, almost disastrous, performance of the Soviet armed forces during the Winter War with Finland in 1939–40, and in the first months following the German invasion of 22 June 1941. It is not necessary in the present context to rehearse the course of the hostilities during what in Soviet usage is still called the Great Patriotic War (1941–5). Despite the eventual Allied victory over Nazi Germany, the results of the conflict for the USSR in economic and human terms were catastrophic and were not fully mitigated or assuaged by the country's newly acquired military and political control of Eastern Europe. Twenty million people dead, massive material devastation, countless towns and villages obliterated, industry in ruins – the sheer horror of this experience of total war left a deep trauma in the psyche of the Soviet people and the Soviet government which has never fully healed. The surprise – despite warnings – of Hitler's attack, the speed of the initial *Blitzkrieg* and the ensuing slaughter and destruction have served only to reinforce the Soviet Union's iron resolve never to be left vulnerable to similar military aggression, from whatever source, in future. It cannot be stated too strongly how much Soviet military thinking, foreign policy and defence strategy have been shaped, and are still conducted, in the light of the country's appalling suffering in the Second World War. Western alarm over 'the Soviet threat' and 'Soviet expansionism' are matched in the USSR by reciprocal fears of 'imperialist aggression' based on a centuries-long experience of Western hostility and dreadful memories of recent foreign occupation. In this respect the armed services, the Communist Party, the government and the civilian population are totally united. Ordinary Soviet citizens are not simply mouthing official platitudes when they speak in quasi-religious terms of their 'sacred duty' (*svyashchennyi dolg*) to defend the motherland (*rodina*).

Apart from the political division of Europe and the Soviet Union's domination of Eastern Europe, the end of the Second World War introduced a number of new factors into the defence policy making process. The wartime State Defence Committee was abolished, popular battle-heroes like Marshal Zhukov were demoted, disgraced, reassigned or, in some cases, arrested, and Stalin – in addition to his positions as General Secretary of the Party, head of government and Minister of Defence – now assumed the grandiloquent military title of Generalissimo. It is fair to say that until his death in 1953, defence policy making, like the making of all other policies in the Soviet Union, was Stalin's own personal prerogative. His rule was arbitrary and absolute. The 'Great Terror' of the 1930s had ensured that men of vision, great individuality or initiative had been removed and replaced by those of an intellectually lower calibre who could be relied on obsequiously to execute Stalin's policies (and in some cases his victims). It was a process which resulted in what one writer has described as the 'survival of the dullest'.[3] Stalin was the acknowledged authority and supreme decision maker on all subjects under the sun from ideology to architecture, from biology to ballistics. And in the latter sphere a significant new element had now entered into the calculation of the country's defence strategy and requirements. That element was of course the need to develop nuclear weapons in response to the United States' possession – and indeed actual use – of the atomic bomb during what had already turned into the preliminary stages of the Cold War. Soviet physicists such as I. V. Kurchatov and his team had in fact been in the forefront of nuclear research and rocket technology both before and during the war, but now a fresh sense of urgency crept in which resulted in the setting up of new scientific institutes and bureaucratic bodies whose task it was – as during the industrial drive of the 1930s – to catch up with and, if possible, overtake the West in this crucial area of the nation's defence. In August 1949, exactly four years after Hiroshima, the first Soviet atomic bomb was tested, and four years later in August 1953 the first thermonuclear bomb was exploded. The nuclear arms race had begun.[4]

The possession of nuclear weapons by both superpowers and the continuing ideological and military confrontation between East and West has undoubtedly been a dominating factor in international relations ever since, and the civil and military leaders of both sides have at all times been forced to take cognizance of the terrible destructive power of the new weapons. A recognition of this power totally to obliterate civilization has not, however, led to a reluctance on either side to develop even bigger and better weapons and more efficient means of delivering them. How much bigger and better these weapons

– nuclear and conventional – should be, how they should be deployed and with what military and/or political objectives in view, are of course central features of a country's defence strategy. In the case of the Soviet Union decisions on these and other defence-related issues are arrived at through a complex variety of institutional and extra-institutional procedures. Against the historical background outlined above, it is now necessary to turn to an examination of the political and military institutions actually involved in the defence policy making process.

The Communist Party

Since the death of Stalin removed the incubus of his personal dictatorship, the Soviet political system has developed a degree of institutional or bureaucratic pluralism of which one of the most obvious features is the simultaneous division, sharing and overlapping of functions between the party and the state apparatus. In this complex, symbiotic relationship it is clear that since the mid 1950s it is the Communist Party of the Soviet Union (CPSU) which has been and continues to be the most important and influential source of political power in the country.[5] In the preamble to the 1977 *Constitution of the USSR*, the Communist Party is acknowledged as the 'vanguard of all the people' (no longer simply the vanguard of the proletariat), and in article 6 its role and functions are defined as follows:

> The leading and guiding force of Soviet society and the nucleus of its political system, of all state organizations and public organizations, is the Communist Party of the Soviet Union ... The Communist Party, armed with Marxism-Leninism, determines the general perspectives of the development of society and the course of the home and foreign policy of the USSR, directs the great constructive work of the Soviet people and imports a planned, systematic and theoretically substantiated character to their struggle for the victory of communism.
>
> All party organizations shall function within the framework of the Constitution of the USSR.[6]

Among these 'party organizations', the most important are the Congress, the Central Committee, the Secretariat and, at the power apex, the Politburo. The Party itself consists of 20 million members out of a total population of 280 million (as of October 1986), that is, roughly 10 per cent of the eligible population, and still operates according to the Leninist principle of 'democratic centralism' whereby the lower bodies in the hierarchical structure of the Party are subordinated to the higher, and adherence to all aspects of party policy, once formulated, is incumbent on every member. Whereas the Party 'determines general perspectives' (that is, formulates policies), it is the state organizations which are formally charged with the task of implementing and executing those policies. However, in practice, particularly in the higher echelons, there is a blurring both of function and personnel, with senior party officials frequently holding government office. Stalin, Malenkov and Khrushchev all held both the top party and government posts, while Brezhnev, Andropov and Chernenko were each simultaneously party leader and also head of state. The party Politburo as at present constituted (1987) includes the Chairman of the Council of Ministers, the Minister of Foreign Affairs, the head of the Committee for State Security (KGB) and, as a non-voting member, the Minister of Defence. It is, therefore, inconceivable that there could be a major clash of interests between the Communist Party and the Soviet government.[7]

1. Congress

In theory the supreme party body is the Congress, which, according to its rules, meets once every five years. Despite their largely ritual aspects, the party congresses are regarded as the most important occasions in the Soviet political calendar, and are attended by an enormous preliminary propaganda build-up. During the week- to two-weeks-long meeting in the Kremlin, important decisions are (unanimously) approved which determine the domestic and foreign policies of the Soviet Union for the coming quinquennium. *Inter alia*, the projections for the forthcoming five-year economic plan are discussed and ratified, and, in so far as defence industry requirements form a major part of the overall plan, the Congress therefore has at least a formal role in considering and endorsing current defence policies. This responsibility is reinforced by Congress's acceptance of the General Secretary's report which includes a review of foreign policy, defence issues and the Party's response to the current state of international relations. In the past, Congress has also received a report from the current Minister of Defence who since 1973 has also been a member of the party Politburo. The most recent meeting of this body (at the time of writing) was the XXVIIth Party Congress which convened on 25 February 1986. All the major Soviet interest groups were represented among the 5,000-odd delegates, including the military and the scientific, technical and academic personnel, and white and blue collar workers in the defence industries. Among other things they heard Mikhail Gorbachev reiterating the peaceful nature of Soviet foreign policy and military doctrine which is 'unequivocally defensive'. At the same time he assured them that while pursuing vigorous initiatives to reduce the threat of war, prevent further escalation of the arms race, lower levels of military capability and ultimately disband all military alliances, nevertheless the Soviet Union 'will not settle for less' than its national security demanded in response to the 'attitudes and actions of the USA and its bloc partners'.[8]

Obviously Congress is too large and unwieldly a body to work out the fine detail of policy formulation, which is left in the hands of the permanent Secretariat and the Politburo. Both of these bodies are technically responsible to the party Central Committee, and the Central Committee membership is in turn selected by Congress. This process has traditionally been merely a rubber-stamping exercise, formally endorsing a list of pre-selected candidates. However, a major feature of the present leadership's policy of 'restructuring' (*perestroika*) and 'democratization' of the whole system of political and industrial management is the gradual introduction of 'genuine' elections, offering a choice of candidates to elective positions in a whole range of economic, government and party organizations.

2. The Central Committee

The Central Committee meets in plenary session not less than twice a year, and both in its membership and its functions is in a sense a microcosm of the quinquennial Congress. At its meetings it reconsiders party policy on a whole range of issues, addresses itself to current problems and approves annual economic plans. This is also the forum in which changes in senior party personnel – in particular Politburo members and party secretaries – are decided. Like Congress, Central Committee membership reflects the 'institutional pluralism' of the present-day Soviet political system and provides some indication of the relative strength of various lobbies and interest groups. At the XXVIIth Party Congress a Central Committee of 307 members was selected of which there were 22 high-ranking military officers (7 per cent); and out of 170 candidate (that is, non-voting) members, 12 held senior military rank (12.5 per cent). These included not only the then Minister of Defence (S. L. Sokolov) and the Chief of Staff of the armed services (S. F. Akhromeyev) but *all* the commanding officers of the various 'theatres of military operations' (TVDs) and the Commander-in-Chief of the Warsaw Pact (V. G. Kulikov) – an indication of the *political* importance of the senior military in the formal machinery of defence policy making.[9]

The decisions of the Central Committee do not have the force of law until presented to and ratified by the country's highest body of state, the Supreme Soviet, or else simultaneously announced by the Council of Ministers (see below). Such ratification is, however, usually automatic. Also automatic, in most cases, is the Central Committee's approval of the policies laid before it for consideration by the Politburo. In the past, however, the Committee has exercised some independent judgment – most notoriously in its refusal to endorse the majority recommendation of the Politburo (then called the Praesidium) that Khrushchev be dismissed from office in 1957.[10] At a very recent Central Committee plenum in June 1987 some extremely important decisions were taken in connection with Gorbachev's proposed radical reform of the economy, as well as the approval of new appointments to (and removals from) the Politburo. It is, however, interesting to note that during a press conference given after the meeting by one of the government's top economic advisers, Abel Aganbegyan, some Western commentators detected evidence of less than total approval by the Central Committee of the General Secretary's proposals – a further indication of the enormously powerful role played by the Central Committee which is no longer invariably bulldozed into meek acceptance of every policy proposal with which it is presented.[11] The party rules also state that between congresses the Central Committee may if necessary convene a nationwide Party Conference to discuss pressing matters of party policy. Such an extraordinary conference was announced to take place in June 1988, its delegates to be elected by secret ballot.

3. The Secretariat

Ever since Stalin became General Secretary of the Communist Party in 1922 (a position, incidentally, never held by Lenin) it is this office which has become the most powerful political position in the Soviet Union (and now one of the two most powerful political positions in the world). When Western media refer to the Soviet 'leader', they do not have in mind the head of the government (that is, Chairman of the Praesidium of the Council of Ministers), still less the head of state (that is, Chairman of the Praesidium of the Supreme Soviet), but the General Secretary of the CPSU. This is a reflection of the paramount importance of the party Secretariat in both the formulation and implementation of policies across the entire spectrum of decision making, both ideological and practical, internally and externally.

The Secretariat is technically the Secretariat of the Central Committee. The individual Secretaries (around a dozen in number) are appointed by the Central Committee, and each is in charge of one or more departments of the Central Committee with a specific area of responsibility and expertise. The Secretariat, based in Moscow, in effect 'runs' the party apparatus (*apparat*) throughout the rest of the country and its staff has appropriately been described as 'the Party's civil service'.[13] It is responsible for formulating policies, supervising the work of government and other public institutions, preparing agenda for senior party organs, recommending appointments to influential positions through the *nomenklatura* system both inside and outside the Party, planning legislation and providing information, intelligence and advice on the basis of which decisions are taken by higher bodies. The Secretariat administers over 20 Central Committee departments, most of them 'shadowing' a corresponding government ministry or ministries. There are, for instance, departments of agriculture, heavy industry, transport, science and education and so forth. There is, however, no single, separate department of defence which monitors the work of the Ministry of Defence. As far as defence policy making is concerned there are no less than three – and possibly four – Central Committee departments with responsibilities in this vital area. They are the Department of Defence Industries which is involved, obviously, in the planning, production and procurement of military weapons; the Department of Machine Construction which has similar interests in both conventional and nuclear weapons and delivery systems; the rather vaguely designated Department of Administrative Organs which deals, *inter alia*, with selection and appointment of senior military personnel; and the Main Political Administration of the Soviet Army and Navy, which is in charge of education, propaganda, ideological instruction and of ensuring the political awareness and preparedness of the entire armed services.

The Main Political Administration (established in 1918 to ensure and maintain the political reliability of the Red Army during the Civil War) is something of a curiosity in the Soviet political system in so far as it is both a party and a state body. That is to say, it is at the same time a department of the Party's Central Committee and also a directorate of the government's Ministry of Defence. It is not, however, strictly speaking, part of the Secretariat and is therefore directly responsible to the Central Committee (and through it to the Politburo) and to the Ministry of Defence. The staff of the Main Political Administration permeates the entire Soviet military and defence establishment from the ministry itself down to the basic units of the armed forces. It runs its own research and training institutes and the Lenin Military-Political Academy, and supervises all military publications. As both a party and a government agency this unique, hybrid body obviously has a highly influential role to play across the whole spectrum of military and defence issues. Similarly, the Central Committee Secretariat's departments of Defence Industries and Machine Construction are deeply involved in the work of the eight or nine ministries which are directly engaged in the production of military *matériel*. In this respect they are an integral part of the defence policy making process.

4. *The Politburo*

Without a shadow of doubt the pinnacle of the political power structure in the Soviet Union is occupied by the Political Bureau of the Central Committee of the CPSU – or Politburo.[14] This is the nerve centre of decision making in all major areas of domestic and foreign policy. To the uninitiated this may be a source of some confusion in so far as the Politburo, while being a party – and *not* a government – agency, in effect *governs* the Soviet Union; in other words it is the policies collectively agreed on and promulgated by the Politburo which ultimately determine every important aspect – economic, social, educational, cultural, legal and military – of life throughout the USSR. This, however, has not invariably been the case throughout its history. Founded, along with the Organizational Bureau (Orgburo) and Secretariat by the VIIIth Party Congress in 1919, its original full voting membership consisted of Lenin, Trotsky, Stalin, Kamenev and Krestinsky. After the collective leadership of the 1920s gave way to Stalin's personal dictatorship, the Politburo was effectively emasculated as a source of political initiative and its members degenerated into little more than Stalin's private entourage who rarely met together in formal session, particularly during Stalin's later years. That is not to suggest or imply that even behind the façade of totalitarianism various interest groups and political figures with their own clienteles did not lobby and manoeuvre for influence or preferential treatment. However, it was not until after Stalin's death that the Central Committee and the Politburo re-emerged as the major source and focus of political power in the Soviet Union.

The size of the Politburo has fluctuated over the years, but has recently hovered around the 20 to 25 mark, including both full (that is, voting) and candidate (non-voting) members, the former usually being in the majority. Until fairly recently nothing was known about the actual procedures and functioning of the Politburo, which were shrouded in secrecy. Our knowledge has, however, been improved following a revealing interview given by a Central Committee official, Valentin Falin, to an American newspaper in 1979,[15] and also since Andropov introduced the practice of publishing brief official communiqués about Politburo business. Although the information given is stripped down to its barest minimum, these bulletins do provide at least a modicum of information about the deliberations and current preoccupations of this most influential political body. (This cannot be said of similarly important bodies in other more 'democratic' systems: the proceedings of the British Cabinet, for instance, are not officially reported.) A perusal of these communiqués confirms that foreign policy and defence matters figure prominently in the Politburo's concerns. To take just one entirely random example, following a routine meeting on Thursday 2 April 1987 it was reported that the Politburo had (a) heard reports by Mikhail Gorbachev, Nikolai Ryzhkov and Eduard Shevardnadze on the result of talks with the British Prime Minister, Margaret Thatcher (it was noted among other things that there were still considerable 'divergencies in principle' between the two states, particularly in terms of reliance on nuclear weapons for national security); (b) discussed the results of a recent meeting of the Foreign Ministers' Committee of the Warsaw Treaty member states; (c) examined the progress of decontamination and reconstruction work at Chernobyl; (d) outlined a package of organizational, technical, economic and scientific measures to improve fundamentally the ecological situation around Lake Baikal in East Siberia; and (e) considered other questions of state construction, personnel policy and cooperation with newly independent countries.[16]

The Politburo holds its regular meetings every Thursday, though may convene more frequently if the urgency or nature of the business demands it. The members receive and discuss various reports prepared for it by the Secretariat, government bodies and other competent agents and officials. On occasion non-Politburo members are co-opted to attend when matters requiring their specialist knowledge or expertise are being considered. These may be, for instance, senior military personnel, leading scientists or academics. Under Brezhnev – and there is no reason to believe that practice has changed significantly under subsequent leaderships – each member was invited to express a view on the topic in hand; these were then summarized by the General Secretary, who chairs the meetings, and eventually a consensus opinion arrived at on the basis of which policy decisions were made. But precisely *how* the consensus is arrived at in the case of more contentious issues, how conflicting opinions are reconciled, what respective weight of authority attaches to the personal view of the General Secretary or that of the relevant specialist, whether the numerical majority view always prevails, etc., is not known. Rarely, however, if ever, – despite the technical distinction between voting and non-voting members – are differences resolved by a vote. In the case of a deadlock, the matter is referred back to the relevant party or government agency for further clarification, and is then reconsidered at the next meeting.

In the crucial area of defence, according to Falin '*all* questions of national security and foreign policy *must* be discussed and *decided* in the Politburo' (emphasis added).[17] It is clear that the military will have a role to play here, though in fact the only professional military officer to be a member of the Politburo is the Minister of Defence, currently Army General D. T. Yazov. In the past, Marshal Zhukov was briefly a member of Khrushchev's Praesidium (1956–7), but it was not until 1973 that those government officials most directly involved in national security and defence were brought into full membership – that is, Marshal Grechko (Minister of Defence), Andrei Gromyko (Minister of Foreign Affairs) and Yury Andropov (Chairman of the KGB). At the time of writing, Gromyko's successor, Eduard Shevardnadze, and the present head of the KGB, V. M. Chebrikov, are both full members, and the ex-Defence Minister, Sokolov, was a candidate member until he was removed in June 1987. His successor at the ministry, General Yazov, also replaced him as a candidate member of the Politburo. There are at present (1987) 14 full members of the Politburo of whom both the Foreign Minister and the Central Committee Secretary for the Defence Industries, L. N. Zaikov, are Gorbachev appointees (1985 and 1986 respectively). The elevation of three new 'Gorbachev men' to full membership at the June 1987 Central Committee plenum has further strengthened the reforming General Secretary's personal position in this all-powerful policy making body.

State and Government

Although the central government agencies described in this section are formally involved in the defence policy making process, the functions of the most senior bodies in this respect have been fairly described as 'symbolic and ratificatory'.[18] However, while this may be true of the Supreme Soviet, other agencies have a much more serious and substantial role to play, in particular the Defence and Defence Industry ministries and the country's top body dealing with national security, the Defence Council (*Soviet oborony*). Under the terms of the Constitution, 'the defence of the Socialist Motherland is one of the most important functions of the State' (which) 'ensures the security and defence capability of the country, and supplies the Armed Forces of the USSR with everything necessary for that purpose'.[19] The major state institutions responsible for discharging that responsibility are as follows.

1. The Supreme Soviet and its Praesidium

Article 108 of the Constitution describes the Supreme Soviet as 'the highest body of state authority in the USSR'.[20] It is the nearest thing to a Soviet parliament. However, it has been properly pointed out that its paramount legislative and executive authority does not mean that it enjoys paramount *political* authority, which is now constitutionally invested in the Communist Party. It is in any case too large an assembly and meets too infrequently to perform anything more than largely formal, almost ceremonial, duties in ratifying policies, decisions, appointments and plans already prepared and effectively decided by other party or government bodies. Frequently, for instance, the wording of official decrees and announcements of the Supreme Soviet is identical with the published reports of the proceedings of the Party Central Committee. This formal process of ratification by the Supreme Soviet is in a sense the Soviet equivalent of the monarch's signature on British Acts of Parliament. However, in so far as many deputies are simultaneously members of other bodies where policies are actually worked out, such as the departments of the party Central Committee or government ministries, then the members of the Supreme Soviet may be said to have a place in the decision making process both in theory and in practice.

The Supreme Soviet is a bi-cameral body consisting of the Soviet of the Union and the Soviet of the Nationalities, the latter representing the political-administrative national regions and republics of the USSR, and each containing 750 members. It meets for a few days at a time twice a year sitting in either separate or joint session. Decisions are invariably unanimous. A 39-member standing committee of the Supreme Soviet, called the Praesidium, is elected at the periodic joint sittings of the two chambers which is 'accountable to it for all its work and exercises the functions of the highest body of state authority of the USSR between sessions of the Supreme Soviet'.[21] The Chairman of the Praesidium performs the duties of head of state. Brezhnev, Andropov and Chernenko each combined this position with that of General Secretary of the CPSU, though Gorbachev has so far kept the two offices separate. The present Praesidium Chairman is the veteran ex-Foreign Minister Andrei Gromyko. Among its multifarious duties as spelled out in the Constitution, the Praesidium of the Supreme Soviet is officially responsible for ratifying or renouncing international treaties; the conferral of the highest military and diplomatic ranks; ordering military mobilization (general or partial); proclamation of a state of war in the event of attack on the USSR or in fulfilment of international treaty obligations; appointment and dismissal of the high command of the armed forces; and the formation and composition of the Defence Council of the USSR. From this list it is clear that the Praesidium is the body which bears full and formal responsibility for the most crucial aspects of the nation's security, even though it does not itself formulate the policies which it is constitutionally charged with implementing. The actual business of defence policy formulation in the highest reaches of the government apparatus is carried out by the Defence Council of the USSR which is formed by, and presumably responsible to, the Praesidium.

2. The Defence Council

Although the precise role, composition and accountability of the Defence Council was a matter of much speculation by Western observers during the 1970s, a somewhat clearer picture has recently emerged, although by no means are all its functions or even membership fully known, as indeed one might expect of such a highly placed body responsible for the most secret matters of national defence and security. The wording of the 1977 constitution has at least cleared up one ambiguity as to its status. It is clearly a state, and not a party, institution, although as elsewhere in the Soviet system, the overlapping membership of state and party bodies means, as explained above, that the Politburo and the Central Committee Secretariat, as well as the government and the armed services are represented on the Defence Council. Brezhnev, Andropov and Chernenko all held the position of chairman of the Defence Council, though whether this was technically by virtue of their position as General Secretary of the CPSU or Chairman of the Praesidium of the Supreme Soviet is unclear. Gorbachev, currently party leader, but not head of state, is at present chairman of the Defence Council, as was Brezhnev even before he became head of state in 1977. Other members almost certainly include the Minister of Defence, the Chief of Staff of the armed services, the Foreign Minister, the Chairman of the KGB, the Central Committee Secretary responsible for the defence industries and the Chairman of the Council of Ministers. Together with the General Secretary this means that at least five members of the Defence Council are also full members of the Politburo as at present constituted. Other senior military as well as party and government figures with specific responsibilities in defence or defence-related areas may also be Council members, and no doubt other outside experts may be called in to attend relevant meetings.

The Defence Council is really the nodal point of the whole network of military and defence planning in the Soviet Union and the co-ordinating centre of all military and administrative expertise and intelligence in this crucial area. Whereas overall political decisions, policy guidelines and objectives are laid down by the Politburo, in defence as in other matters, it is within the Defence Council and in the light of Politburo decisions that actual, concrete issues are discussed, resolved and articulated for practical implementation by the armed services, procurement agencies, defence industries and other competent bodies. And again, because of the overlapping personnel involved, it is hardly conceivable that the Politburo and the Defence Council could ever be at loggerheads over any issue of substance. Nor is the Council likely to be the arena for any serious conflict of interests between its civilian and military membership. Although the latter is more strongly represented – as one might expect – in the Defence Council than in the Politburo, the civilians, according to Falin, are in the majority. The Defence Council has within its purview the whole gamut of military and national security issues including the structure, organization, deployment and combat readiness of the armed forces; intelligence gathering operations; senior appointments; choice and acquisition of weapons systems; development of military doctrine and theory; and the provision of advice and/or instructions to Soviet representatives in international arms-control negotiations. In the event of a major war its role would no doubt be paramount in coordinating and conducting the entire national war effort: it would become, in effect, the Soviet war cabinet. The role of the Defence Council is, therefore, absolutely central to the whole defence decision making operation.[22] There are, however, other important government agencies to be considered.

3. *The Council of Ministers*

The Council of Ministers of the USSR is 'the highest executive and administrative body of state authority in the USSR',[23] that is, it is the country's government. It is formed, like the Defence Committee, by the Supreme Soviet to which it is directly accountable and to which it must regularly report. Its membership consists of the Chairman (often referred to as the Soviet Prime Minister), the First Vice-Chairmen and Vice-Chairmen, all government ministers and chairmen of the State Committees of the USSR. In addition, the chairmen of the Councils of Ministers of the fifteen Union Republics which make up the USSR are *ex officio* members. It is, therefore, a fairly large body which seldom meets in plenary session. On the other hand its Praesidium, or standing committee (consisting of the Chairman, First Vice-Chairmen and Vice-Chairmen), meets, like the Politburo, on a regular weekly basis. The Council of Ministers has an extremely wide range of responsibilities, as defined by the Constitution, in directing the overall economic, social and cultural development of the USSR. Through its many ministries, it is this body which in effect 'runs' or manages the Soviet Union and its decrees have the force of law. As far as defence matters are concerned, it is mainly through the Defence Industry ministries (as well as the Ministry of Defence itself), the Committee of State Security (KGB) and the Praesidium's Military-Industrial Commission that the Council of Ministers is involved in the country's national security. Article 131 (5) of the Constitution also states that it shall 'exercise general direction of the development of the Armed Forces of the USSR, and determine the annual contingent of citizens to be called up for active military service'. It should also be noted that whereas the Praesidium does not include the Minister of Defence or any professional military personnel, nevertheless among the eleven Vice-Chairmen who sit on the Praesidium are the chairmen of the State Planning Committee (Gosplan), the State Committees for Science and Technology (GKNT), Material and Technical Supply (Gossnab) and the Military-Industrial Commission (VPK) – a fact which clearly reflects the Praesidium's strong interest in defence-related issues.

Of all these bodies, the most important in defence matters is the Military-Industrial Commission of the Praesidium of the Council of Ministers. As its title suggests, this is where the requirements of the Defence Ministry and the armed forces, and the ability of the defence industries to supply them are coordinated before its projections and reports are passed on to the Defence Council, and ultimately to the Politburo, for decision. The Military-Industrial Commission will obviously work in close collaboration with the relevant department in the Central Committee Secretariat. Although the Commission does not actually formulate defence policies, the technical information and specialized advice and intelligence – on, for instance, armaments research and development – contained in its reports must obviously constitute a vitally important input into the deliberations of the Defence Council and the decisions of the Politburo.

The Military-Industrial Commission will doubtless include in its membership the chiefs of the nine defence production ministries. These are usually identified as the ministries of Defence Industry, Aviation Industry, Electronics Industry, Radio Industry, Communications Equipment Industry, Shipbuilding Industry, Machine Construction, Medium Machine Construction and General Machine Construction – the last two having responsibility for nuclear weapons and missile production. While some of these also turn out products for the civilian sector, other apparently purely 'civilian' industrial ministries (for example, Machine Tool and Tool Building, Instrument Making, Automation Equipment and Control Systems) also produce finished goods or components with a direct or indirect military application. This is only one of the reasons why it has always been notoriously difficult to calculate exactly what proportion of industrial production, and ultimately of the whole national economy, goes on defence.[24]

What is certain, however, is that the defence budget forms an integral part of the overall five-year economic plan worked out by Gosplan, debated and approved by the Party Congress and promulgated by the Supreme Soviet. It is then the task of the various defence industry ministries (like all the other economic ministries) to translate the requirements of the plan into actual production in its hundreds of factories, design bureaux and enterprises. At the moment the whole of the Soviet economic system is undergoing a massive restructuring process which, among other things, envisages that large sectors of the economy will be forced to tender and compete for orders and be paid according to results which will depend to some extent on market forces, rather than relying on centrally planned or imposed government orders. While the consequences of this radical transformation of the traditional Stalinist command economy are problematical and the focus of intense speculation both in the West and in the Soviet Union, it is out of the question that the defence industries will cease to be under the direct control of the state. According to Aganbegyan in the interview referred to above, by the 1990s 'the share of the economy governed by direct state contracts with the enterprise will fall to about 25 to 30 per cent.' He then went on to emphasize that state contracts would cover mainly the defence sector and strategic sectors of the economy, including energy and communications.[25] The Council of Ministers and its agencies will therefore continue to act as the executive arm of the defence policy making process for the indefinite future.

Academic Institutions
So far we have dealt with the political, rather than military, organizations responsible for defence. Before turning to examine what role is played by the military itself, it is worth mentioning briefly that apart from the purely government and party organs just described, other civilian institutions and outside bodies also have a small, but appreciable, role to play in defence policy making particularly in the fields of weapons research, strategic analysis and risk and threat assessment.

The most important intelligence agency in the Soviet Union is, of course, the KGB, which, along with the military's own intelligence service (GRU – see below) has among its many other functions that of

ALAN WOOD

monitoring and gathering information on technical, scientific, military and political developments elsewhere in the world that will directly affect all kinds of Soviet security considerations. However, apart from these two crucial bodies whose operations are by their very nature cloaked in secrecy, other organizations and even individuals have an indirect role to play which may be increasing in importance. While the defence industries have their own research and development institutions, other forms of advanced research in science and technology which have an obvious military potential – and are thereby relevant to the nation's defence capabilities – are carried out in the universities, institutes of higher education and, more especially, the various branches and institutes of the prestigious Academy of Sciences of the USSR (ANSSSR). While such areas as nuclear physics, space research, computing and materials technology obviously have military implications and therefore impinge directly or indirectly on the nation's defence, so too is the work of such other academic bodies as the Institute of World Economy and International Relations (IMEMO) and the Institute for the Study of the USA and Canada (IUSAC) whose expert staff and research papers provide the most elevated political organs with valuable, up-to-date analyses of world-wide developments which may affect the security interests of the Soviet Union. The director of the last-named institute, Giorgy Arbatov, is known to be an influential figure in senior government and party circles, and other top academics and scientists are among the membership of major policy making bodies such as the party Central Committee. Those with relevant expertise who are not formally members of such bodies are frequently invited to attend meetings in a consultative capacity. The Armenian, Abel Aganbegyan, referred to above, was until recently Director of the Siberian branch of the Academy of Sciences' Institute of Economics and Organization of Industrial Production (IEiOPP) at Novosibirsk and is now one of the driving forces behind Gorbachev's economic reform programme. Other staff of the same institute, notably Academician Tatyana Zaskavskaya, have been responsible for compiling memoranda on the country's economic problems which have been considered at the very highest levels.[26] The programme of economic restructuring which has been partially influenced by their recommendations is of course not without its security implications in so far as the country's defence capabilities, and the policies which determine them, are directly linked to the strength and productive efficiency of the national economy as a whole.

The Military

It goes without saying that in the Soviet Union, as indeed in every other nation, the senior military has a crucial role to play in both the planning and, on the bottom line, the execution of the country's defence policy. Much has been written in the past about the tension or conflict of interests which may or may not exist between the political masters and the military leadership of the Soviet Union.[27] The degree of conflict has often been exaggerated and it is fair to say that the ultimate political objectives of both civilian and military leaderships are identical. The ubiquitous activities of the Central Committee's Main Political Administration of the Soviet Army and Navy helps to guarantee this situation, and the very high party membership rates among high-ranking officers tends to confirm it. Unquestionably, some leading military figures have been more influential, outspoken or even politically ambitious than others, but in the final analysis it is the overwhelmingly civilian Politburo of the Central Committee of the CPSU which decides policy, and periodic speculations in the West about the likelihood of a 'military coup in the Kremlin' seem at best to be simply interesting intellectual exercises. It would also be over-simplistic to think in terms of a bellicose and arms-hungry military ranged confrontationally against a more pacific and financially parsimonious political establishment. Before considering the present state of civil–military relations under Gorbachev, however, it is necessary to examine briefly the institutional and operational framework within which the military contributes to the policy making process.

1. The Ministry of Defence and the General Staff

The Ministry of Defence, accountable to the Council of Ministers, and through it to the Supreme Soviet, is the leading administrative institution with overall responsibility for the implementation of the Soviet Union's defence and military policy. Like the other ministries, it is a highly centralized bureaucratic agency based in Moscow, and controls the country's entire defence system from the training of conscript soldiers, through developing military theory to deploying the Soviet nuclear arsenal. Unlike other ministries, though, and unlike the Defence Ministries in the Western alliance, the Soviet Ministry of Defence is staffed entirely by uniformed, serving, professional military officers. A *partial* exception was the case of Marshal D. F. Ustinov, Minister of Defence from 1976 until his death in 1984, who, despite his military title, had spent almost his entire career as a bureaucrat in the

ALAN WOOD

defence industries, rather than as a professional soldier. He was, however, succeeded by a serving officer, the then Army General and a First Deputy Minister of Defence, S. L. Sokolov, who held this important post until relieved of his portfolio in June 1987 immediately after the surprise landing of a German light aircraft near Red Square. His replacement, General D.T. Yazov, is also a career military man who fought in the Second World War and was, until just before his promotion, Commander-in-Chief of the increasingly important Far Eastern Military District of the Soviet Union. The minister has three First Deputy Ministers, one of them Chief of the General Staff (see below) and another Commander-in-Chief of the Warsaw Pact Forces. The Main Military Council, or Collegium, of the ministry, consisting of its top officials and the five service chiefs, is responsible for supervising the general direction and development of the armed forces, recruitment, training (both military and political) and the integrated activities of all branches of the military machine.

While the Collegium is concerned largely with administration, overall *operational* matters are the responsibility of the General Staff. This is the central repository of military intelligence, information and planning, as well as the generator for the practical implementation of policies throughout the armed services in line with current defence policy requirements. Its ability to receive, store and evaluate information, and thence to trigger the appropriate active and operational responses throughout the system it controls has led to its being frequently referred to as not only the head, but also the 'brain' of the armed forces.[28] The General Staff has several different subsections, or directorates, with responsibility for specific areas. Among the most important of these is the Main Intelligence Directorate (GRU), the military's own intelligence gathering and evaluation agency. Along with intelligence collected by the rival organization, the KGB, concerning the military effectiveness, weapons development and also political disposition of potential enemies, the work of the GRU is obviously crucial in helping the relevant authorities to determine the country's defence needs, including weapons requirements. It is, therefore, a vital tributary to the mainstream of defence policy making.

The Main Operations Directorate (GOU), as its name suggests, is the organ responsible for the planning and practical implementation of military operations including training and deployment of troops, military and naval exercises and, in the final event, the conduct of actual war. For example, it is thought that the GOU was responsible for planning and directing the military intervention of Warsaw Pact troops in Czechoslovakia in 1968 – from the military point of view an efficiently and successfully conducted exercise. As soon as the initial force deployment was complete, operational command was handed over from the Warsaw Pact to the Soviet General Staff. One Western analyst has maintained that the Operations Directorate is the 'most important of the General Staff's suborgans', and suggests that it 'is now also concerned with developing targetting and war plans and helping to formulate general military policy.'[29] If this is the case, then the GOU is an extremely important factor not only in the implementation, but also in the formulation of defence policy and decision making as a whole.

Military doctrine, as opposed to strategy, is in the hands of the General Staff's Military-Scientific Directorate. Set up in 1962 in response to the enhanced role of nuclear rocketry in the country's defence, this organ is responsible for the development of military theory and the conceptual principles which determine how the nation's defence capabilities should be exercised. The work of these, and its other, directorates at the theoretical, operational and intelligence levels, as well as their expert technical knowledge of the various weapons systems available, means that the General Staff is without rival as the very best informed body on military and defence matters in the Soviet Union. There is so far no civilian organization or institution with equivalent or countervailing expertise, and to an almost exclusive degree, therefore, the other central policy making institutions such as the Defence Council and the Politburo must rely for much of their information on data supplied to them by the General Staff. As decisions can only be taken on the strength of available knowledge, the near-total monopoly of military-technical information enjoyed by the senior staff of the armed services obviously gives the military leadership an enormously powerful voice in the defence strategy of the Soviet Union. It is easy to see, for instance, how vital decisions on, say, arms control or an actual military initiative (for example, in Afghanistan) would have to be taken by the politicians in the Politburo on the basis of military intelligence gathered by the GRU, backed up by reports on combat readiness and forecasts of the military effectiveness of an operation prepared by the GOU. And it is of course possible that the military experts may not always put their political masters completely in the picture. A notorious example of this occurred during the SALT negotiations in the early 1970s when a senior military officer in the Soviet delegation asked the Americans not to divulge technical details of *Soviet* military capabilities to the Soviet civilian negotiators, on the grounds that such information was the military's own affair![30]

It is inevitable that in contributing to the defence policy making process there will be occasions when the chiefs of the armed services do not see eye to eye, and when inter-service rivalry manifests itself in seeking preferential treatment, enhanced funding or differing tactical approaches. In such circumstances, the General Staff, or in the event of deadlock, the Collegium, are the forums in which these disputes are reconciled and an agreed policy recommended to the higher authorities for decision. The General Staff is also the major channel of liaison and mediation between the country's military and political leaderships. Given all these important functions, not only does the crucial role of the General Staff as an institution become clear, but so too does the enormous influence enjoyed in the highest political circles by whoever is Chief of the General Staff. Between 1977 and 1984 this position was held by the forthright and outspoken Marshal N. V. Ogarkov, a man who is said to have 'dominated Soviet military politics', especially in the early 1980s.[31] The nature of his influence and the reasons for his dismissal are discussed below within the overall context of civil–military relations. First, however, it is appropriate at this point to see what military forces the General Staff actually has at its disposal.

2. The Armed Forces of the Soviet Union

The General Staff controls the five separate branches of the fighting services. These are: the Ground Forces ('the Army'), the Navy, the Air Force, the Air Defence Forces and the Strategic Rocket Forces. Each of them has its own Commander-in-Chief who is also a Deputy Minister of Defence.

The Ground Forces were traditionally regarded as the 'senior service', until the requirements of the thermonuclear missile age brought the Strategic Rocket Forces into existence and called into question the need to maintain massive conventional land forces. Khrushchev, in particular, downgraded the Ground Forces, both numerically and institutionally, depriving them of a separate command. They have since recouped their strategic importance and prestige, and as well as conventional weapons also now deploy their own short-range nuclear armoury under the immediate control of the combat branch known as the Rocket and Artillery Forces. There are, in addition, four other combat branches: the tank/armoured forces, air defence, motorized infantry and airborne troops. These are deployed throughout the 16 military districts of the Soviet Union, each with its own commanding officer, and in four Groups of Forces in Eastern and Central Europe.

In the past, the Navy has had its own separate ministry ('Admiralty'), but since 1953 has been subordinated, like the other services, to the unitary Ministry of Defence. Like the Ground Forces, too, it has five combat divisions: surface, submarine, coastal defence, naval aviation and naval infantry, and carries its own nuclear weapons in submarine and surface vessels and in naval aircraft. The Soviet Navy, under the now-retired Admiral Gorshkov, greatly expanded in size, technical sophistication and global coverage during the 1960s and 1970s, and shows no signs of its importance diminishing in the present coordinated defence strategy of the Soviet Union. There are four major fleets, the Black Sea, Baltic, Northern and Pacific, but its vessels are to be found throughout the oceans of the world.

The Air Forces of the Soviet Union are an independent service, but in the event of war would probably be operationally subordinate to other commands. Of its three main 'wings', Long Range Aviation, which comprises the Soviet Union's manned nuclear bombers, and Military Transport Aviation will come under the direct control of the Ministry of Defence, while Frontal (that is, Tactical) Aviation will come under the relevant Ground Force command, according to which theatre they are operating in, or over.

The second youngest of the services is the Air Defence Force (in Russian, literally, Anti-Air Defence) founded in 1948 to protect the country from all forms of aerial attack whether from aircraft, ground- or sea-, and more recently, space-launched missiles. Apart from the Defence Minister himself, it was, naturally, the Chief of the Air Defence Forces, Marshal A. I. Koldunov, who bore the brunt of the government's anger and embarrassment at the penetration of Soviet airspace by the young West German pilot Mathias Rust when he landed his Cessna light aircraft in the centre of Moscow at the end of May 1987. Before his dismissal, Koldunov had previously held the post for nine years, including the time when the Korean airliner was shot down over Sakhalin after violating Soviet airspace in 1983.

Finally, the most recent addition to the Soviet armed services are the Strategic Rocket Forces, founded in 1959, and created as part of the major rethinking that was going on in military doctrine and 'force posture' to take account of latest developments in missile technology and the need to gain strategic parity with the United States when the likelihood was that any further major war would quickly escalate into, or even begin as, one between opposing nuclear rocket systems. Although, as noted above, other branches of the armed services have their 'own' nuclear weapons, it is the Strategic Rocket Forces which maintain control of all the Soviet Union's medium-range and inter-continental ballistic missiles and their nuclear warheads (MRBMs and ICBMs). Operational command is vested in the Minister of Defence, though any decision to launch them would undoubtedly have to be taken at the very peak of political authority, by the Politburo.

Civil–Military Relations

Much has been written in the West, as noted elsewhere in this chapter, on the nature of the relationship between the political (especially the party) and military hierarchies in the Soviet Union. That relationship has been variously described as both 'adversarial' and 'symbiotic'. Although it is not the purpose here to review the enormous literature or rehearse the arguments on the subject, nevertheless a few general observations on the present state of play under Mikhail Gorbachev's administration are germane to the present discussion.

The belief that the political–military relationship is inherently antagonistic has been most forcefully put by Kolkowicz, thus: 'the relationship between the Communist Party and the Soviet military is essentially conflict-prone and thus presents a *perennial* threat to the political stability of the Soviet Union' (emphasis added).[32] Elsewhere he talks of the frustration felt by 'an up-to-date military machine that is forced to wear the horse-collar of ideological and political control'.[33] Such a view has been, in this writer's opinion, successfully challenged by other Western analysts who have argued that 'a more accurate assessment of the institutional values of the two entities suggests congruence, not conflict.'[34] There are sound historical, as well as ideological and conceptual grounds to support this conclusion. On only one occasion in modern history – the 'Decembrist' conspiracy of 1825 – has the Russian military, acting on its own, offered a political challenge to the civilian regime, and that of course ended in fiasco. That is not to say, of course, that there have never been major diferences of opinion or even confrontation between the military and the government, but these constitute the exception rather than the norm. In recent times, Khrushchev had a somewhat erratic relationship – as one would expect of his mercurial and idiosyncratic style – with the armed forces, sometimes relying on them for political support, sometimes antagonizing them through his impetuous foreign and domestic initiatives. Under Brezhnev's leadership a more stable pattern seems to have been established and the General Secretary enjoyed a particularly close relationship with his Minister of Defence, Marshal Grechko, whom he elevated to full membership of the Politburo in 1973, and Marshal Ustinov, who succeeded him in 1976. It was during the Brezhnev years that the Soviet Union attained rough military (including nuclear) parity with the United States and was able from this position of strength to enter into negotiations which led to the Strategic Arms Limitation and Mutual Balanced Force Reduction talks and the whole process of détente which culminated in the Helsinki accord on security and cooperation in Europe in 1975.

As mentioned earlier, a new subjective factor entered into Soviet military politics in 1977 with the appointment of N. V. Ogarkov as Chief of the General Staff and First Deputy Minister of Defence. Against the prevailing trend, Ogarkov openly clashed with his superior, Defence Minister Ustinov, publicly challenged national defence policies (particularly on détente and arms control) and unashamedly argued for increased spending on the military and for a greater role for the military both in routine and crisis decision making. A combination of these personal and policy factors was probably the reason for his sudden removal from office and reassignment to other duties in September 1984. He was not, however, disgraced; he still holds a senior appointment (Commanding Officer of the Western Theatre of Military Operations) and continues to be a full member of the Central Committee. An important book on military strategy by Ogarkov was also published in 1985, an indication that his opinions are still held in some respect by the civilian and military authorities (it could not have been published without the approval of the Party's Main Political Administration). In it he argued, basically, that the West is not to be trusted, and will only negotiate under pressure from a militarily powerful Soviet Union. From this it follows, he says, that 'the strengthening of the defence capabilities of the USSR is an objective, vital necessity.'[35] The use of the word 'strengthening' (rather than simply *maintaining*) defence capabilities would seem to indicate that Ogarkov, even from the wings, was still warning about a false sense of national security and advocating enhanced budgetary provision for the country's defence.

It is, therefore, possible that the major reason for his ouster was to prevent him from succeeding the already ailing Ustinov as Defence Minister. It has been suggested that the members of the Politburo, who were already limbering up for the post-Chernenko leadership succession, may not have relished the prospect of his assertive and obtrusive military presence as either Minister of Defence or potential member of the Politburo.[36] However, as late as summer 1986 some Western analysts were still speculating about the possibility of Ogarkov's recall to the centre of military policy as Minister of Defence on the departure (through death, retirement or, as it turned out, dismissal) of Marshal Sokolov.[37] In the event neither Ogarkov's nor any of the other names canvassed – Akhromeyev (Ogarkov's successor as Chief of General Staff), Kulikov (Commander-in-Chief, Warsaw Treaty Organization forces), Ivanovsky (Commander-in-Chief, Ground Forces) or the civilian Zaikov (Central Committee secretary for defence industries) – was selected, and the appointment of the lesser-known General Yazov may indeed be an indication of Gorbachev's determination to maintain a low profile for the military and to exclude an assertive, Ogarkov-like soldier from the most senior political circles.

Gorbachev's overall policy of increasing the country's economic efficiency and industrial productivity – as well as improving the quality of social amenities – has obvious ramifications for the Soviet Union's defence capabilities. Although defence industries have always received favoured treatment, nevertheless a general improvement in the country's total productive capacities – through management restructuring, quality control, cost-effectiveness, computerization, etc. – will have a positive knock-on effect on the military sector. In the long run, as Stalin realized full well, only a vigorous modern economy and a strong industrial base can sustain the country's perceived military requirements. Looked at from another point of view, an emphasis on improving consumer goods, housing, educational, medical and social facilities may be construed as detracting – or subtracting – from the defence allocation. There is little evidence, however, that Gorbachev's economic objectives, as set out in the *Guidelines for the Economic and Social Development of the USSR for 1986–1990 and for the Period ending in 2000*,[38] or the programme for the restructuring of the country's economic management adopted at the June 1987 meetings of the Central Committee and the Supreme Soviet, have been, or are likely to be, seriously challenged by a military leadership which feels badly done by in terms of budgetary provision. Both the Party and the government have reiterated their determination to 'ensure that the Soviet armed forces have at their disposal all the necessary means to perform their constitutional duty of reliably defending the socialist Fatherland'.[39]

In his keynote speech to the June 1987 plenum of the Central Committee – a speech which has been described as the most important statement by a Soviet leader since Khrushchev's denunciation of Stalin in 1956 – Gorbachev declared, 'on behalf of the Politburo and the Defence Council, I firmly state that there should be no doubt either in the Party or among the people about the ability of the armed forces of the USSR to defend the country.' At the same time, however, and in the aftermath of the aircraft in Red Square incident, he used the occasion to issue a sharp rebuke to the military for 'laxness of discipline, lack of due order, ... negligence, mismanagement and irresponsibility ... The violation of Soviet air space ... reminds us once more how strong and tenacious the negative trends exposed by the XXVIIth Party Congress turned out to be in our society, and even in the army.'[40] The sacking of the Defence Minister and the chief of the national Air Defence Forces has already been noted. It was followed soon after by an announcement that the officer specifically in charge of the capital's own air defences, Marshal Konstantinov, had been dismissed and several of his staff expelled from the Communist Party. They were accused of demoralizing their troops by bullying, idleness and corruption. Whether this represents, as the report suggests, 'further signs of a major shake-up in the Soviet military', remains to be seen.[41] Certainly none of the security services, including the civil militia and the KGB, is 'immune from the present purge of corrupt and incompetent officials. General Zhigilo, for instance, formerly head of the prestigious military engineering school in Kaliningrad, was recently fired, kicked out of the Party and pilloried in the press for embezzlement, ostentatious living and malfeasance in office.[42]

There may indeed be reservations in some military circles about Gorbachev's proposals for instance on disarmament and arms control (including his famous statement of 15 January 1986 advocating total abolition of nuclear weapons). The recent resumption of nuclear testing by the Soviet Union after an 18-month unilateral moratorium probably reflects the military's exasperation and fear that, in the absence of a reciprocal response from the United States, the country's security was being undermined. If this is the case, then it is another example of how the high command's monopoly of military-technical information and threat assessment can exert military pressure on the political decision makers. There is probably some private concern, too, about the way Gorbachev's economic priorities may adversely affect the military budget. None of this, however, indicates that there is any likelihood of a serious departure from the traditional pattern of military-political relations, with the politicians firmly in control. Ogarkov was something of a maverick and there was no sign of any institutional or even factional backing for his idiosyncratic opinions, nor did he openly challenge the Party's right to make the ultimate decisions. In any case, the new programme of the CPSU adopted at the XXVIIth Congress states unequivocally: 'The Communist Party's leadership over military development and the armed forces is the cornerstone for bolstering the defence of the socialist homeland. It is under the Party's guidance that the country's defence and security policy, and the military doctrine, which is purely defensive in nature, are formulated and implemented.'[43] Short of some dramatic unforeseen domestic crisis or a dangerous deterioration in East–West relations, it seems clear, therefore, that the military will remain the loyal and like-minded executant of the Party's will and continue to cooperate constructively through the established channels in shaping the country's defence policies.

Conclusion

An examination of the institutional mechanisms which make up these 'established channels' has been the main concern of this chapter. It remains now to consider some non-institutional factors and to draw some general conclusions.

To describe the system through which defence policy is made is not to identify what that policy actually consists of. However, it seems inappropriate not to consider briefly the 'what' as well as the 'how'. Ever since the 1917 Revolution Western observers have argued over the motives behind, and the objectives before, the Soviet Union's foreign, military and defence policies. Crudely put, the argument boils down to this: is the USSR principally motivated by the ideological goal of establishing world communism by exporting or encouraging revolutionary movements abroad, thereby posing a direct menace to other nations' peace and security ('the Soviet threat'); or has she always sought, and does she still seek, merely to guarantee the safety of her borders, the integrity of her national territory and sea-boards, and to protect herself and her allies from the threat of foreign aggression? There is no doubt that in ideological terms the CPSU is still dedicated to the ultimate triumph of international socialism – as reiterated in the new Party Programme. The concept of exporting revolution on the point of a bayonet, or the tip of a missile, has however long since gone by the board, and it is quite evident that it is the immediate national interests of the Soviet Union itself that is the number one priority, rather than the cause of world revolution. The shattering experience of the Second World War and the risk of nuclear obliteration make it unthinkable that the USSR would embark on any kind of military adventure where it did not feel that its own national security was at stake or seriously affected. In comparison with Western military forces around the world, Soviet troops had seen markedly less active combat since the Second World War until the military intervention in Afghanistan in 1979. Even that operation should be seen as an exercise in maintaining the security of what the government sees as a vulnerable segment of its southern frontier, rather than as part of a grand strategy of Soviet 'expansionism'.

This does not mean, however, that military doctrine excludes active preparation for fighting, and winning, war. Soviet strategists maintain in fact that it is the high level of Soviet military preparedness and defence readiness that has been the best guarantee of peace in Europe for the last forty years or more. During the 1960s there was even a debate among Soviet military theorists about the 'winnability' of an all-out nuclear conflict with the West.[44] More recently, the emphasis in both top political and military circles has been on preventing nuclear war and on reaching solid disarmament agreements with the United States, without of course in any way diminishing the nation's short- or long-term security. In the section of the Party Programme headed 'Main Goals and Directions of the International Policy of the CPSU', the 'provision of auspicious external conditions for the refinement of socialist society and for the advance to communism *in the USSR*, removal of the threat of world war, and achievement of universal. security and disarmament' is placed at the top of the list of priorities (emphasis added). Bottom of the list, significantly, is a clause on 'international solidarity with communist and revolutionary-democratic parties, with the international working-class movement and with the national-liberation struggle of the people'.[45]

How are these goals to be achieved? As noted in a previous section there is obviously a close correlation between defence capability and economic performance, though this does not mean that the Soviet Union's undoubted status as a military superpower implies that it is also an economic superpower. In fact, the high levels of military build-up during the 1970s were accompanied by a general slowing-down of the economy overall. Deficiencies in planning, pricing, management and distribution, poor quality control, lack of accountability, corruption, intra-sectoral rivalries over resource allocation and technological lag have all been identified in official Soviet sources as contributing to what has been described as a 'pre-crisis' economic situation in the mid 1980s. It is in an attempt to grapple with all these problems that the recent economic restructuring programme has been launched by Mikhail Gorbachev. While in no way wishing to lower the country's defences, a scaling down of military requirements arising from a satisfactory settlement on arms reductions would obviously greatly facilitate the fulfilment of the domestic social and economic programme. In his report to the XXVIIth Party Congress in 1986, Gorbachev specifically linked disarmament with economic benefits. Contrasting Soviet interests in this respect with those of the 'U.S. ruling class and the military-industrial complex', he declared, 'for them disarmament spells out a loss of profits and a political risk; for us it is a blessing in all respects, economically, politically and morally.'[46]

Any progress in this area is, however, unlikely to involve a major shift from the 'most favoured sector' status enjoyed by the Soviet military and the defence industries. No Soviet leadership would even contemplate any course of action which would jeopardize the country's ability to defend itself and its allies and diminish its military-based authority in its dealings with the United States, NATO or China or in protecting its interests wherever they were felt to be threatened. The interface between military doctrine (that is, setting out the theoretically substantiated political objectives of defence policies) and military science (the business of translating those objectives into practice – recruitment, training, deployment, fighting battles, etc.), the relationship between the politicians and the marshals, the balancing of priorities between competing sectors of the economy must all be understood in light of the country's historical vulnerability to attack, the fear of encirclement and the 'siege mentality' referred to above. The implicit warning in the title of Ogarkov's 1985 book, *History Teaches Vigilance*, is still an emotive integer in the calculations and equations of the Soviet civilian and military policy makers.

There is, however, an important professional and generational factor to be taken into consideration here. Although the system of 'military-patriotic education'[47] in the Soviet Union ensures that the horror and destruction of the Great Patriotic War are not forgotten, nevertheless a new generation of political leaders is in the process of taking over authority which had no direct, personal involvement in or experience of that conflict, except as young children, in contrast to the previous generation of leaders, the majority of whom had seen active service on one front or another. To what extent this will have a bearing on the attitudes and judgments of those now in power is difficult to estimate. Also the great technological sophistication of modern weapons systems means that the professional knowledge and expertise of scientists, academics, researchers and civilian specialists will encroach more and more on the military's monopoly of technical information and offer alternative perspectives. The military, though, will continue to produce and promote its own highly qualified 'technocrats in uniform'.

This is not to suggest that the high command will, or can, be elbowed on to the margins of defence decision making, and its privileged social status, popular prestige, as well as financial rewards, are unlikely to be in any way downgraded. But it could well be that the increased political role of the military fostered under Brezhnev and to a lesser extent by Andropov and Chernenko has for the time being diminished. Gorbachev is at any rate determined to enhance the CPSU's control of the military, as the new Party Programme again makes clear:

> The CPSU deems it vital in the future to *increase* its organizing and directing influence on the armed forces' activities ... broaden the role of and influence of the political bodies and party organizations of the army and navy and ensure that the army's blood relationship with the people will become still stronger [emphasis added].[48]

Despite the prognostications of some American pundits doubting the longevity of the present regime, Gorbachev is likely to remain in the saddle for a long time to come. Unlike Western politicians he does not have to worry about parliamentary accountability or the vagaries of a fickle electorate. As far as defence is concerned, this is certainly one area where the regime can count on just about one hundred per cent popular support. Not even the so-called 'dissident movement' has articulated any *major* criticism of the Soviet Union's military power or policy. Nor is there likely to be a challenge to Gorbachev's position from within the military establishment. If, as one Western expert has suggested, 'For the present the role of the Soviet military at the highest levels of decision-making can best be described as subdued, but restive',[49] it is unlikely that this 'restiveness' will be transformed into defiance, coordinated resistance or open opposition. Gorbachev is also gradually cutting out the old wood in the Politburo and the party-government *apparat*, replacing it with people of his own generation, background, outlook and aspirations, and the basis for a neo-Stalinist reaction to the course which has been charted is being systematically and systemically eroded in every branch of the party, government and military establishment.

The Soviet Union is not at a crossroads or even a major turning-point in its history, as has been suggested. It is, however, at an extremely interesting juncture and the future is pregnant with intriguing possibilities. There is a new-style leadership which, apart from anything else, is totally innocent of and untainted by any personal complicity in the terror of the Stalin years. On every front, economic, managerial, intellectual, technological, social, educational and military, there is a spirit and a process of rethinking and restructuring seriously and purposefully at work. Internationally, too, things are changing. There are prospects of real progress not just in the control, but actually in the elimination, of certain categories of nuclear weapons after Gorbachev's commitment to the so-called 'double-zero global formula' in the intermediate nuclear force (INF) negotiations in Geneva (July 1987). Abandonment of the Soviet Union's previous insistence on maintaining a hundred SS-20 missiles in her Asian territories not only adds a new ingredient to the preparation of some kind of INF treaty, but is also symptomatic of the USSR's awareness of the Eastern dimension in her international relations, particularly those with China and Japan.[50] The twenty-first century has been described as the 'Pacific century' and the rocketing commercial, demographic and industrial importance of the 'Pacific basin' or 'Pacific rim' countries has been widely commented on. Here is not the place to discuss this phenomenon, but the Soviet Union, by virtue of her vast economic resources, mineral wealth and communications networks in Siberia and the Far East, obviously has a key interest in developments in the Pacific region as a whole, military and defence aspects included.[51]

There are exciting prospects ahead across the whole spectrum of Soviet policy and behaviour, both domestically and internationally. The new dynamism in the Kremlin co-exists, however, with the old forces of stability, inertia and suspicion of change. Least likely to change in any radical way, even if the policies themselves do, are the processes, structures and mechanisms by which those policies are decided and made. It seems safe to assume, therefore, that the institutional values and relationships between party, government and military actors in the process of Soviet decision making reviewed in this chapter will remain in operation for the foreseeable future.

Notes

1 J. V. Stalin, *Problems of Leninism* (Moscow, 1947), 213.

2 On the purge of the Red Army, see J. Erickson, *The Soviet High Command: A Military-Political History, 1918–1941* (Boulder, CO, 1984).

3 For a discussion of this process of 'unnatural selection', see A. Amalrik, *Will the Soviet Union Survive until 1984?* (1970).

4 The early development of Soviet nuclear weapons is succinctly discussed by D. Holloway, *The Soviet Union and the Arms Race* (New Haven, Conn., 1983), 15–28.

5 Membership, structure, functions and performance of the CPSU are analysed in detail by R. J. Hill and P. Frank, *The Soviet Communist Party*, 2nd edn (1983).

6 *Constitution (Fundamental Law) of the Union of Soviet Socialist Republics*, Novosti Press Agency (Moscow, 1977) (hereafter, *Constitution* ...).

7 On Party–state relations and the Soviet political system in general, see J. H. Hough and M. Fansod, *How the Soviet Union Is Governed* (Cambridge, Mass., 1979); D. Lane, *State and Politics in the*

USSR (1985); Hill and Frank, *The Soviet Communist Party*, 104–21.

8 'Political report of the CPSU Central Committee to the 27th Congress of the Communist Party of the Soviet Union', *Pravda*, 26 February 1986. (The full text in English translation is to be found in *Soviet News* no. 6313, 26 February 1986.)

9 D. R. Herspring, 'The Soviet military in the aftermath of the 27th Party Congress', *Orbis*, Summer 1986, 303.

10 On the attempt to remove Khrushchev, including the role of the military, see R. W. Pethybridge, *A Key to Soviet Politics: The Crisis of the Anti-Party Group* (1962).

11 See reports in the *Observer*, 28 June 1987 and the *Guardian*, 27 June 1987.

12 Report 'On the Party's tasks in fundamentally restructuring management of the economy', TASS, 25 June 1987 (English translation in *Soviet News*, no. 6381, 1 July 1987).

13 M. McAuley, *Politics and the Soviet Union* (1977), 200.

14 On the working of the Politburo, see Hough and Fansod, *How the Soviet Union is Governed*, 466–73; Hill and

Frank, *The Soviet Communist Party*, *passim*; N. Temko, 'Soviet insiders: how power flows in Moscow', in E. P. Hoffman and R. F. Laird (eds), *The Soviet Polity in the Modern Era* (New York, 1984), 167–91.

15 *Washington Star*, 16 July 1979.

16 *Soviet News*, no. 6369, 8 April 1987.

17 *Washington Star*, 16 July 1979.

18 Edward L. Warner, III, *The Military in Contemporary Soviet Politics: An Institutional Analysis* (New York, 1977), 19.

19 *Constitution* . . . , articles 31 and 32.

20 *Ibid.*, article 108.

21 *Ibid.*, article 119.

22 The political role of the Defence Council is discussed in E. Jones, *The Defence Council in Soviet Leadership Decision-Making*, Occasional Papers no. 188, Kennan Institute for Advanced Russian Studies (Washington, DC, 1984).

23 *Constitution* . . . , article 128.

24 On defence spending, see Holloway, *The Soviet Union*, 109–30, and P. Hanson, 'Estimating Soviet defence expenditure', *Soviet Studies*, July 1978, 403–10.

25 See note 11 above.

26 P. Hanson, 'The Novosibirsk Report: comment', *Survey*, Spring 1984, 83–7; the translated text of Zaslavskaya's report is to be found *ibid.*, 88–108.

27 See, for instance, R. Kolkowicz, *The Soviet Military and the Communist Party* (Princeton, NJ, 1967); T. J. Colton, *Commissars, Commanders and Civilian Authority* (Cambridge, Mass., 1979); Warner, *The Military*; W. E. Odom, 'The party connection', *Problems of Communism*, Sept.–Oct. 1973, 12–26; Y. Avidar, *The Party and the Army in the Soviet Union* (Jerusalem, 1983).

28 The phrase was first used as the title of Marshal B. M. Shaposhnikov's history of the formation of the General Staff, *Mozg armii*, 3 vols (Moscow, 1924); the same title was used more recently in an article written by Marshal Kulikov, Chief of the General Staff between 1971 and 1977, *Pravda*, 13 November 1974.

29 K. Currie, 'Soviet General Staff's new role', *Problems of Communism*, March–April 1984, 36.

30 J. Newhouse, *Cold Dawn: The Story of SALT*, (New York, 1973), 55–6.

31 Herspring, 'The Soviet military', 297.

32 Kolkowicz, *The Soviety Military*, 11.

33 *Ibid.*, 341–2.

34 Odom, 'The party connection', 16.

35 N. V. Ogarkov, *Istoriya uchit bditelnosti* (Moscow, 1985), 80.

36 Herspring, 'The Soviet military', 299.

37 *Ibid.*, 314–15.

38 English translation in *Soviet News*, no. 6320, 16 April 1986.

39 S. F. Akhromeyev, as quoted in Herspring, 'The Soviet military', 313.

40 English translation in *Soviet News*, no. 6381, 1 July 1987.

41 *Krasnaya zvezda*, as reported by Reuters, *Guardian*, 18 June 1987.

42 Announcement in *Pravda*, as reported in the *Guardian*, 25 March 1987.

43 Draft programme of the CPSU, English translation in *Soviet News*, 30 October 1985.

44 Holloway, *The Soviet Union*, 29–64.

45 *Draft programme of the CPSU*.

46 *Pravda*, 26 February 1986; *Soviet News*, no. 6313, 26 February 1986.

47 For a brief discussion of 'military-patriotic education' in the Soviet Union, see Holloway, *The Soviet Union*, 160–30.

48 *Draft programme of the CPSU*.

49 D. R. Herspring, 'Soviet military politics', *Problems of Communism*, March–April 1986, 97.

50 As this chapter was going to press a new treaty eliminating intermediate range nuclear weapons was signed by the USA and the USSR, in December 1987.

51 For the most up-to-date analysis of the economic and strategic role of Siberia and the Soviet Far East, see A. Wood (ed.), *Siberia: Problems and Prospects for Regional Development* (1987), esp. chs 7, 'Military and Strategic Factors', by John Erickson, and 9, 'Siberia and the World Economy', by John Stephan.

5

West Germany

REGINA COWEN

Introduction

For the past twenty years it has been accepted conventional wisdom to speak of the Federal German political system as a 'penetrated' system, one whose defence and foreign policies lack a distinctly national political input. Almost invariably, political and scholarly work has been guided by the uniqueness of the German case. This perceived uniqueness is explained by reference to Germany's past and the circumstances surrounding West German accession to the North Atlantic Alliance. It is further elaborated by detailed observations of West German economic recovery, the country's influential position within the European Community and its emergence as a major political actor on the international scene. These observations are then compared with West Germany's persistently low defence profile – the predictable paradox of real political power and unrealized military leverage and potential is established. Analysis then proceeds to review the challenges to the paradox. Scenarios are devised exploring a German swing towards neutralism, a possible Soviet domination, the potential for a militarily self-sufficient Federal Republic, or the prospects for an active West German pursuit of reunification. Concluding remarks often raise the spectre of uncertainty over West German continued and faithful alliance membership. Suggestions are made to forestall potential and to counter actual trends in West German politics. These range from closer intra-alliance consultation to solidifying a joint European pillar in NATO with the aim of aligning West German defence thinking even closer with alliance preferences.[2]

The purpose of this review of the main characteristics of the traditional approach to West German security politics is to demonstrate its decreasing utility in the analysis and management of current and future security problems that beset the alliance and, by implication,

West German security planning. Unless this traditional approach is modified, analysis of West German defence policy making will remain locked into what we already know about it, without providing us with the tools to assess and appreciate new developments and their management by West German policy makers. The key to conceptual reform lies in recognizing that West Germany occupies a special but no longer unique place within the Atlantic Alliance. This is not meant as an argument against the present-day relevance of historical events. What it does mean, however, is that history alone should not continue to be our sole guide to an understanding of West German defence policy. The Federal Republic's uniqueness has been decreasing with a corresponding rise in defence and security problems that affect either the alliance as a whole or its European members collectively. Policy problems arising out of the superpower arms control impasse, the increasing cost of weapons procurement, the introduction of new technology and tactics into alliance strategy, the domestic dimension of the arms control process and effective allied defence cooperation, have proliferated both in numbers and importance. Although each country deals differently with each of these issues, there is a commonality of perspectives among European NATO members. European views differ greatly from those held by a US administration. Europe has not succeeded in carving out a formal role for itself in the security field yet it has identifiable security interests of its own. West German policy makers share these interests and have been actively engaged in their representation and presentation through the appropriate alliance channels.

The Atlantic Alliance is not a strait-jacket for German policy makers – another misconception that has contributed to keeping the concept of West German 'uniqueness' alive. The idea of alliance constraints upon German security policy making is largely based on the assumption that other NATO members have a defence identity beyond their alliance commitment. This is the case for the United States, Britain and France. The USA has global defence interests and responsibilities; Britain and France have obligations arising from their former colonial policies; the three also maintain a nuclear capability. West Germany has no other defence commitments but those associated with alliance membership and provided for by the Federal German constitution. To date, there has not been a single verifiable attempt by a West German government to change the nature of German alliance commitments. What has emerged, and this is something quite different, is a sustained attempt by the West Germans to increase their bargaining position in intra-alliance politics in order to see German national interest reflected in alliance policies. And West German national interests there are.

West Germany's long-time uniqueness was due to political and military circumstances well captured in Karl Kaiser's observation: 'The two German States are not regimes that created foreign policies but foreign policies that created political regimes.'[3] While this had profound implications for West German external and internal political organization and policy formulation, it did not preclude domestically based foreign and defence policy objectives from being raised.

To many observers, NATO has reached a political crossroads. Defence issues currently discussed by NATO fall into two broad categories. One is a largely technology-driven debate about the relationship between offence and defence, and questions the West's traditional reliance on strategic offensive forces.[4] The other, reflecting an increased political saliency of nuclear weapons in the domestic policies of member states, is a debate about ways and means of de-emphasizing the roles nuclear weapons play in alliance military strategy.[5] There is much in both debates that has refocused policy makers' attention on West Germany. West Germany epitomizes, in the eyes of many, not West German but shared alliance problems. The US defence commitment is extended to Western Europe as a whole, not just to Germany. Should this change, all of Western Europe will be affected. Changes in military strategy particularly involving an upgrading of conventional forces and its well-known potential effects on the nuclear–conventional forces mix could again affect all of Western Europe. West Germany is more sensitive to these changes than other European NATO members; not because of its history, which is responsible for the existence of the Federal Republic, but because it is NATO's front-line member most likely to suffer both the political and military brunt of perhaps drastic, uncoordinated changes in alliance defence policy.

The objective of this chapter is first to shed some light on West Germany's decreasing uniqueness and to identify those elements of Germany's immediate post-war history that are indeed of permanent relevance to West German defence thinking and policy making. In the second section, the organization of defence policy making is examined in order to explain the nature and character of interaction between the West German defence organization and NATO. It will explain the domestic and international purposes of West German defence policy making structures and assess their effectiveness. The third and final section will suggest that while there is a considerable degree of defence expertise at the political level, the institutional infrastructure in the Foreign Office and the Ministry of Defence still largely reflects political concerns dating back to the 1950s and 1960s, such as those relating to political control over the armed forces and political rehabilitation of the

Federal Republic. In order to be able to address current and future alliance' problems, West Germany will need to develop a politically more courageous and an institutionally more creative approach to defence policy making.

History, Yesterday and Today

After 30 years of membership in the Atlantic Alliance, the German government can point to an impressive record of German defence contributions to the defence of Central Europe: all German combat units are assigned to NATO in peacetime; Germany provides 50 per cent of NATO's land forces, 50 per cent of the ground-based air defence system and 30 per cent of all combat aircraft; in the Baltic region, the German Navy fields 70 per cent of NATO's naval forces and 100 per cent of NATO's naval air forces. The Bundeswehr (Federal Armed Forces) comprises 495,000 troops of which 12 divisions are maintained at the highest readiness and availablity status. In order to offset the effects of a steadily falling birth-rate on troop levels in the 1990s, the present government took the not uncontroversial decision to raise the military service period from 15 to 18 months. In the decade to 1985, the Federal defence budget increased steadily from DM 31.2 billion in 1975 to DM 49.0 billion in 1985 with projected 1986 budgeting totalling DM 51.3 billion. While growth in real terms, after inflation, has not consistently met SACEUR's call for a 3 per cent real annual expenditure increase, the inflation rate has fallen from just above 4 per cent in 1982 to well under 2 per cent in 1985 and some positive growth of the German defence budget seems assured for the medium term.[6]

Despite these efforts, German defence policy has repeatedly been the subject of critical political and academic scrutiny – and not without reason. The principal key to an understanding of West German defence policy does not lie so much with an appreciation of defence outputs – they are indeed substantial and effective – as with an examination of the motivations and intentions that make up the background to defence policy formulation and the processes by which defence resources are translated into policy objectives. In other words, defence outputs alone are not an acceptable basis upon which West German defence policy should be judged. Almost invariably, all of Germany's allies in NATO – and the Soviet Union – share this view, which is largely rooted in the aggressive militarism of Wilhelminian Germany and the Third Reich, followed by the division of Germany into an eastern and a western state and the subsequent incorporation of both states in their respective alliance organizations. In practical terms, this prevents either German state pursuing a military policy that does not conform with the parameters laid down by the United States or the Soviet Union. Yet, while the division of Germany served the most immediate political objectives of the USA and the Soviet Union, the succeeding forty years have not gone all the way to dispel the doubts in East and West that a militarily stable status quo along the Central European front has only postponed an eventual settlement of 'the German Question'.

If not fearing German reunification, both East and West are sensitive to the nature of the political dialogue that has been developing between the two Germanies during the 1970s. West Germany's allies are concerned about the strength of West German commitment to improving relations with East Germany and Eastern Europe generally and are uncertain as to West Germany's long-term *Ostpolitik* objectives that might weaken her allegiance to the Atlantic Alliance. The Soviet concern with inter-German relations is primarily one of political spill-over from West to East Germany. Economic and cultural relations between the two Germanies have been growing steadily over the past decade and the Soviet Union, always sensitive to the links between economic development and calls for political reform, is certain to watch potential political implications of German–German relations very carefully.

Lingering doubts in East and West as to where West Germany stands in the ongoing East–West struggle are exacerbated by the integration of nuclear weapons into each side's deterrence posture and by the structure of the Western alliance itself. In many ways, German defence policy epitomizes both the paradoxes and compromises of post-war Western defence policy. Indeed, it might be argued that irrespective of West Germany's historical legacy, that country's internal and external political attitudes and behaviour are of crucial importance to the continued viability of NATO's existence and allied defence policy towards the Soviet Union. The post-war European constellation of forces brought about the division of Germany, but the subsequent and continued relevance of this historic event to the Atlantic Alliance does not exclusively stem from the division itself, but was also caused by the way Germany's NATO allies perceived her position within the alliance, and by the introduction of nuclear weapons into military strategy. History notwithstanding, the German national question is alive and important to the alliance today not because it commands an intrinsic moral imperative but because the entire Western defence strategy rests upon continued positive West German political commitment to NATO.

The circumstances in which West Germany joined the Atlantic

Alliance have been thoroughly researched elsewhere and require little elaboration.[7] What is of importance here are those circumstances connected with Germany's accession to NATO which have had a lasting impact upon alliance and German defence policy formulation. There are several major factors that have governed the West Germany – NATO defence relationships from the outset: geography, the American security guarantee and NATO's defence policy.

Geography has always played a crucial role in German defence thinking whether embodied in Bismarck's 'Schaukelpolitik' or the Rapallo agreement with the Soviet Union. Membership in NATO promised a safe Western border for the first time ever and NATO strategy promised to ward off a Soviet or Warsaw Pact military threat from the East. With West Germany in NATO, not only did its Western border become safe, it also became permeable, anchoring the new Federal Republic in the social and political value system of Western democracies. Such was the initial bargain: revocation of occupation status and the granting of full sovereign rights to West Germany in exchange for political and military integration (in all but name) into the organizations of the Western allies. The dilemma of German geography appeared, for the Federal Republic at least, to have been solved through an ingenious combination of sovereignty and integration.

A second development brought about by the Federal Republic's geographical inclusion in the Western alliance was a transfer of Western defence objectives on to the West German political agenda. Meeting NATO's military requirements dominated West German defence thinking and planning for the best part of the first decade of West German membership in the alliance. West German conventional rearmament took precedence over a discussion of national defence policy considerations; indeed, with the exception of the Von Bonin defence concept, national defence alternatives did not emerge and the Adenauer government certainly did not encourage any such developments. West Germany's defence obligations under its NATO commitments had been clearly defined: the Federal Republic was to establish an army of half-a-million troops within three years between 1955 and 1958.[8] For a number of reasons, of which more is said below, West Germany did not achieve prescribed manpower levels until 1965. Essentially, though, Germany's early years in NATO did not see German conceptual input in alliance defence thinking and strategy developments. While there was an obvious domestic uneasiness regarding prompt and vocal German articulation of national defence interests beyond existing NATO guidelines, it would be mistaken to conclude that abstinence from a domestically conceived defence policy was a mere tactical ploy by Adenauer aimed at reassuring Germany's new allies of his country's 'good behaviour' in defence matters. Rather, the visible absence of domestic defence thinking was due to the total collapse of the old political order. Defence policy making suffered from the dislocation of political interests as much as did domestic and foreign policy making. Just as domestic policy (*Innenpolitik*) was exclusively focused on economic reconstruction, and foreign policy on *Westpolitik*, so was defence policy perceived as a narrowly defined task. With commercial, industrial, social and political interests beginning to define their roles and finding their places within the new democratic political structures and processes, German-centred policy considerations in all these fields began to be articulated.[9] Once the basic conceptualization of West German political and military orientation had been accomplished (and it had been a largely Adenauerian concept of the relationship between sovereignty and controlled rearmament within the Western alliance), West German political resources were used in a task-orientated fashion. Further conceptualization was simply not required in order to fulfil the given objectives of economic reconstruction and NATO defence obligations.

Another facet of West Germany's geographic inclusion in NATO is its exposed front-line position. Although NATO is intent upon defending NATO territory as close to the inter-German border as possible, the fact is that in case of war German territory on both sides of the battle-line would be devastated beyond recognition. Whether conventional or nuclear, armed conflict in Central Europe would result in the defence destroying the territory it defends. This defence dilemma cannot be resolved but, far more importantly, its relative significance for routine defence policy planning in Germany and within the alliance can and has been reduced. The dilemma over German defence by no means implies instability along the Central Front. Such instabilities as there are, or as conceivably might come about, are those of force structures and postures on either side, changes in military strategy or technological breakthroughs, perhaps in the field of anti-submarine warfare or such as envisaged in the Strategic Defense Initiative (SDI). In other words, the German defence dilemma exists but stability along the Central Front is not impeded by this dilemma but by changes in those factors that govern the degree of political saliency accorded to it. Above all else, the American political commitment to the defence of Europe is of crucial importance in persuading the West Germans that their defence dilemma can be lived with. The long-standing American commitment to the defence of West Germany has been the single most important factor in preventing the West Germans defence dilemma from turning into a security dilemma.[10] It has allowed West Germany to develop democratic political processes and organizations in a largely controlled political environment. The US defence commitment is symbolized by the deployment of some 233,000 US servicemen in the Federal Republic and an almost equal number of US dependants. Beyond the stationing of conventional forces, the US had deployed short- and medium-range nuclear weapons on West German soils, largely in order to offset a perceived Warsaw Pact conventional superiority. The US–German defence relationship must, of course, be seen within the wider context of the US–German political relationship. It is the latter that informs the former, not the reverse. West German commitment to political cooperation with the United States has been consistently supported by a majority of West Germans. Even at the height of the recent INF-stationing controversy, over two-thirds of the West German population voiced their support for continued West German membership in NATO. In March 1983 the Conservative Christian Democrats (CDU) were returned to power, their pro-INF agenda being well known to the public. To date, these elections are the most conclusive indicator to the real balance of opinion within the Federal Republic. The INF (Intermediate Range Nuclear Forces) controversy, a burgeoning German peace movement and the increased political saliency of nuclear weapons in the domestic politics of a number of European countries brought the lingering doubts of Germany's allies about a perceived drift of German politics once again to the foreground.[11] Josef Joffe's reflection on this debate offers a succinct summary of how the majority of West Germans probably felt during this time:

> There may be less than meets the headlines. For the observer, journalist, or academic, pathology is always more enticing than health. Hence the fascination with a [peace] movement ... that has suddenly rekindled the old German uncertainties tends to obscure some far more benign (and banal) facts about contemporary West Germany.[12]

Indeed, foreign preoccupation with German domestic politics cannot escape a certain sense of irony surrounding the issues. Democratic pluralism, particularly in matters of defence, should be seen as a healthy sign of the West German post-war success story. Instead, it is often regarded as an unhealthy deviation from the model. One banal fact is that the majority of Germans have never seriously demanded a basic change in West Germany's political orientation. The Social Democrats (SPD) had to take account of this new majority in the 1950s and were eventually forced to change their political priorities from reunification to alignment with the West. The apparent rivalry between

126

Gaullism and Atlanticism in the 1960s reaffirmed the German alliance
with the United States. It was well understood by Germans that until
Europe had truly emerged as a political and military counterweight to
both the United States and the Soviet Union, German security would
have to rest upon close cooperation with the United States.[13]

Most persuasive of West German steadfastness in its Atlantic relations is
the record of failure that has characterized Soviet attempts to disrupt
the US–German accord. The Soviets have failed at both ends of the
spectrum: neither tantalizing visions of German reunification, nor
threats to freeze German *Ostpolitik* and the inter-German dialogue, have
in any recognizable way been able to shift the consensus of the West
German majority away from its Atlantic convictions.[14]

Challenges to West Germany's political orientation that have periodically arisen from a domestic context have been successfully weathered
by the country's leadership. The West German Communist Party has
not entered the Federal parliament and is not likely to do so in the
future. Communist systems as exemplified by those in Eastern Europe
and the Soviet Union continue to hold little appeal. Nationalist
sentiments do not constitute a political force either. Calls for reunification or for a return of other formerly German territories on the one
hand and calls for a politically more assertive Federal Republic on the
other, do not command electoral support. The domestic legitimacy of
the current governmental system is only contested by such political
fringe groups as are found in any modern democracy. The Green Party,
or the Greens, as it and its grass-root support is often referred to,
express a curious combination of more democracy and more independence for the Federal Republic. More democracy, because they see
the compromises of coalition governments as a betrayal of the electorate's
mandate and as a dilution of the people's 'real' political will. More
independence, because they see West German security interests at best
diverted and at worst perverted through membership in the Atlantic
Alliance. This profound moral opposition to nuclear power and nuclear
weapons makes it difficult for the older political parties to explore and
discuss nuclear and conventional force issues with them. The Greens'
persistent refusal to work towards political compromise may speak
well of the force of their conviction but does remarkably less so for
their acceptance and adoption of established and proven democratic
processes.[15] In the longer term, support for the Greens at the ballot box
is more likely to stem from their stance on environmental matters than
their defence policy. Such environmental disasters as the nuclear
accident at Chernobyl and the more recent chemical waste spillage into
the Rhine river may well be reflected in an increased share of the Green

vote. Although the CDU-led government has taken steps to improve the protection and preservation of the environment, and the SPD has called for even more stringent measures, the older parties' 'sudden' environmental concern is largely viewed as one of tactical manoeuvring pursued to broaden their electoral appeal. On defence policy itself, the Greens and the peace movement have had relatively little direct impact. Their achievements in the defence area as a whole have, however, been far from negligible. Irrespective of whether one agrees with the ideas and ideals of the peace movement, the fact is that it has brought about, through its activities on and off the streets, two important modifications to the German domestic defence agenda. First of all, the increased saliency of nuclear weapons in the management of East–West relations has been brought home to many ordinary people in the Federal Republic. Consequently, calls for a more broadly based political approach to the East–West conflict are now more frequent than ever before. Secondly, nuclear arms control as an instrument both to moderate the superpower competition and to decrease the likelihood of miscalculation by either side, has now a strong political constituency across party political lines. Popular awareness of what is perceived to be an ever more dangerous arms race, coupled with a widespread belief that arms control can and should fulfil a risk-reducing function, has to be taken seriously by the West German government. The established political parties have reacted quite differently to this challenge. For the CDU, as the major governing party, a large part of the answer to the problem of popular concern lay in a renewed reaffirmation of the US–German relationship. Much of this effort has shown itself in Chancellor Kohl's firm public support for the Reagan arms control negotiation stance and the equally firm criticism of the SPD concept of a *Sicherheitspartnerschaft* (security partnership) with the Soviet Union. Less publicly though, the Kohl government has on many occasions impressed upon US policy makers the need for political dialogue with the East. A discussion of West German arms control attitudes as part of the Federal Republic's security policy is presented below. Suffice it here to point to the Kohl government's most illuminating examples of the continuing importance attached to the US–German relationship.

The Strategic Defense Initiative launched by President Reagan in March 1983 challenged the basic framework of East–West security. The threat of nuclear retaliation, the backbone of deterrence and the Atlantic Alliance is, if technically feasible, to be replaced by a shield of layered defences capable of intercepting and destroying enemy missiles well before they reach their targets.[16] There are grave doubts even among SDI supporters that it will be technically feasible to extend a defensive capability to Western Europe. Even if it were possible to shield Europe from such missiles as the SS–20 or even the ones of much shorter range like the SS–21, 22 and 23, NATO Europe would still be faced with Warsaw Pact conventional forces. The German government, however, is most worried about the more general instabilities that SDI might cause between the USA and the Soviet Union: an exacerbated arms race in offensive and defensive forces, a virtual stalemate in arms control negotiations at all levels of negotiation and a decoupling of US security from that of West Germany and Europe as a whole.[17] Yet despite its profound reservations about the political and strategic wisdom of SDI, the Federal government signed an agreement with the USA concerning the transfer of SDI-related technologies, and West German industrial participation in the research programme, knowing full well that the factual contents of the agreement were far exceeded in importance by the fact of the agreement itself. Bonn observers of the long-drawn-out negotiations felt that there had never really been an opportunity for the German government not to conclude an agreement with the USA once negotiations had begun. In other words, the German government, rather than withdrawing from negotiations which at no stage offered more than a token share of SDI funds to German industry, feared that a breakdown of negotiations might be interpreted as West German official rejection of the whole SDI concept. After the INF débâcle, safeguarding Atlantic relations was given preference over West German security concerns.[18]

The Social Democratic Party has not made pro-Atlanticism part of its political opposition agenda. The party is still deeply split over defence policy although the choice of Johannes Race, an SPD moderate, as Chancellor candidate did suggest for a short while that the SPD had recovered its political centre, lost towards the end of the Schmidt government.[19] Heavy losses in recent regional elections in Hamburg and Bavaria, however, dimmed the party's prospects of a return to power in 1987. Many in the SPD see the Green Party posing a serious challenge to issues and areas the SPD has traditionally regarded as within 'its' domain – *Ostpolitik* being a case in point. The centre of the SPD has always understood that *Ospolitik* cannot succeed without a successful *Westpolitik*. The Greens do not accept this premise and the SPD left wing, disillusioned with the arms control process and the current leaders in Washington, has made a number of Green ideas its own. The SPD on the whole, however, has not lost sight of its principal allegiance to the United States and is not likely to adopt measures leading to either a disavowal of Germany's role in the alliance, denuclearization of NATO strategy or the withdrawal of American forces from Germany. The SPD has so far not developed an appetite for radical changes in Germany's defence posture; its defence proposals tend to be aimed primarily at modifying NATO strategy by working towards a no-first-use policy and demilitarized corridors along the Central Front.[20] Without question though, the SPD as a major political party faces severe problems. Its greatest challenge, however, does not stem from the Greens but from the Christian Democrats, a fact not often recognized by outside observers. A CDU government today embodies many of the Schmidt-led SPD government policies of the latter 1970s. Particularly in the areas of defence and national security, it has been the CDU rather than the SPD which has consistently followed the designs worked out by the SPD more than a decade ago. Those who call on the SPD to recapture the political centre should not overlook the fact that for the time being, that very centre is well and truly occupied by the CDU. Whether an overwhelming CDU election victory will lead to a greater assertion of right-wing elements in the CDU and of the Christian Social Union, the CDU's Bavarian sister party, remains to be seen. This possibility should, however, not be excluded from any current assessment of West German domestic politics.

Since the formation of the Federal Republic, a usable majority of West Germans have not supported extremist political views. With a constitution that requires political parties to obtain 5 per cent of the popular vote before it can be legally represented in the Federal parliament, coalition governments have established a political centre that has both breadth and depth and is not easily shaken.[21] At present, the left wing of the SPD is experiencing the steadfastness of the centre; the right wing of the CDU and the CSU may yet have to do so.

After geography and the Atlantic relationship, the third characteristic of West Germany's approach to the North Atlantic Alliance is guided by West German attitudes to NATO strategy. Specifically German attitudes make themselves felt in primarily three areas: an emphasis on NATO strategy's deterrent role, the détente and defence imperatives of the 1967 Harmel Report and the coupling of West German and European defence to that of the United States. These German interests are not officially contested by Germany's allies but there are important variations of balance and interpretation. Over the years, German defence strategy requirements have remained remarkably unchanged. Since in the event of armed conflict in Europe West Germany would most likely not survive, successive West German governments have sought to maintain a seamless web between West German and US security from attack. Regarding NATO strategy, West Germany has been eager to forestall or counter any developments that potentially carry the risk of limiting war to Europe, leaving the territories of the two main protagonists, the Soviet Union and the United States, intact.[22] While US deterrence thinking has moved increasingly towards the attainment of credible military options, the Federal Republic has consistently stressed the uncertainties pertaining to nuclear use and the potential for escalation to the strategic level once war has broken out. That, plus West Germany's long-standing support of NATO's nuclear first-use option, is believed to have had the desired deterrent effect upon Soviet military planning.[23] Equally important though, past modifications to NATO strategy, while nominally meeting the US demands for more military options, have not alleviated the risk of inadvertent nuclear escalation. The Germans could still argue credibly that deterrence was intact *and* maintain a cooperative relationship with the United States. NATO's strategy of Flexible Response, formally adopted in 1967, epitomizes a successful harmonization of different interpretations of how to deter a Warsaw Pact attack most effectively. Yet, although often ignored, it epitomizes even more West German readiness to stick with its Atlantic partner even when that partner's developing security thinking threatens to undermine the German interpretation of the mechanisms of deterrence.

Other examples in support of West Germany's preference for good Atlantic relations exist. One of the earliest can be found in the late 1950s and early 1960s when West Germany had to come to terms with the fact that if it continued to remain an obstacle to US–Soviet *rapprochement*, it would come out as loser all round. A persistent West German claim that the German question was at the root of East–West tensions and therefore needed to be settled before the establishment of a political dialogue with the East, came to be viewed by the United States as largely true – but increasingly of less priority. West Germany was running the risk not only of getting nowhere with its hardline approach to East Germany and the Soviet Union, but of endangering US political support if and when the German question returned to the US agenda. In the event, the Federal government recognized that US and West German interests were not identical, but that perhaps they could be complementary. Subsequently, the Federal Republic embarked upon its own *rapprochement* with the East.[24] Another example is provided by the West German response to the Strategic Defense Initiative, mentioned earlier. While Flexible Response left the German view of deterrence intact, SDI in its original conception of a defensive shield over the United States threatened to sever US from West German security, and undermine the German view that the key to deterrence rests upon the risk of nuclear escalation to the strategic level.

Nevertheless, the Kohl government lent its support to the defence research initiative hoping, along with the rest of Western Europe, that SDI research will show the technical unfeasibility of a defensive shield against nuclear attack.[25]

It was suggested at the beginning of this section that Western European members of the North Atlantic Alliance share a particular perception of how the alliance provides for their security. All Western European countries rely on the US nuclear umbrella to deter the outbreak of war in Europe. They are also convinced that European security depends upon the continued vulnerability of the continental United States. The Federal Republic as a European alliance member subscribes to this general European position. The above discussion, however, has identified some specifically West German sensitivities and concerns. Its geographic location makes the Federal Republic especially vulnerable, despite Soviet ability to threaten all of Europe equally. This perception of vulnerability is enhanced by NATO's strategy which assumes an initially conventional phase, should war break out in Europe. Much of the conventional threat to West Germany is offset by the US security guarantee and NATO's nuclear first-use option. In order to solidify the US commitment, West Germany has consistently aimed for a cooperative political relationship with the United States. Because of the essentially symbolic nature of the US commitment, many West Germans believe their security to depend as much upon a political consensus with the United States as upon actual and visible US forces and weapon systems deployed in the Federal Republic. Indeed, West Germans are aware that a continued visible demonstration of the US defence commitment may well depend upon the maintenance of a basic political accord between the two countries.

For historical reasons, and because of West Germany's dependence upon the combined defence efforts of its allies, the Federal Republic suffers more from political discord in the alliance than any other of its members. Political disarray in the alliance accentuates West Germany's vulnerability and dependence, inviting Soviet pressures to deepen political rifts in the alliance and weakening the West German ability to conduct and manage *Ostpolitik*.

Much of the character of West German NATO membership over the next five to ten years will be determined by the collective ability of the alliance to maintain and modernize its defences while at the same time efforts to improve the political East–West climate are being made.

The Defence Policy Making Apparatus

An analysis of West German defence policy making proper reveals an interesting dichotomy between the obviously complex circumstances of

West German security and a defence policy making process that is highly formalized and routinized.[26] Defence policy is conducted within the confines of political guidelines laid down by the Federal Chancellors according to article 65 of the Basic Law.[27] These guidelines are phrased in the most general political terms and are in no way meant to substitute for policy. Indeed, the legal powers of the Chancellor vis-à-vis his ministries are restricted to the setting of political guidelines. Article 65a of the Basic Law places peacetime command authority over the armed forces (Bundeswehr) with the Minister of Defence alone. Should the Federal Republic ever become the object of an armed attack, command authority is transferred to the Federal Chancellor in accordance with article 115b of the Basic Law.[28]

The dominance of the Foreign Office in handling security affairs is all-embracing. Although the Ministry of Defence formulates its own communications to West Germany's military staff at NATO, all exchanges need to be coordinated with the Foreign Office. Likewise, reports by staff officers on international assignments at NATO or MBFR are channelled through the Foreign Office to the Ministry of Defence. The latter's responsibility for force structure and military strategy does provide it with a decision making input for all those security issues handled by the Foreign Office that have clear implications for force structure and strategy. The so-called *Mitzeichnungsrecht*, the right of concurrence, gives the Ministry of Defence its powers. Should differences between the MOD and the FO not be resolvable at the working level, the respective ministerial state secretaries take up the matter.[29] In the FO, *Fachreferate* (desks) constitute the working level. Their staffs are small and their workload is either very broadly or very narrowly defined. The Arms Control Office, headed by an Ambassador, has four desks with two foreign service officers each. There is the disarmament and arms control desk that follows world-wide developments with particular responsibility for START (previously SALT) and INF. Another broadly focused desk is concerned with non-proliferation, test bans, B–, C– and R– (Biological, Chemical and Radiological) weapons and the UN Geneva Disarmament Committee, while still another is charged with United Nations disarmament efforts. The only desk with a clear European focus is the one on security, disarmament and arms control in Europe with primary responsibility for Mutual Balanced Force Reduction (MBFR). Routine policy making issues are addressed by the FO's Political Department, especially by the Atlantic Alliance and Defence desk with a staff of two military officers. Both departments are responsible to a Secretary of State. Although there is a high degree of professionalism in the Foreign Office, the number of people intimately knowledgeable about defence and security questions and able to bring their expertise to bear on routine decision making is extremely small. There is a distinct and increasing lack of technical expertise, particularly with respect to defence technological developments and attendant problems of strategic implications. The small size of the defence community within the FO (there are at most a round dozen people, probably fewer, who can claim a broad and specific appreciation of defence and alliance politics) does not seem to have changed much over the past ten to fifteen years, though some inter-desk reshuffling of responsiblity does seem to have taken place. Helga Haftendorn mentions a transfer of Conference on Security and Cooperation Europe (CSCE) responsibility from the Atlantic Alliance desk to General East–West Relations desk in the East European Division of the FO. This transfer of tasks, she suggests, was primarily due to an increasing requirement to coordinate CSCE policy with West Germany's Eastern European relations.[30] The FO planning staff has no formal policy planning responsibility, although its work may involve more specific attention to security problems. It is primarily tasked with advising the minister on a broad range of issues. Its present head, Konrad Seitz, however, is highly respected for his expertise in the security field.

The Ministry of Defence combines a high degree of military and political expertise.[31] Among staff divisions (Führungstab der Streitkräfte, FuS), Divisions II and III with their respective desks are intimately involved in threat assessment and strategy planning. The two divisions work closely together but it is Division III with its desks on Military Political Factors (III 1), Military strategy (III 2), Military Relations with NATO and West European Union (III 3), Armament Planning (III 4), Arms Limitation and Control (III 5) and Operational Factors (III 6) that represent the defence expertise of the ministry. The head of Division III represents the Federal Republic in NATO's High Level Groups. All staff divisions are responsible to the Inspector General, Germany's highest ranking military officer. He acts as military adviser to the minister and is responsible for Bundeswehr force planning. The planning staff in the MOD has a far greater conceptual input into ministerial planning than its Foreign Office counterpart. It is headed by a civilian with a military deputy and its members are drawn equally from both the military and civilian staffs. It assists the minister in long-term defence and force planning and is in this capacity the only body with a distinct long-term policy orientation in the official West German defence establishment.

The Chancellor's Office has little formal input in defence and security policy making. At the working level, Group 21 works on East–West relations generally and Group 23 on questions of defence and arms control/disarmament. Their work is, however, usually of an advisory nature, and the Chancellor's Office cannot issue directives to either the FO or MOD working levels.[32]

In her discussion of the West German security policy making system, Helga Haftendorn criticizes 'the high level of bureaucratisation and compartmentalisation within the departments'.[33] She concludes that much of this is due to a 'primarily legal or military disposition on the part of many staff members' which in turn 'leads to a certain narrowness of approach, either decidedly legalistic . . . or dominated by threat perceptions and thus emphasising relative force capabilities'.[34] She observes further that 'the system of preparing and coordinating decisions at the working level is so complex that both top officials and political leaders, although kept informed on most matters, are seldom involved in routine processes (or in cases of decisions which are considered to be routine), except for formal confirmation.'[35] This leads her to argue that the weakness of the system shows itself most clearly when it provides only one or a limited set of policy options to political leaders. Undoubtedly, over-bureaucratization and compartmentalization of issue areas can be found in the security policy making organization of any West German NATO ally. The routinization of decision making and its concentration at the working level reflects an emphasis on standard operating procedures no different from the general organizational behaviour of other Western institutions. Standard operating procedures are also responsible for the limited policy options available to the political leadership. What both Helga Haftendorn and Catherine Kellcher[36] underestimate, however, is the impact domestic and international factors have had on the initial West German defence policy organization and its present-day appearance.

In order to examine these factors, two arguments will be put forward. First, the West German defence organization appears to be far more like its Western European counterparts than is generally appreciated. Secondly its weaknesses, organizational and procedural, do not stem from over-bureaucratization or routinization of defence policy decision making but from the persistence of political rationales that guided the establishment of the West Germany defence organization in the 1950s. There are essentially two political rationales that have informed West German defence policy making. The first is the primacy of politics, which dramatically altered the balance of power between civilian and military control of national security in favour of political authority. The second is the need to achieve an intra-alliance distribution of power through networks of interdependence that would allow West Germany to emerge as a politically equal partner.

The primacy of politics played a crucial role in the organization of the Ministry of Defence in the mid 1950s and the role accorded to the service chiefs and the Inspector General within the ministry. Ministerial structures and procedures were deliberately devised in order to forestall service rivalry, prevent the emergence of the military staffs as a force within the ministry, and curtail staff influence upon procurement and budgetary decision making. These combined measures assured the politically desired redefinition of the role of the Chiefs of Staff and the Inspector General and a fragmentation of military representation in the MOD. The position of the Inspector General, the highest serving military officer in the Federal armed forces, is a particularly weak one and exemplifies that rank does not need to be commensurate with authority. The Inspector General heads the Armed Forces Staff Department which draws its staff from the three services. The Armed Forces Department represents the interests of the armed forces as a whole, especially vis-à-vis the other two main ministerial departments, the Administrative Department and the Armaments Department. The Armed Forces Department is thus formally removed from the administration of and defence procurement for the Bundeswehr. The same applies to the three service Chiefs of Staff. The Inspector General, responsible to the minister for force planning, can in this capacity issue directives to the service chiefs but is not their departmental or military superior. Indeed, the service chiefs' responsibility for operational readiness is to the minister alone and they have direct access to him. Between the Chiefs of Staff, the Inspector General and the ministry's civilian departments, communication is based on the 'principle of dialogue'.[37] This is a German version of intra-ministerial bargaining where, without formal authority, the service chiefs and the Inspector General are encouraged to search for consensus with the civilian departments upon which policy decisions would be based. The problem with this kind of organization and communication has always been that it presupposes a basic consensus between military and civilian departments that can be improved through the principle of dialogue. This basic consensus did not exist when the Ministry of Defence was created. In fact, by fragmenting the military interests in the MOD and narrowly defining the tasks of the military departments, the primacy of politics very quickly led to an institutionalized one-way street of communication well exemplified through the organization of the Ministry of Defence, intended to prevent a possible resurgence of organized and politically influential military interests.

The disadvantages and weaknesses of institutionalized political control over military staffs, however, made themselves felt in a persistent under-appreciation of military expertise in force and procurement planning. Suggestions for reform made by the military staffs were seen as challenges to the primacy of politics. In August 1966, when the exclusion of the staffs from policy decision making began to threaten the operational readiness of the Air Force for which he was responsible, Lieutenant General Panitzki resigned, claiming insufficient consultation prior to a ministerial directive allowing armed forces personnel to join a trade union. His resignation was symbolic of the emerging incompatibility between rigorous political control over the military staffs and an increasingly complex defence planning environment.[38]

Faced with a potentially permanent loss of military expertise in crucial areas like force planning, procurement and military technology, the government began a series of reforms aimed at improving the services' bargaining position within the ministry without actually transferring decision making powers from civilian to military departments. In September 1968 the decree on 'Federal Armed Forces Planning in the Ministry of Defence' was issued. Its purpose was to acheive a comprehensive integration of defence policy, armed forces planning and equipment planning. In January 1971 a sweeping reform of the defence procurement sector was initiated in order to improve procurement efficiency. These decrees brought about a closer involvement of the military staffs in armed forces and procurement planning but did not alter the basic relationship between the staffs and civilian departments. The services did achieve the establishment of the position of system officer or manager. He would be responsible to his service chief and charged with the management of all processes necessary for effective procurement of a major weapon system. Yet he had no powers of decision at any stage of the procurement process and had to proceed according to the principle of dialogue. Despite this obvious weakness in the position of the system officer, it was an important step towards a permanent involvement of the military staffs in defence procurement, an area vital to the fulfilment of their original brief: operational readiness.[39]

Generally speaking, the political priorities that guided the initial establishment of the Ministry of Defence have not been changed. The effectiveness of the military staffs' input into procurement and military planning tends to depend more on the calibre of staff officers than upon ministerial organization. The position of system officer signifies the only functional orientation of the ministry, otherwise largely run by a mixture of hierarchical and horizontal dependencies. A functional integration of defence resources has not come about. Neither has much been achieved with regard to force planning and arms control policy. While there is considerable expertise in both subjects in the Inspector General's department, staff have little formal opportunity to shape the conceptual input in arms control policy.

There can be little doubt, however, that more informal communication between the military at the working level and their colleagues in the Foreign Office and the Chancellery does take place. The extent to which informal contacts influence policy is, of course, difficult to assess. At the working level, the MOD's contribution to arms control policy making is restricted to the right of concurrence where strictly military matters are concerned. There is little evidence in support of an organizational response by the West German government to the increasingly close links between arms control and force planning on the one hand and the impact of sophisticated defence technology upon strategic and regional stability and arms control negotiating options on the other. Much of the expertise at the working levels in the Foreign Office and to some extent in the MOD is concentrated on CSCE and MBFR. It is, of course, the case that in both CSCE and MBFR the Federal Republic is directly involved in negotiations, while there is no direct involvement in other East–West negotiating forums. West German policy input in the latter are therefore restricted to NATO channels, particularly within the Defence Planning Committee and the North Atlantic Council. Regular high-level visits to Washington, usually involving the Chancellor and either or both the Foreign Minister and the Defence Minister, allows the Federal Republic to present its interests to US policy makers; members of the US arms control negotiating team at Geneva frequently brief European governments on the state of the talks and progress at the negotiating table.

Policy makers in the mid 1950s and early 1960s were not aware of the potential rivalry between the two policy objectives of political control over the armed forces and West German political rehabilitation. In fact, the two were thought to be complementary: political control over the Bundeswehr was believed to further Western recognition of the Federal Republic's commitment to democratic norms. This policy approach proved effective while West German governments subscribed to the view that defence policy making was primarily a process of administering the West German military contribution to NATO. Political rehabilitation also made it imperative that West Germany was not seen to be too outspoken in matters of defence. Other circumstances helped to maintain a low defence profile. Most first-generation defence equipment for the armed forces was procured from the United States, reducing the role of West German defence procurement agencies to that of administering equipment supply contracts. Offset agreements for allied troops stationed in West Germany were to a large extent realized through West German acquisition of defence equipment from the respective countries. Yet it was soon recognized, particularly by the then Minister of Defence Franz Josef Strauss, that political rehabilitation would only make sense if based on partnership among political equals. West German dependence upon defence equipment from the allies would only perpetuate its political inferiority. For Strauss, the answer lay in promoting domestic defence production. First, however, formidable economic and technological problems had to be attended to. During rearmament, the Federal economy was working at full employment levels and defence production would have withdrawn skilled labour from the civilian sectors. The NATO target of 12 Bundeswehr divisions within three years (between 1955 and 1958) was already threatening to cause structural economic problems. Despite sharp criticism from NATO, Adenauer decided in 1956 to realign domestic economic priorities with NATO obligations and extended the period of West German rearmament.[40]

Once the decision in favour of domestic defence production had been made, the government very quickly became aware of the technological gap that separated West German Second World War defence technology from that of the allies. In order to make domestic defence production an economically viable undertaking, German industry had to be provided with the requisite know-how. Consequently, the government acquired defence production licences, notably for the US F-104 Starfighter aircraft, and began to explore possibilities for joint procurement ventures with Britain and France. It was at this stage that the two strands of West German defence policy began to conflict with each other. Decisions at the political level had not led to a functional reorganization at the working levels. Timely and economical procurement of technologically sophisticated equipment in support of the government's political objective of equality with Britain and France required a functional reorientation of what was an essentially administratively oriented organization of procurement. While administration of procurement had been due to the purchase of first-generation equipment from abroad, it had also been useful in limiting the role of the armed forces in procurement decision making. With domestic defence production and defence cooperation with the allies under way, however, it was no longer possible to do without active armed forces involvement. Military expertise had to be taken into account if West Germany was truly committed to defence research, development, production and maintenance of equipment. The problem was that active involvement of the armed forces was seen as a relaxation or even abrogation of the primacy of politics. A discussion of the latter has already shown how the government thought it could enlist military expertise without expanding the role and the authority of the military. Several procurement crises, such as the one during the Starfighter procurement, the ill-fated attempts at developing a vertical-short-take-off-and-landing aircraft and the financial shortfalls that beset the Multi-Role Combat Aircraft (MRCA) Tornado procurement in 1980 and 1981, can largely be traced back to a continuing dysfunctional allocation of responsibilities at the working levels.[41]

The Need for Reform

The tension that continues to exist between the institutionalization of the primacy of politics and West Germany's well-evidenced commitment to a domestic defence production base in support of *Westpolitik* also shows itself in a wider defence context. At the working levels, officials in the Foreign Office and the Ministry of Defence are busy implementing past policy objectives and little creative energy is left to examine new challenges. West Germany's basic security requirements are as fully met as they are ever likely to be in an age of strategic parity and corresponding questions about an alliance strategy based on the threat of nuclear retaliation. As far as future alliance political management is concerned, West Germany needs to institutionalize a defence planning system that incorporates the experience of the present system *and* a responsiveness to new issues. Such responsiveness could be achieved in the first instance through clear political directives on the priorities of future defence planning. Secondly, the government should draw on a much larger pool of defence expertise than it does at present. The primacy of politics should not remain a one-way street of control for military officers; they have a valuable contribution to make. On a small scale, officers are seconded to work on the parliamentary staffs and each year three officers, one from each service, join the civilian researchers at the Foundation for Science and Policy in Munich. This one year gives officers the opportunity to address the more conceptual problems of national security. This enterprise could be expanded relatively easily and might also include secondment to universities with a research interest in the security field. Thirdly, both the Foreign Office and the Ministry of Defence should provide more opportunities for mid-career people from different professional backgrounds to join existing staffs. Requirements would, of course, depend upon how well existing resources in both ministries can be made to work together more effectively. However, a better appreciation of US domestic politics and processes in the Foreign Office, for example, as well as of the politics of nuclear weapons would be useful in any case. The principal aim of a new defence policy planning system should be that of institutionalizing at the working levels a variety of defence expertise.

This would both increase and improve policy options offered to political leadership and make defence expertise less dependent upon a small circle of defence experts. West German basic security interests have remained unaltered and are unlikely to change. An exposed geographical position demands a deterrence strategy credible at both the conventional and the strategic nuclear level. NATO strategy must ensure equal security for all member states. The US political commitment to the defence of West German territory must be maintained. There seems to be, however, much less conceptual clarity among West German policy makers regarding the potential effects of new technology and new strategic thinking upon West Germany's basic security requirements. This lack of clarity at the West German policy making level is especially evident when the political relationship with the US appears to be challenged by changes in US strategic thinking and US arms control negotiating positions. The Strategic Defense Initiative and the President's apparent willingness to consider an eventual abandonment of ballistic missiles at the recent Reykjavik Summit found the West German government in considerable unease. Both SDI and an abandonment of nuclear weapons threaten West Germany's basic security interests. Yet the Federal government supports both SDI *and* the US negotiating stance. This paradoxical approach is explained by West Germany's preference for safeguarding its Atlantic relationship as the cornerstone of security. Prior to SDI, West Germany was able to maintain a security consensus with the United States and see its basic security requirements fulfilled. The problem for the future, however, seems to be that the Atlantic partnership can no longer be insulated from other developments in the security area. West Germany will need a more creative and courageous approach to its defence problems. Continued cooperation with the United States in the security field is essential. In order to strengthen its bargaining position vis-à-vis the United States and forestall foreign and domestic criticism of West German unilateralism in defence issues, the Federal government would be best advised to work through bilateral European contacts and within the Western European Union framework.

If NATO is to remain an alliance for defence and détente, and there is no credible alternative in sight, its effectiveness will depend upon how well its members are able to realign defence necessities with political objectives. For the Federal Republic, the task will be one of persuading in the first instance its Western European neighbours of West Germany's long-term security objectives of stable political and military East–West relations. Assuring West Germany's allies of its own political predictability will be of vital importance. At the same time, West Germany and the rest of NATO Europe should strive to achieve at least a maximum consensus on those defence issues that have a direct bearing upon their security.[42] In the long run, only a European position jointly arrived at will stand a chance to influence US policy making. The issues on a European agenda should include an analysis of threat perception on either side through force planning, a wide network of politicial and economic contacts with the East, and political and military confidence-building measures, based on the already worthwhile achievements of the recently concluded Conference on Disarmament in Europe at Helsinki.

A joint European security agenda would allow the Federal Republic to be conceptually involved in identifying and defining security problems that affect all European NATO members. At the same time, it would clarify West German security interests to its neighbours. It would decrease perceptions of West German uniqueness among them by anchoring West German security thinking in a Western European conceptual defence and détente consensus.

West Germany has been very successful in institutionalizing control over its armed forces, politically, legally and organizationally. West German political rehabilitation within the Western state community has been another success story. Challenges to West German security are unlikely to spring from either an independent and politically assertive officer corps or a breakdown of Western European political and economic cooperation. Existing security policy making structures in West Germany are still mainly focused on traditional defence and foreign policy concerns. There is no need to abandon these policy making structures but they need modification in accordance with a dynamic security environment. West Germany has clearly identifiable security interests. Their continued realization is a West German and alliance-wide interest. West Germany and its European allies must make the political resources available to reach a consensus on largely new but shared security problems in order to safeguard their most basic security requirements within the alliance framework.

For the major part of West Germany's membership of NATO, West German security has been maintained through a constellation of political circumstances and military forces that asked of the West

Germans little more than a political commitment to alignment with the West. A West German defence policy input was not demanded and the West Germans themselves were not ready to formulate a German input into alliance defence policy making. While German basic security interests were soon actively pursued at the political level, the organization of defence policy making was created largely in order to achieve other objectives. These objectives have been met and resources should now be harnessed to provide a greater West German conceptual input into alliance defence policy planning.

Notes

1 The thesis of a 'penetrated system' was first put forward by Wolfram Hamrieder in *West German Foreign Policy 1949-1963*; here quoted from P. Noack, *Die Aussenpolitik der Bundesrepublik Deutschland*, 2nd revised and expanded edn (Stuttgart, 1981), 7.

2 This predictable course of argument is particularly evident in C. M. Kelleher, 'The defense policy of the Federal Republic of Germany', in D. J. Murray and P. R. Viotti (eds), *The Defense Policies of Nations* (Baltimore, Md and London, 1982), 268–96. Also see W. F. Hahn, *Between Westpolitik and Ostpolitik: Changing West German Security Views* (Beverly Hill, Calif. and London, 1975), notably chs 1 and 9. Another example is provided by Wolfram Hanrieder, 'West Germany', in W. F. Hanrieder and G. P. Auton, *The Foreign Policies of West Germany, France, and Britain* (Englewood Cliffs, NJ, 1980), 3–94.

3 K. Kaiser, *German Foreign Policy in Transition*, 1, quoted in Noack, *Die Aussenpolitik*, 7.

4 For a more detailed discussion of the present offence–defence debate see R. Cowen, *The Strategic Defense Initiative and the Atlantic Alliance: Doctrine Versus Security* (New York, forthcoming). Among the many SDI-related publications, one of the most comprehensive analyses is still the

Stanford University Special Report by S. D. Drell, P. J. Farley and D. Holloway, *The Reagan Strategic Defense Initiative: A Technical, Political, and Arms Control Assessment* (Stanford, Calif., 1984).

5 J. D. Steinbruner and L. V. Sigal (eds), *Alliance Security: Nato and the No-First-Use Question* (Washington, DC, 1983), particularly ch. 8 by Krell *et al.* on 'The no-first-use question in West Germany', pp. 147–72. Also see K. Kaiser *et al.*, 'Nuclear weapons and the preservation of peace: a German response', *Foreign Affairs*, 60 (Summer 1982).

6 The Federal Minister of Defence, *The Role of the Federal Republic of Germany in Nato* (Bonn, 1982), 11. For figures after 1982 see D. Marsh, 'Burden of non-nuclear army', *Financial Times*, 20 November 1986, 6.

7 Arnulf Baring, *Aussenpolitik in Adenauers Kanzlerdemokratic* (Munich, 1969); G. Wettig, *Entmilitarisierung und Wiederbewaffnung 1943-1955* (Munich, 1967); for a more general assessment see D. N. Schwartz, *Nato's Nuclear Dilemmas* (Washington, DC, 1983).

8 R. Cowen, *Defense Procurement in the Federal Republic of Germany: Politics and Organization* (Boulder, CO, 1986), 6–14.

9 *Ibid.*, 14–18.

10 Kelleher, 'Defence policy', 269.

11 Persuasive argumentation against this drift can be found in Gebhard Schweigler, 'The domestic setting of West German foreign policy', in U. Nerlich and J. A. Thomson (eds), *The Soviet Problem in American–German Relations* (New York, 1985), 21–61. The post-INF political atmosphere in Europe is cogently assessed by S. S. Szabo, 'European opinion after the missiles', *Survival*, 27, no. 6 (Nov.–Dec. 1985), 265–73. Gerd Langguth's *The Green Factor in German Politics* (Boulder, CO, 1984) provides a useful assessment of the Greens' background as a political movement and the societal support they enjoy.

12 J. Joffe, 'The Greening of Germany', *The New Republic*, 14 February 1983, 22; here quoted from Schweigler, 'Domestic setting', 27.

13 This is their key argument in C. M. Kelleher, 'The Federal Republic and Nato: change and continuity in the 1980s', in R. G. Livingston (ed.), *The Federal Republic of Germany in the 1980s* (New York, 1983), 8–12.

14 Very useful summaries of Soviet political motives and tactics towards influencing West German foreign and domestic policy making are provided by J. Van Oudenaren, 'Soviet assessment of trends in the alliance', and G. Wettig, 'The present Soviet view on trends in Germany', both in H. Gelman (ed.), *The Future of Soviet Policy towards Western Europe*, R–3254FF/Nato (Santa Monica, Calif., September 1985).

15 There are differences of opinion in the Green Party regarding its political aims within and outside parliament. The Greens themselves distinguish between 'Fundis' (fundamentalists) and 'Realos' (realists) with the former rejecting parliamentary democracy and the latter aiming 'to make parliamentary democracy more trustworthy and transparent' (Kelly, Langguth, *The Green Factor*, 69–78).

16 US Congress, Office of Technology Assessment, *Ballistic Missile Defense Technologies*, OTA–ISC–254 (Washington, DC, September 1985), especially ch. 6 on 'Crisis stability, arms race stability and arms control issues', 119–36.

17 'Bei der Bonner SDI–Anhörung uberwiegt die differenzierte Ablehnung', *Frankfurter Allgemeine Zeitung*, 11 December 1985, 4. 'In Bonn Lauft alles zu auf Verhandlungen über eine deutsche SDI–Beteiligung', *FAZ*, 10 December 1985, 2. 'After Reykjowik, trans-Atlantic strains will row', *International Herald Tribune*, 4 November 1986, 4. 'Most Nato defense chiefs back U.S. and Reykjowik and endorse SDI', *IHT*, 23 October 1986, 3. 'Kohl urges conventional arms sub', *IHT*, 23 October 1986, 3.

18 Private interviews with West German Foreign Office officials, Bonn, April 1986.

19 In his September 1986 parliamentary farewell address, Helmut Schmidt reflected on international and domestic political developments, touching on *Ostpolitik*, arms control, the relationships with Washington and Paris, and lamenting the complacency of the Kohl government in these fields – all of which are of vital importance to West German security. Schmidt claimed that the Kohl government had 'temporarily abdicated its influence over the shape of the West's overall policy'. 'Helmut Schmidt sums up: Ostpolitik, arms and allies', *International Herald Tribune*, 15 September 1986, 4. Many similar concerns are voiced by Christoph Bertram, scrutinizing Kohl's election slogan 'More of the Same' for evidence of active policy making. He suggests that 'during the last four years the Kohl government has preferred to draw on assets rather than invest in the future.' 'Should West Germans really get more of the same?', *IHT*, 22 January 1987, 6. The fact that the Kohl government can draw upon political assets is a tribute to the Schmidt chancellorship and may also explain why the present government so firmly occupies the West German political centre without, as yet, having had to come up with policy initiatives of its own.

20 There has been a flurry of activity in

the security field initiated by the SPD. Amongst them, the intellectually most interesting ideas can be found in: A. von Bulow, 'Defensive entanglement: an alternative strategy for Nato', in A. J. Pierre (ed.), *The Conventional Defense of Europe* (New York, 1986), 112–51. The chapter contains many of von Bulow's ideas expressed at greater length in an earlier and much-disputed SPD working paper entitled 'Alptraume West Gegen Alptuaume Ost'. Also see H. Ehmke, *Some Reflections on Europe's Self-Assertion* (Bonn, January 1984), particularly sections 2 and 3 on the alliance and the world economy respectively. The SPD and the East German SED have adopted an *Outline of an Agreement to Establish a Zone Free of Chemical Weapons in Europe* (Bonn, 1985), in which the SPD working group did not work through existing government channels.

21 It is generally believed that the political centre relies as much on effective coalition government as on effective opposition parties. The grand coalition of the mid 1960s between the CDU and the SPD deprived parliamentary opposition of its voice and pushed government critics to the political fringes. A Grand Coalition today would most certainly strengthen popular support for the Greens and most likely result in political polarization.

22 On this point see A. J. Pierre (ed.), *Nuclear Weapons in Europe* (New York, 1984), particularly Pierre's introduction, pp. 1–14, and Karsten Voigt's chapter 'Nuclear weapons in Europe: a German Social Democrat's perspective', pp. 98–118.

23 Krell *et al.*, 'The no-first-use question in West Germany', 150–2.

24 Noack, *Die Aussenpolitik*, 68–71.

25 For one of the most sober assessments of the technological challenges SDI is meant to tackle, see D. Walker, J. Bruce and D. Cook, *SDI: Progress and Challenges, Staff Report submitted to Senator William Proxmire, Senator J. Bennet Johnston, and Senator Lawton Chiles* (Washington, DC, 17 March 1986).

26 *Grundgesetz für die Bundesrepublik Deutschland*, Beck'sche Edition 47, rev. edn (Munich, April 1981), 47.

27 *Ibid.*, 45.

28 *Ibid.*, 79–80.

29 H. Haftendorn, 'West Germany and the management of security relations: security policy under the conditions of international interdependence', in E. Krippendorf and V. Rittberger (eds), *The Foreign Policy of West Germany* (London and Beverly Hills, Calif., 1980), 12.

30 *Ibid.*, 13 and 15.

31 Subsequent description and analysis are based on a series of private interviews with West German MOD and FO officials notably in 1981, 1982, 1984 and 1986.

32 Private interviews

33 Haftendorn, 'West Germany and the management of security relations', 27.

34 *Ibid.*, 28.

35 *Ibid.*, 12.

36 Haftendorn supports the notion of a penetrated system for the post-war period ending in 1955 with West German accession to NATO. She suggests that during subsequent years, direct penetration has been 'replaced by a coordinated, partially integrated international decision-making network'. Growing interdependence in the security, economic and political fields has, according to Haftendorn, led to a decrease of outside political control of West Germany while the policy making restraints caused by interdependence fulfil essentially the same function. This approach is persuasive, given West Germany's obviously high degree of integration in all kinds of Western organization; yet it does not explain why the West German defence organization appears to be as badly equipped to handle defence decision making as Haftendorn so ably demonstrates. Interdependence as a theory does not successfully replace that of penetration. If interdependence had indeed been a decisive factor in defence organization, West German defence organization would not display largely domestically rooted political priorities. Haftendorn, 'West Germany

and the management of security relations', 7–9. Kelleher shares Haftendorn's view of an over-bureaucratized and fragmented security policy but places greater emphasis on a myriad of circumstances, all relevant in some degree, that have contributed to West Germany's present defence organization. The breadth of her approach, almost inevitably, leads her to highlight the uniqueness of the West German case and a consequential emphasis on points of tension in West Germany's relationship with NATO and the United States at the expense of an analysis of routine defence policy management. Kelleher, 'Defence policy', 283–8 and 293–4.

37 An analysis of how the principle of dialogue governs the relationship between the armed forces staff and the civilian MOD departments can be found in Cowen, *Defense Procurement in the Federal Republic*, 56–7 and 71–3.
38 *Ibid.*, 83–93.
39 *Ibid.*, 128–35.
40 *Ibid.*, 6–14.
41 *Ibid.*, 279–87.
42 S. R. Sloan, *Nato's Future: Toward a New Translantic Bargain* (Washington, DC, 1985), 189–91. Sloan recommends a 'European security assessment' similar to the one called for by the French Prime Minister after the Reykjavik Summit. 'Chirac calls on Western Europe to draw up own security charter', *International Herald Tribune*, 3 December 1986, 1–2.

6
France

JOHN FENSKE

This essay briefly describes the sources, institutions, current outcomes, and future of French defence policy. The underlying argument is that the central tenet of French defence policy – the largest possible autonomy of decision for France – holds great promise but also poses serious problems. The promise lies in the hope that, at some point in the indefinite future, the keeping alive of a strong political will to autonomous power can serve as the basis for a grouping of European powers with greater independence vis-à-vis their American protector. Problems arise in the form of conflict between intentions and resources: France does not have today the financial or human resources needed to fulfil all its military and diplomatic ambitions, and while the aggregate resources of the European Community suggest the possibility of attaining the same league as the superpowers, it is difficult to reconcile the constant demand of French authorities for their own autonomy of decision with the growing imperative of European cooperation.[1]

Sources

An essay on contemporary French defence policy must give central prominence to the heritage of General Charles de Gaulle, if for no other reason than the fact that he is still frequently invoked by the French themselves. Two seminal quotations suffice to display the lines of force that continue to shape current deliberations on defence in France. In November 1959, soon after becoming President of the new French Fifth Republic, de Gaulle outlined the tasks facing military leaders and planners:

> The defence of France must be French. This is an imperative that has not always been very well understood these last few years, a fact of which I am quite aware. It is necessary that our defence become French once again. For a country like France, if war is to be fought, it must be our war. Our

147

effort must be our own. If it were otherwise, our country would be in contradiction with everything she has been since her origins, with her role, with the esteem she has for herself, with her soul. Of course, French defence could be, if the occasion arose, combined with that of other countries. That is in the nature of things. But it is essential that our defence be our own affair, that France defend herself by her own efforts, for her own reasons, and in her own manner.[2]

As a corollary to the fundamental principle of national independence, he went on in the same speech to prescribe the construction of an indigenous *force de frappe*, or nuclear 'striking force'. In a press conference three years later, he announced his two infamous 'noes': to Britain's entry into the Common Market and to the American proposal of French participation in the ill-fated MLF, or Multilateral (Nuclear) Force. Again, the tension between the twin imperatives of autonomy and alliance is foremost in his words:

It is evident that a country, in particular our own, in this age cannot, would not be able to, conduct by itself a large-scale modern war. In the historical period we now find ourselves, our need of allies is self-evident. But for a great people there is also need of liberty to decide and act for oneself, as well as to possess the means of fighting for that liberty. This is a strict necessity, for alliances do not have absolute virtues, no matter what feelings are behind them. If one loses spontaneously, even for a moment, the liberty to decide and act for oneself, one greatly risks never again recovering that liberty.[3]

Whence this ticklish obsession with autonomy of decision, with independence, with the primacy of *national* defence? A longer treatment of the subject would discuss the imprint of centuries of efforts to create a centralized state in France, beginning with the Capetian kings a full millennium ago. This essay restricts itself to some of the lessons of recent French history, that is, since the Second World War.[4]

De Gaulle came to power in 1958 for the second and final time as a direct result of the Fourth Republic's inability to withstand the throes of the Algerian War. He arrived in office convinced, as he had been already at the end of the Second World War, that France needed a stronger executive if she were ever again to 'be herself', which to him meant to 'be great'. He saw the recent past of his country strewn with tokens of decline: the military defeat of the Second World War, due in part to a rigid, backward-looking doctrine against which he had remonstrated in vain; the humiliation of the occupation years, scarcely obscured by the heroic resistance efforts he had inspired and guided from London; the defeat and withdrawal in 1954 from colonial possessions in Indochina, followed swiftly by troubles closer to home in

Algeria. Above all, there were the endless petty political struggles of the Fourth Republic parliamentary regime, which had constantly vitiated the potential of France for greatness.

Two episodes from the Fourth Republic are worth recalling, since they are often cited still today in explanation of current French defence policy. First is the debate over the European Defence Community, or EDC, which sorely divided the political elites in the early 1950s. The EDC Treaty would have instituted a supranational European army as a framework for the rearming of West Germany. Though originally a French plan, it meandered four years through the French political system until finally refused by Parliament in August 1954. French politicians and officials look at the EDC as a lesson in the need for national consensus on refusing attempts at supranational institutions, and more generally on issues imposed by the outside world, especially in the pre-eminently *national* area of defence.

The second episode is the Suez Crisis of October 1956. France, Great Britain and Israel together planned and began a military operation to take back the Suez Canal, which had recently been nationalized by Egypt. Under intense pressure from the superpowers, including threats of atomic punishment by Moscow, they stopped and withdrew. It is generally agreed that this crisis marked the birth of certitude within a significant (and ultimately triumphant) portion of the French political elite that an independent atomic force would be necessary if France were to avoid a repetition of this humiliating retreat.

De Gaulle sought to remedy the ills of the Fourth Republic by giving his country a new image of itself, an image rooted in effective symbols of unity and modernization, foremost among them a strong executive and atomic weaponry.[5] While the European and Atlantic partners of France could applaud the first innovation, the decision to build an independent atomic arsenal touched off an interminable quarrel with the Atlantic Alliance.[6] What to Alliance partners looked like a diversion of scarce resources into military projects of dubious value, was for France an essential part of regaining a truly *national* defence.

De Gaulle believed that the era of superpower parity, foreshadowed by the launching of Sputnik in October 1957 and especially evident after the Cuban Missile Crisis of October 1962, provided new space for manoeuvre by medium powers. With the homeland of each superpower clearly menaced by the nuclear weapons of the other, the atom could impose its paradoxical military stability: the very risk of nuclear destruction obliged the superpowers to avoid confrontations having a serious chance of escalation to all-out war. Thus began France's 'love affair with the atom',[7] for its own mastery of nuclear weapons allowed it to exploit the political breach opened up by the reciprocal neutralization of the superpowers.

In 1962, American Defense Secretary McNamara presented the 'flexible response' proposal as a way to enhance the credibility of NATO's overall military posture. France instead saw the new strategy as a trap threatening the independence of its nascent nuclear-weapons capability and therefore insisted on the ways the American proposal would compromise European interests. The Alliance had relied up to this point on 'massive retaliation', that is, on the threat to respond to Soviet aggression, even to a purely conventional attack, with strikes against the USSR by the American strategic nuclear arsenal. The impetus for flexible response came from the increasing vulnerability of the US homeland to Soviet retaliation. The introduction of 'tactical' or 'theatre' nuclear weapons seemed to offer an intermediate step on the escalation ladder that would make a NATO nuclear response appear more credible than all-out nuclear war, while keeping present the danger that fighting might lead there anyway. The Americans maintained that such measures would plug leaks in the 'umbrella' of 'extended deterrence' held over NATO Europe. De Gaulle and his spokesmen counter that flexible response was further proof that the umbrella was being gradually withdrawn.

There has always been a conundrum behind the reassuring notion of responding flexibly to aggression: such a strategy is credible to the extent that it promises limiting war to the theatre, that is, to Europe; but the defence elites of NATO Europe count on it as a means to 'couple' their defence to the American strategic nuclear arsenal.[8] The West Europeans have tended to believe that only a clearly perceived risk of involving the American arsenal is a serious enough deterrent to avert any war at all from taking place on their soil. A common-sense view of national interests would suggest that Americans prefer a definition of 'flexibility' permitting the territory of the United States to be spared, while Europeans favour one posing the greatest possible risks to the Soviet Union.

In 1967, one year after France's withdrawal from the NATO military command structure, NATO officially endorsed flexible response, thus agreeing to paper over an unresolvable dilemma between 'dominance' (believing that escalation, even within a war 'gone nuclear', can be controlled) and 'uncertainty' (seeing instead the ultimate deterrent value in 'the threat that leaves something to chance', that is, in the prospect of uncontrollable escalation). France meanwhile came down decisively on the side of uncertainty, for such a position offered a double advantage: it corresponded to the best strategy for a small nuclear power vis-à-vis a superpower, and it gave France a way to contest American hegemony within the Alliance.

Consider now the geopolitical position of France relative to the two other European members of the Atlantic Alliance covered in this study. Like France, the United Kingdom is also a nuclear power, yet tied to the United States (the French are always quick to point out) by a 'special relationship' of 'Anglo-Saxon' complicity, therefore possessing European credentials more suspect than one might infer from traditional British insularity alone. West Germany is doubly handicapped by the settlement of the Second World War: forever looking towards the other Germany and working to keep open the possibility of ultimate reunification, and at the same time denied (by self-imposed restrictions, international agreements and Soviet threats) the right to possess the only weapon that might permit a self-sufficient defence posture, hence its attachment to an American military presence in Europe. Because of its relative independence from the American protector, France sees itself as the only natural choice for the role of speaking and acting freely on behalf of European interests.

The preceding discussion of sources suggests four principal sets of influences on the defence policy making process in France. First is the political tradition of executive-branch dominance, instituted by de Gaulle and synonymous with the Fifth Republic. In the international sphere, the corollary of this tradition is a constant vigilance to preserve national independence. The Fourth Republic bequeathed to the Fifth a nuclear-weapons programme that quickly bore fruit, but it is implausible that the Fourth, with its parliamentary politics and its habit of reliance on NATO, would have 'used' nuclear weapons to restore French greatness in the manner of the Fifth. Second, despite the stress on independence, relations with the superpowers remain central, and the East–West 'correlation of forces' a paramount concern. The German *glacis* and the American nuclear umbrella have together allowed France to strike various poses of independent defence and diplomacy. When the USSR begins to look more threatening or the German buffer less stable, then France must act, as it has in recent years, to restore equilibrium.

Europe itself is a third influence on policy making. Geography, trade, the ambition to command greater resources, the existence of the Soviet Union and its East European allies, the need to react to a weakening commitment or growing competition from America, all point ineluctably to the importance of strengthening Europe as a political entity. The fourth and final influence is inherent in the other three: the increasingly pressing contradiction between French national resources and ambitions, or the parallel one between the desirability of a European dimension and the insistence on French autonomy. All efforts to find a common European political will must deal ultimately with the question of defence, and for the moment this question finds no answer. The problem is most succinctly put by one of the stock responses in the catechism of French officialdom: 'Nuclear weapons cannot be shared.'

Institutions and Actors

This section reviews the following institutions and actors with respect to their roles in defence policy making: Parliament, President, Defence Council, Prime Minister, Secretariat General for National Defence, Defence Ministry, Foreign Affairs Ministry.[9] In addition, the influence of political parties and outside experts is also briefly discussed. The discussion is mainly about *where* the key decision makers sit: *how* decisions are made is notoriously difficult for an outsider to investigate in France, particularly so in the areas of defence and diplomacy. The reader should assume that many lines of control and consultation exist beyond the formal and better-known channels mentioned here.[10]

1. Parliament

A newcomer to French defence policy might first notice that the subject has aroused native passions every few years in the Fifth Republic. This occurs because Parliament and hence the public know about the choices of the executive branch mainly from presentation and discussion of the multi-year programming law (*loi de programmation*) and subsequent extensions.[11] As discussed above, one of the central innovations of the Fifth Republic was the movement of power from the legislature to the executive, and defence is one sector in which this trend is highly evident.[12]

The National Assembly has a National Defence Commission, and the Senate a Foreign Affairs and Defence Commission, which report on the programming laws; together with the Finance Commissions in both houses, they also report on the yearly finance bill in which funds approved in the programming law are actually disbursed. The constitution of the Fifth Republic, however, gives Deputy and Senator little leverage to get more information or to force the government to take action, unless Parliament can find allies within the administration (or is sought by them). One example of successful parliamentary interference with the executive concerns planning for a sixth ballistic-missile submarine. President Giscard d'Estaing attempted to increase the share

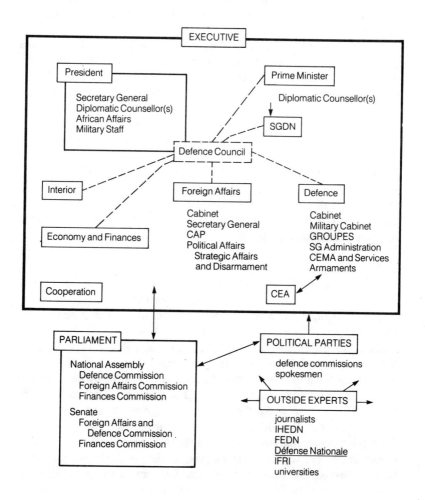

Figure 6.1 Institutions and actors: defence policy making in France

of the defence budget devoted to conventional armaments and found some of the money by delaying construction of the submarine. But in September 1978, under pressure from the Gaullist half of his majority coalition in Parliament, Giscard reversed this decision and included money for the sixth submarine.

The programming law describes defence policy in only the most general of terms, and the spending categories give the executive enormous discretion. Parliament has scarce resources available for research of complex technical issues and cannot interrogate relevant officials or military personnel without authorization from the executive branch. Various procedural rules allow the government to force through a bill (by limiting debate, or by calling for a vote of confidence) as well as to reject unwanted amendments, even to ignore ones that have been approved. The only significant checking or oversight functions allowed Parliament are, first, reports by parliamentary commissions on military-spending laws, and second, the right to put oral and written questions to the ministers, though in practice few of these are devoted to defence and foreign affairs.

2. President

During the first 28 years of the Fifth Republic, it had been fairly accurate to locate the power of the French executive in the presidency. In March 1986, parliamentary elections brought together a majority of Deputies from the right under a socialist President. At the time of writing, an unprecedented constitutional and political experiment is unfolding, in which a President and a Prime Minister from opposite sides of the political spectrum hold office simultaneously – a situation the French call 'cohabitation'. Although the tradition established by de Gaulle had been to make defence and foreign affairs into a 'reserved domain' for the President, the constitution in fact gives the Prime Minister considerable autonomy, and the new constellation of executive power under 'cohabitation' shows presidential powers in many areas to be considerably diminished. One should expect, however, a return to usual practice if the President is once again recognized as leader of the parliamentary majority. In any event, 'cohabitation' does not appear to have significantly altered the predominance of the executive branch in defence matters.

The French President is chief of the armed forces and the only one authorized to order firing of nuclear weapons. To assist him in these functions, he has the Presidential Military Staff (*Etat-Major Particulier*): on the one hand, this staff provides the principal means of communication with the military hierarchy, including keeping 'the button' ready; on the other hand, depending upon the style and mandate of the Chief of the Presidential Military Staff (*Chef d'Etat-Major Particulier* or CEMP), this group can also take on advisory and policy making responsibility. Two recent CEMPs, General Guy Méry under Giscard and General Jean Saulnier under Mitterrand, have gone on to become Armed Forces Chief of Staff (*Chef d'Etat-Major des Armées* or CEMA).

The President appoints the Prime Minister and (on the recommendation of the latter) the Defence Minister and the Foreign Affairs Minister, as well as all other members of government, subject to the requirement of parliamentary support. Ministers then report to the Prime Minister. The President is responsible for monitoring international agreements, in particular for negotiating and ratifying treaties. The President also has the right to declare a national emergency, which would give him extraordinary powers.

The President is assisted and counselled in all his work by the Secretary General of the Presidency (*Secrétaire Général de la Présidence de la République* or *SG de l'Elysée*), a position roughly equivalent to the American presidential 'Chief of Staff'. There is also a special assistant for diplomatic affairs (*Conseiller Diplomatique*) who organizes and counsels on the mass of military and diplomatic issues arriving constantly; this position is remotely akin to the American 'National Security Adviser'. However, neither of these key officials has ever been given the authority, visibility, or organizational weight found in the American counterpart, and typically the positions have been held by self-effacing, mid-career civil servants. Other presidential advisers may also handle defence and diplomatic issues. In particular, there is a secretariat for African affairs, which also fall within the purview of the Cooperation and Foreign Affairs Ministries.

3. *Defence Council*
The Council of Ministers, chaired by the President, has nominal authority for defence policy, though in practice its approval is a formality. The highest body deliberating specifically on defence matters is the Defence Council (*Conseil de Défense*), also chaired by the President, and on his initiative called to meet at irregular intervals. Composition of the Defence Council varies according to the matter under deliberation, though by law it includes the President, the Prime Minister, the Defence Minister, the Foreign Affairs Minister, the Interior Minister, the Economy and Finances Minister, and the Armed Forces Chief of Staff. The President is assisted in Defence Council meetings by the Chief of the Presidential Military Staff and the

Secretary General of the Presidency. The Secretariat General for National Defence (described below) prepares the agenda. Also frequently present are the three service chiefs, the Armaments Delegate General, the head of the Atomic Energy Commissariat, and the Commissariat's Director of Military Applications.

4. Prime Minister

The Prime Minister is able to contest traditional presidential predominance in defence matters because the constitution explicitly makes him 'responsible for national defence' and subsequent decrees give him the powers necessary to carry out decisions of the Defence Council. In prior practice, the Prime Minister gave way to the President in matters of policy, restricting his own role to the operational aspects of defence. Under 'cohabitation', the Prime Minister has upgraded his private staff of diplomatic and military experts and made several challenges to the prerogatives of the President.[13]

5. Secretariat General for National Defence

The SGDN (Secrétariat Général de la Défense Nationale) is attached to the Prime Minister's office. Only a small group within the SGDN is responsible for preparing Defence Council meetings and assuring implementation of its decisions. The bulk of the 600 or so employees are concerned with reflection on defence-related issues, such as the state of foreign military forces, potential crises, interministerial coordination, protection of state and industrial secrets. As part of these tasks, the SGDN also has responsibility for the Interministerial Intelligence Committee, which coordinates the various counter-espionage and foreign intelligence activities.[14]

6. Defence Ministry

The organizational chart of the Defence Ministry naturally includes several bodies of high importance for defence policy making: the Ministerial Cabinet, the Strategic Planning and Studies Group, the military Chiefs of Staff, and the Armaments Delegate General.

The Ministerial Cabinet includes a Director and several Technical Counsellors (Conseillers Techniques), high-level civil servants whose jobs and powers are chiefly a function of their own interests and talents. A separate Military Cabinet provides access to the military hierarchy and forces. There is also a Secretary of State for National Defence (Secrétaire d'Etat à la Défense Nationale), but traditionally the policy making role of this position has been rather limited. Defence Civil Servants (Haut Fonctionnaires de Défense) are assigned to those ministries having defence-related functions (such as Transportation and Foreign Affairs) in order to provide liaison with the Defence Ministry, though formal and informal contacts exist at many levels.

The Strategic Planning and Studies Group (*Groupe de Planification et d'Etudes Stratégiques*, with acronym GROU.PES or GROUPES, pronounced 'Group S') has a venerable history, having begun in the early 1960s as the Centre for Forecasting and Evaluation (*Centre de Prospective et d'Evaluation* or CPE), the means by which de Gaulle adapted the French military to its new nuclear vocation. Consisting of about 25 members, GROUPES is headed by an Armaments Engineer (*Ingénieur Général de l'Armament*), who is assisted by officers representing the three services. The mandate of GROUPES is to serve as the Minister's 'think tank' in matters of general strategic concern (for example, the implications of the American Strategic Defense Initiative), as well as to conduct specific studies of future weapons-systems research and acquisition. GROUPES is one of the more obvious candidates for the role of principal institutional memory with regard to defence policy.

The Chief of Staff of the Armies (CEMA) has operational responsibility for the three services.[15] In time of crisis or war, CEMA can expect to be named the Chief of the General Staff of the Armies (CEMGA). In collaboration with budget specialists from the ministerial cabinet and with the Secretariat General for Administration, CEMA combines and arbitrates the budget requests from the three service chiefs. Inter-service rivalries, however, can carry the battle to higher or other levels: it is uncommon, but not unknown, for a service chief to plead his case against CEMA or the Minister in the Defence Council; and leaks, interviews, and the carefully worded statement are becoming standard weapons in defence of a service's share of the budgetary pie. The military chiefs also have responsibility for defining the working relationship between France and NATO, subject to the proviso that the ultimate decision to commit forces or permit allied access to French territory be left to the political authorities.

The Armaments Delegate General (*Délégué Général pour l'Armement* or DGA) has responsibility for a vast industrial domain: research, development, and production of new weapons; supervision of arsenals and defence industries; and international activities, such as import, export, and coproduction.[16] With 310,000 employees (6 per cent of industrial employment), the arms industry has a significant macro-economic impact. The state looks to armaments as well for maintaining competence in high-technology realms. In keeping with its status of mini-superpower, France is the number three arms merchant in the world, holding roughly 10 per cent of global markets, which represents about 40 per cent of French arms production. The DGA is also the formal link between the Defence Ministry and the Atomic Energy Commissariat (*Commissariat à l'Energie Atomique* or CEA), which has a traditional interest in the role of nuclear weapons in defence policy.

7. Foreign Affairs Ministry
The Ministerial Cabinet and the Secretary General of the Foreign Affairs Ministry can be expected to have an interest in the definition of defence policy.[17] However, the task of following defence and arms control issues falls principally to the Political Affairs Office (*Direction des Affaires Politiques*) and to one of its subdivisions, the Strategic Affairs and Disarmament Service (*Service des Affaires Stratégiques et du Désarmement*). This latter service handles diplomatic relations with NATO and the West European Union, bilateral military cooperation (in particular, with the Federal Republic), and multilateral projects (such as the European Fighter Aircraft project). There is also a separate 'think tank', reporting to the Minister, that is often concerned with the political and strategic implications of defence policy: the Forecasting and Analysis Centre (*Centre d'Analyse et de Prévision* or CAP).

8. Political Parties
Each of the four major political parties maintains a defence commission and one or more specialists to study issues and produce position papers.[18] Retired senior military personnel often lend patronage or contribute ideas, though they tend to shun public exposure. Politicians interested in joining or heading one of the relevant parliamentary commissions are usually the ones most active within a party. However, there is little evidence to suggest that the party commissions have any direct influence on executive-branch decisions. Rather, the parties fulfil indirect functions, such as providing a forum for public debate, preparing and educating future ministers and presidents, and floating 'trial balloons' on issues such as European defence cooperation.

9. Outside Experts
Until the last ten years or so, the expression 'outside expert' might well have been considered an oxymoron in France, since the bureaucracy likes to think (with good reason) that it monopolizes expertise on a subject so vital to the state. The 1980s have witnessed a steady growth in the quality and scope of public discussion on defence issues, though it would be premature to speak of a 'strategic community' in France, except perhaps for the semi-secret one within the executive. Since 1948

civilian notables have been invited to attend seminars of the Institute for Higher Studies in National Defence (*Institut des Hautes Etudes de Défense Nationale* or IHEDN, under the authority of the SGDN), where they can study contemporary defence issues, meet future military leaders, and hear speeches by high officials.

The Foundation for the Study of National Defence (*Fondation pour les Etudes de Défense Nationale* or FEDN) is an official institution, funded by the Defence Ministry, that promotes publication of defence-oriented work.[19] The quasi-official monthly *Défense Nationale* prints articles by outside experts and retired military officers, as well as a steady trickle of official speeches and articles. A more independent body is the French Institute for International Relations (*Institut Français des Relations Internationales* or IFRI), with its quarterly journal *Politique Etrangère*.[20] Universities are also gradually developing programmes on defence and related matters.[21]

Current Policy

1. Budget

Taking a cue from the adage, 'expenditure is policy', this section begins by looking at the two most recent defence-spending laws: the one approved under a government of the left in spring 1983, covering the period 1984–8, and, more briefly, the second approved under a government of the right in the autumn of 1986, covering the period 1987–91. Information available at the time of writing suggests that the 1986 law continues with roughly the same priorities as the 1983 law, and that a new budget should be expected following the presidential election scheduled for 1988.[22]

The 1983 law approved spending 830 billion francs (current value) over the five years 1984–8, 142.1 billion of which in 1984. This represents approximately 15 per cent of the total annual budget in France and 3.9 per cent of PIBm (*Produit Intérieur Brut marchand*), which is a subset of Gross Domestic Product (about 88 per cent of GDP). Using NATO definitions, the French defence effort as a share of GDP was, for 1984 budgets, intermediate (4.1 per cent) between the efforts of the United Kingdom (5.4 per cent) and the Federal Republic of Germany (3.3 per cent).[23]

2. Equipment and Manpower

The budget corresponds to declaratory policy in that it gives priority to the development of nuclear forces. About 20 per cent of the total defence budget (representing one-third of capital expenditures within that budget) go to the strategic and tactical nuclear forces. In May 1985, a new ballistic-missile submarine went into service with a new series of missile, the M–4, apparently incorporating MIRV technology.[24] With six warheads per missile, and 16 missiles per submarine, the new submarine carries 96 warheads, versus 16 on older boats, which are being modified to take the M–4. France now claims to keep three submarines on patrol continuously; thus, when the M–4 modifications are complete around 1993, the ballistic-missile submarines should provide France with 288 warheads on station, out of 480 total.

France also maintains airborne and land-based strategic nuclear forces, though they are both considered highly vulnerable and receive far less funding than the sea-based deterrent. There has been serious talk, but no decision yet, about developing a mobile land-based strategic component, which could be either a ballistic missile or a cruise missile. The equipment budget for 1987–91 reaffirms the priority of ballistic-missile submarines over a mobile missile – a curious episode of the cohabitation experiment, in which the President prevailed over the Prime Minister.

The current generation of tactical nuclear weapons is also being modernized. First, a medium-range air-to-ground missile (*Air-Sol Moyenne Portée* or ASMP) is being deployed as a replacement for gravity bombs and will also be used to rejuvenate the airborne strategic nuclear forces. Second, a medium-range ballistic missile, the Hadès, will enter service around 1992, thus extending the range of targeting from the current 120 kilometres (the Pluton missile) to over 350 kilometres. The Hadès will be put under direct control of the CEMA, instead of the battlefield commander. In addition, France has kept open the option of deploying the enhanced radiation warhead ('neutron bomb'), and there have been suggestions that the Hadès would be equipped with this warhead.

The 1984–8 programming law instituted a reorganization of the land army with two major aspects. The land army is to be cut by 22,000 troops, with a 1988 force-level goal of 290,000 (an additional 13,000 are to be cut from other services and civilian administration). On the other hand, a new unit called the Rapid Action Force (*Force d'Action Rapide* or FAR) was created, in some sense more than compensating for the reduction in troop strength.[25] French officials have made it clear that, while their traditional concerns about maintaining autonomy of decision rest intact, the FAR is intended as a signal of increased solidarity with the Alliance. Viewed from NATO head-quarters, the most welcome innovation is probably that the FAR provides *mobile* forces *in addition to* the French First Army, capable of intervening in

Central Europe or elsewhere.[26] Much is made of the one air-mobile division (out of five total) and its anti-tank helicopters; on the other hand, it should be noted that French 'divisions' are in fact comparable to two NATO brigades (two-thirds of a division).

3. Doctrine

The 'military doctrine' or 'declaratory policy' supposedly guiding these expenditures comes in a direct line of descent from the instructions given to the nation by de Gaulle, representative samples of which were quoted earlier in this essay. The very essence of all defence policy in France is autonomy of decision, especially so as defence is the area of state effort intended to provide the ultimate guarantee of that autonomy. These fundamentals were introduced into French defence planning through the efforts of men like Generals Gallois, Beaufre, and Poirier, and grafted onto existing institutions through the work of the CPE, predecessor to the GROUPES.[27] The CPE's early work was codified under the leadership of Defence Minister Michel Debré, one of de Gaulle's closest associates, in a 1972 White Paper that, for lack of a replacement, is still valid today. In practice, analysts consider the programming law, and especially the preamble outlining general considerations, as being the most recent authorized version of defence policy. Speeches by the President, ministers, the CEMA, and other high officials add detail and occasional modification to the body of policy established by the programming law.[28]

The 1972 White Paper described a model for considering French defence needs that divides the world into three circles. The first circle is France, also known as the national sanctuary, because of the inviolable status said to be conferred upon it by the threat of nuclear retaliation. The second circle includes the immediate approaches to national territory, in particular the territory of neighbouring allies and especially the Federal Republic of Germany. The third circle is everywhere else in the world, including France's overseas departments and territories, as well as former colonies with which it has defence agreements.[29]

The atom bomb was said to confer an 'equalizing power' (*pouvoir égalisateur de l'atome*) upon any country capable of exploding a sufficient quantity of these weapons on the territory of an enemy, even a much stronger enemy. Sufficiency is the criterion dictated by a strategy called 'deterrence of the strong by the weak' (*dissuasion du faible au fort*): the weak power, not pretending to match the far greater arsenal and operational capabilities of a strong enemy, can nevertheless deter attacks on the 'national sanctuary' by putting at risk a fraction of the enemy's homeland at least equal to the gain the enemy would hope to get by attacking the weak. France has traditionally claimed to have an 'anti-cities' strategy (often called 'counter-value' in American strategic parlance), because it is supposedly the most efficient way to pose risks. Thus, France seeks only a minimal deterrent capability, and comparison of risk with the war aims of the strong suggest the additional nickname 'proportional deterrence'.[30] This is a 'non-war strategy', for to begin an engagement with the strong is to lose it: 'in the nuclear age and for a power such as France, the only possible victory is in staying at peace.'[31] Hence the importance of having the correct declaratory policy, of not suggesting in any manner the actual possibility of using nuclear weapons, other than their virtual use as a menace reserved for the defence of national territory and the ultimate survival of the nation.

The most obvious criticism of this strategy is that it amounts to an all-or-nothing threat: either the enemy leaves France inviolate (a 'sanctuary') or it suffers as much damage as the French strategic forces are able to deliver – the rub being that a 'strong' enemy like the Soviet Union would almost certainly retain sufficient nuclear forces, even if France attacked first, to destroy France utterly – or, as is said in France today, to 'vitrify' the entire country. The first solution to the all-or-nothing problem was found in the use of non-nuclear forces immediately outside the national frontiers (specifically, the parts of the French First Army stationed in Germany) that would serve as a means of testing the enemy's ultimate intentions in a 'national deterrent manoeuvre'. The purpose of such forces is explicitly not to attempt the impossible of matching the conventional capabilities of the strong enemy, but the far more modest goal of giving the French chief of state information about aggressive intent against the national sanctuary.

As a further response to criticism of the all-or-nothing nature of French strategy (and perhaps because the land army, too, wanted to have atomic weaponry), tactical nuclear weapons (*Armement Nucléaire Tactique* or ANT) were introduced into the French arsenal beginning in the early 1970s. They were accommodated by the notion of 'vital interests' – which include the whole of the national sanctuary, but are not limited to it – and became part of the 'national deterrent manoeuvre' assigned to the First Army. French ANT have traditionally been described as having an utterly different role from that of NATO's tactical nuclear weapons under the flexible response strategy: rather than being a kind of 'superartillery' intended to compensate for losing the conventional battle, French ANT are reserved for a single militarily significant 'ultimate warning' strike (*ultime avertissement*) against enemy forces. In order to emphasize further the nearly automatic link to the French strategic arsenal, ANT were recently rebaptized as 'pre-strategic' weapons.

The expression 'vital interests' has often been used in ways that could be construed as the timid beginnings of a French version of 'extended deterrence'. There is a margin around the national sanctuary, of uncertain value and indefinite contours, which France refuses to specify in advance as covered by the nuclear forces, but which could be a site where 'vital interests' are at stake. Thus, there is no guarantee that France will respond to aggression outside its boundaries as it would to an attack on French soil. Nevertheless, a potential aggressor must keep clearly in mind that there is also no guarantee that France will not use its ANT in defence of 'vital interests' outside national territory. Despite the abstract formulation, it is clear from context that the most likely location of 'vital interests' outside France would be in West Germany.

4. NATO and Other Allies
While the foregoing outline of French military doctrine describes not only a nuclear priority, but also a subordination of conventional-force efforts to the 'national deterrent manoeuvre', in practice France has maintained abundant contacts with NATO ever since leaving the integrated military command in 1966. In 1967 the Ailleret-Lemnitzer Agreement, and in 1974 the Valentin-Ferber Agreement, established plans for the participation of French troops alongside NATO, if the political authorities so decide. French elites willingly maintain the convenient fiction that France is 'outside NATO' as a way of saying that it is not in the NATO integrated military command. They have been telling their people more frequently in recent years that France is a faithful member of the Atlantic Alliance, bound by the North Atlantic Treaty to come to the aid of other signatories subject to aggression. On the other hand, they do not talk any more than necessary about France's continued membership in many NATO structures, including the North Atlantic Council (the top decision making body) and the air defence warning system NADGE (NATO Air Defence Ground Environment).[32]

The land-army reorganization announced in 1983, especially the creation of the FAR, attempts the juggling act of simultaneously reducing troop strength, cutting expenses, modernizing, and providing more 'polyvalent' forces. NATO and Germany are rightly sceptical of the total additional firepower they can hope for as a result of these innovations. However, the FAR constitutes a clear political signal of increased willingness to affirm solidarity instead of insisting on the primacy of the national sanctuary and the possibility of remaining a non-belligerent during hostilities between NATO and the Warsaw Pact.

JOHN FENSKE

The 'polyvalence' of the FAR alludes to its potential for intervention outside Europe as well, principally on behalf of French interests in Africa, the Caribbean and the South Pacific. Two especially sensitive distant points to protect are Kourou, French Guyana, where the Ariane civilian missiles are launched; and Mururoa Atoll in the South Pacific, site of France's underground nuclear testing programme. Of great importance to Paris are the French-speaking former colonies strung across north and central Africa, as evidenced by the troops stationed there, and especially by the interventions over the past decade in Zaïre, the Central African Republic and Chad.[33] Providing a less confining alternative than either superpower is one of the most frequent reasons given for maintaining French interests in Africa. The concrete form of this alternative is often a handsome arms contract and considerable influence with the client state.[34]

5. Defence Politics

Viewed from other Alliance capitals, one of the most enviable aspects of French defence policy is the surface unanimity of political elites and the acquiescence of the populace, a situation the French proudly call their 'national consensus on defence and foreign policy'.[35] France is unique among Alliance countries in the weakness of its peace movements, and no doubt the official policy of a 'non-war strategy' is soothing in comparison with the conventional battles and limited nuclear wars evoked by discussions of NATO doctrine. Other explanations advanced for the French consensus include the independent stance 'outside NATO', the public perception that France is protected by its own nuclear weapons rather than American ones, the lack of American military presence on French soil, the influence of Catholic and statist traditions, and the 'inoculation effect' due to heavy influence of the pro-Moscow French Communist Party in most mass peace demonstrations.[36]

The Future

French defence policy in the latter half of the 1980s will steer a course avoiding the caricatures recently applied to it by British and French weekly news magazines: 'The French are ready to cross the Rhine' and 'Defence: France is out of breath, out of ideas.'[37] Authorized voices have still not dispelled all ambiguity about French participation alongside NATO in case of a Soviet attack, yet there has been an un-mistakable evolution towards greater Alliance solidarity. The problem is that other Alliance members, particularly West Germany, believe that greater solidarity on a verbal level ought to translate into greater budgetary efforts in favour of continental conventional defence, while France still feels strongly the pull of other priorities. Chief among these conflicting priorities is development of the national nuclear arsenal. Maintaining a presence outside Europe is another priority with a large claim on resources, as is evident in the decision embodied in the 1987–91 budget to build two nuclear-powered aircraft carriers.

De Gaulle's spectacular moves to increase France's freedom of manoeuvre took place during the heyday of the atom, when 'pure deterrence', 'mutual assured destruction', and 'uncertainty'[38] presided over relations among the great and medium powers. The 'equalizing power of the atom' allowed France to achieve a voice in Europe and the Alliance out of proportion to its economic and demographic weight. Military doctrine could be constructed upon principles such as the 'national sanctuary' without seriously disturbing the East–West equilibrium because the American–Soviet atomic stalemate was so stable. France could thus ignore with impunity the complaints of Alliance partners, concentrating instead upon its nuclear programme and relations with African clients.

The historic occasion seized by de Gaulle and turned to the advantage of French grandeur has all but come to a close. Three spheres of international relations have witnessed revolutions that put new strains on France's foreign and defence policies.[39] First, the peaceful balance between the superpowers in Europe has given way to fears among West European defence and foreign policy elites that the Soviets have built and continue to augment an intimidating military machine, both conventional and nuclear, insufficiently matched by the West.[40] De Gaulle's confident assertion that American interests were not identical with European interests, that the Americans would not put their own territory at risk in order to save Europe, is more generally accepted today. But vindication of his prescience is of little comfort to France, for much of the liberty to take an independent stance had been due to the same American nuclear umbrella that de Gaulle and others so assiduously disparaged. Moreover, America is seen as less interested nowadays in Europe, culturally and especially commercially, since the Pacific Basin – East Asia, Central and South America – has been steadily gaining in importance.

The second revolution with which France must contend today concerns its European partners, foremost among them the Federal Republic of Germany. In the early 1960s, French preoccupation with an independent, national defence could be accommodated as something irksome but not catastrophic. Today the same insistence would be perceived as implicitly neutralist, running counter to a growing desire in Western Europe for a unified voice within the Alliance and in East–West relations. French elites have justified their increased attention to 'solidarity' by pointing to the necessity of anchoring the Federal Republic more firmly in the West. Some have exaggerated the danger of West Germany's being tempted by another 'Rapallo' (a French national myth in the same class as 'Yalta'), that is, a separate deal with the Soviet Union to the detriment of the rest of Europe. Nevertheless, there are indeed political currents in Germany and other European countries that risk compromising the future of a European power base by acceding to the persistent, patient Soviet efforts at intimidation. France is especially concerned about the long-standing Soviet demand for inclusion of French and British nuclear forces in American–Soviet arms control talks.

The third revolution concerns military doctrine and related technology. The golden age of peace guaranteed by the mere existence of nuclear weapons now appears irretrievably gone: the USA and the USSR are engaged in a new 'arms race' even more demanding than the one that built their nuclear arsenals. Doctrine and technology are now converging on increased flexibility and operational credibility; the emphasis is on miniaturization and greater precision through advances in guidance, electronics and computing; and some of the particular labels attached to these changes are FOFA (Follow-On Forces Attack, the official name for a recent addition to NATO's Flexible Response), ET ('Emerging Technologies'), and SDI (Strategic Defense Initiative). France is hit triply hard by this revolution, for it puts pressure squarely on 'deterrence of the strong by the weak', calls for increased resources in all sectors of military equipment and technology, and makes imperative a greater presence in space.[41]

Most analysts in France are convinced that while French defence policy has not forsaken the basic principles laid out in the 1972 White Paper, there has been perceptible 'movement' in response to a changing environment. The FAR (see above) in particular was meant, all at the same time to be compatible with established doctrine, to introduce more modern technology into the land army, and to respond to a longstanding request by the Alliance for an enhanced conventional contribution. Four years after creation of the FAR, French officials recognize privately that it did not improve Alliance relations as much as hoped for. Other recent measures intended to demonstrate solidarity with allies have also been disappointing: the half-hearted revival of the West European Union (WEU), Franco-German military consultation, and joint weapons production projects (Franco-German helicopter, and the combat aircraft among several European countries).[42]

While official statements continue incantation of the approved formulas, practice has apparently moved on. The nuclear part of the defence budget retains priority, but within that part, tactical nuclear weapons have been receiving an increasing share: Hadès, the neutron bomb, the ASMP. Strict adherence to professed doctrine would call for only a small number of these battlefield weapons, since a truly 'ultimate warning' would require no more than needed for a unique, militarily significant salvo. Indeed, French theory on the use of tactical nuclear weapons is often described as the antithesis of NATO's Flexible Response, with 'flexibility' assimilated to 'warfighting' – that is, to accepting the failure of deterrence. The strategic nuclear force also shows signs of evolution, for if 'pure' or 'proportional deterrence' were the object, it would be hard to justify the additional efforts made to master MIRV technology, as opposed to simply improving penetration.[43] It is noteworthy that the Defence Minister in the period 1986–8, a former head of the Atomic Energy Commissariat, suggested that the neutron bomb might offer a solution to the 'Maginot Line' character of the strategic nuclear arsenal: his words do not constitute an official policy change, but the very fact of his remarks is astounding.[44] More frequently and more urgently, the French are asking themselves nowadays how their military power might be useful beyond the confines of the 'national sanctuary'.[45]

At the beginning of the Fifth Republic, French politics called on military strategy to provide the nation with greater liberty of action. The resulting principles and habits of defence policy making are thought by many in France today to have lost their original rationale and become an infringement on politics. No one argues with the abstract proposition that France or any nation should strive to preserve the freedom to decide on its own. The difficulty is that French people and their elites increasingly view their independence as inextricable from that of their European neighbours and allies. The next few years should witness budgetary and doctrinal battles over defence policy, the outcome of which will determine whether France is able to close the gap between aspiration and orthodoxy.[46]

Notes

1 Throughout this essay, frequent use has been made of the following works: D. S. Yost, 'France's deterrent posture and security in Europe', *Adelphi Paper*, nos. 194–5 (Winter 1984–5); P. Hassner, 'France, deterrence and

Europe', *International Defence Review*,
no. 2 (1984); 'La France et la sécurité
de l'Europe', *Politique Etrangère*, 48,
no. 2 (Summer 1983); and '1936–1986,
50 ans de politique étrangère de la
France', *Politique Etrangère*, 51, no. 1
(Spring 1986).
2 Charles de Gaulle, *Discours et messages*,
III (Paris, 1970), 126. Here and
elsewhere, translation into English is
by the author. For analysis and
appraisal of de Gaulle's heritage, see S.
Hoffmann, *Decline or Renewal? France
Since the 1930s* (New York, 1974), and
P. G. Cerny, *The Politics of Grandeur:
Ideological Aspects of de Gaulle's
Foreign Policy* (Cambridge, 1980).
3 Charles de Gaulle, *Discours et messages*,
IV (Paris, 1970), 71–2 (press
conference of 14 Jan. 1963).
4 A good chronological account is given
in A. Grosser, *Les Occidentaux* (Paris,
1978), which was published in English
as *The Western Alliance* (1980); see also
his *Affaires extérieures: la politique de la
France 1944–1984* (Paris, 1984). For a
book with a clear argument about
France's place in the geopolitical
structure of post-war Europe, see A.
W. DePorte, *Europe Between the
Superpowers* (New Haven and London,
1979). See also M. M. Harrison, *The
Reluctant Ally* (Baltimore, 1981).
5 S. Hoffmann, 'La France face à son
image', *Politique Etrangère*, *51*, no. 1
(Spring 1986). See also *L'Aventure de la
bombe: de Gaulle et la dissuasion
nucléaire* (Colloque de l'Institut
Charles-de-Gaulle, Paris, 1985).
6 R. Aron, 'Le grand dessein du
général', *Mémoires* (Paris, 1983); D. N.
Schwartz, *NATO's Nuclear Dilemmas*
(Washington, 1983); L. Ruehl, *La
Politique militaire de la Vᵉ République*
(Paris, Fondation Nationale des
Sciences Politiques, 1976); W. Kohl,
French Nuclear Diplomacy (Princeton,
1971); W. Mendl, *Deterrence and
Persuasion* (1970).
7 Hassner, 'France, deterrence and
Europe'.
8 L. Freedman, 'Flexible response and
the concept of escalation', *RUSI and
Brassey's Defence Yearbook 1986*
(1986).

9 Information of a general nature on this
subject can be found in H. Haenel, *La
Défense nationale* (Que Sais-Je, no.
2028, Paris, 1982); and in the official
brochure, *L'Organisation de la défense
de la France* (Dossier d'information no.
81, March 1986, Ministère de la
Défense, Service d'information et de
relations publiques des Armées).
10 One of few books on foreign policy
decision making in France is S. Cohen,
La Monarchie nucléaire (Paris, 1986).
For information on style and principles
of the French bureaucracy in general,
consult E. N. Suleiman, *Politics,
Power, and Bureaucracy in France: the
Administrative Elite* (Princeton, 1974);
and S. Mazey, 'Public policy-making
in France: The art of the possible',
West European Politics, 9, no. 3 (July
1986).
11 A *loi de programme* (as in 1986)
concerns only equipment, whereas a *loi
de programmation* (as in 1983) covers
both equipment and operations.
12 M. Jeannin, 'La planification militaire
en France', *Regards sur l'actualité*, no.
104 (Sept.–Oct. 1984), as well as his
doctoral thesis, 'La Planification
militaire (thèse, Doctorat d'Etat en
Droit, Université de Paris–II, 1983);
D. S. Yost, 'French defense
budgeting: executive dominance and
resource constraints', *Orbis*, 23, no. 3
(Fall 1979).
13 There have been some illuminating
quarrels over defence policy between
President and Prime Minister under
'cohabitation'. See, for example, J.
Isnard, 'Le stratège et l'ordonnateur',
Le Monde, 7 Nov. 1986; and D. de
Montvalon, 'Dissuasion: le choix des
armes', *L'Express*, 31 Oct. 1986.
14 *Comité Interministèriel de
Renseignement*, which coordinates
efforts of the *Direction de la Surveillance
du Territoire* (DST, similar to the
American FBI's counter-espionage
division), the *Direction Générale de la
Sécurité Extérieure* (DGSE, similar to
American CIA and military
intelligence), and smaller intelligence
bodies.
15 The three service chiefs are: *Chef
d'Etat-Major de l'Armée de Terre*

(CEMAT, land army), *Chef d'Etat-Major de l'Armée de l'Air* (CEMAA, air force) and *Chef d'Etat-Major de la Marine* (CEMM, navy).

16 P. Dussauge, *L'Industrie française de l'armement* (Paris, 1985); J.-C. Victor (ed.), 'Armes', *Autrement*, no. 73 (Oct. 1985); D. Greenwood, *The Organisation of Defence Procurement and Production in France* (Aberdeen Centre for Defence Studies, Aberdeen Studies in Defence Economics, no. 14, Feb. 1980); *Délégation Générale pour l'Armement* (May 1985, Ministère de la Defense, Service d'information et de relations publiques des Armées); E. A. Kolodziej, *Making and Marketing Arms: The French Experience and Its Implications for the International System* (Princeton, 1987).

17 Cohen, *La Monarchie nucléaire*. From May 1981 to March 1986, the Foreign Affairs Ministry (*Ministère des Affaires Etrangères*) was called the External Relations Ministry (*Ministère des Relations Extérieures*).

18 P.-M. de la Gorce, 'Dissuasion française et défense européenne', *Le Monde Diplomatique*, Sept. 1985; J. Klein, 'Le débat sur la défense en France', *Stratégique*, no. 24, IV (1984); J. Howorth and P. Chilton (eds), *Defense and Dissent in Contemporary France* (London and New York, 1984). See also *Le Monde*, 28 June 1985, 1–2.

19 FEDN publishes a quarterly journal, *Stratégique*, as well as a series of publications by independent authors (the *Cahiers*).

20 IFRI, formed in 1979, is the French counterpart of the Council on Foreign Relations (USA), the Royal Institute of International Affairs (UK), and similar organizations in Italy and the Federal Republic of Germany.

21 One of the best examples of sustained academic effort is the yearbook *Arès – Défense et Sécurité*, published by the University of Grenoble.

22 Detailed information about nearly all aspects of defence in France, including the budget, can be found in the 'Chroniques' section of the monthly *Défense Nationale*. See also J. Howorth, 'Resources and strategic choices; French defence policy at the crossroads', *The World Today*, 42, no. 5 (May 1986).

23 F. Heisbourg, 'Défense et sécurité extérieure', *Politique Etrangère*, 50, no. 2 (Summer 1985).

24 There has been some confusion whether the M-4 has merely MRV (multiple re-entry vehicle) instead of MIRV (multiple independently targetable re-entry vehicle) technology, but the best evidence in the public domain suggests MIRV. See the discussion in D. S. Yost, 'French nuclear targeting', in D. Ball and J. Richelson (eds), *Strategic Nuclear Targeting* (Ithaca, NY, 1986), 138–9. See also *Le Monde*, 22 May 1985, 8.

25 D. S. Yost, *France and Conventional Defense in Central Europe* (Boulder, CO, 1985); L. Poirier, 'La Greffe', *Défense Nationale*, 39 (April 1983).

26 'NATO's Central Front', *Economist*, 30 Aug. 1986; General B. Rogers, 'Renforcement de l'OTAN: le rôle de l'Europe', *Politique Etrangère*, 51, no. 2 (Summer 1986).

27 P. M. Gallois, *Stratégie de l'âge nucléaire* (Paris, 1960), published in English as *The Balance of Terror* (Boston, 1961). A. Beaufre, *Introduction à la stratégie* (Paris, 1963) and *Dissuasion et stratégie* (Paris, 1964). L. Poirier, *Des Stratégies nucléaires* (Paris, 1977) and 'Le deuxième cercle', *Le Monde Diplomatique*, July 1976, repr. in *Essais de stratégie théorique* (Cahier No. 22, Paris: Fondation pour les Etudes de Défense Nationale, 1982).

28 Most key speeches can be found in *Défense Nationale*, with commentary in the national press such as the daily *Le Monde* and the weekly *L'Express*. The White Paper is titled *Livre Blanc sur la Défense Nationale* (2 vols, Paris: Ministère de la Défense Nationale, 1972–3).

29 It should be noted that Gallois gave a faithful exegesis of official policy only in the early 1960s. He believes there are but two circles, France and everywhere else, which is his way of saying that there can be no alliances in the nuclear age. See his books *L'Adieu*

aux armées (Paris, 1976) and *Le Renoncement* (Paris, 1977).

30 For a complete discussion, see Yost, 'French nuclear targeting'.

31 Poirier, 'Le Deuxième cercle'.

32 For more detail on the France–NATO relationship, see Yost, *France and Conventional Defense*, 13–14 and *passim*.

33 J. Chipman, 'French military policy and African security', *Adelphi Paper*, no. 201 (Summer 1985); D. S. Yost, 'French policy in Chad and the Libyan challenge', *Orbis*, 26, no. 4 (Winter 1983); P. Lellouche and D. Moïsi, 'French policy in Africa', *International Security*, 3, no. 4 (Spring 1979).

34 E. A. Kolodziej, 'French arms trade: the economic determinants', *SIPRI Yearbook 1983*; Victor (ed.), 'Armes'.

35 R. Fritsch-Bournazel, 'France: attachment to a non-binding relationship', in G. Flynn and H. Rattinger (eds), *The Public and Atlantic Defense* (Totowa, NJ, 1985).

36 P. Lellouche (ed.), *Pacifisme et dissuasion* (Paris, 1983); J. Howorth, *France: the Politics of Peace* (1984); D. Colard, 'Le Pacifisme à la française', *Arès – Défense et Sécurité*, 7 (1984–5).

37 'The French are ready to cross the Rhine', *Economist*, 13 July 1985, and 'Spécial défense: la France s'essoufle', *L'Express*, 30 May 1986.

38 Freedman, 'Flexible Response'.

39 Hassner, 'France, deterrence and Europe'.

40 For examples of reactions among French elites, see J. Fourré *et al.*, *La France face aux dangers de guerre* (Paris, 1981); and R. Aron, *Les Dernières années du siècle* (Paris, 1984).

41 P. Boniface and F. Heisbourg, *La Puce, les hommes et la bombe* (Paris, 1986); J. Fenske, 'France and the Strategic Defence Initiative', *International Affairs*, 62, no. 2 (Spring 1986).

42 L. Benecke *et al.*, 'Franco–West German technological co-operation', *Survival*, 28, no. 3 (May/June 1986), 234–44; K. Kaiser and P. Lellouche (eds), *Le couple franco-allemand et la*

défense de l'Europe (Paris, 1986); F. Gorand, 'La politique de sécurité européenne de la France de 1981 à 1985 et après', *Commentaire*, 9, no. 33 (Spring 1986).

43 See the discussion of the *oeuvres vives* ('vital works') modifications to French targeting in Yost, 'French nuclear targeting'.

44 Interview with Defence Minister André Giraud in *L'Express* (see n. 37 above). For more on the question of French tactical nuclear or 'pre-strategic' weapons, see A. Adrets, 'Les relations franco-allemandes et le fait nucléaire dans une Europe divisée', *Politique Etrangère*, 49, no. 3 (Autumn 1984); and discussion of Adrets' article in the two issues following.

45 For example: E. Copel, *La Puissance de la liberté* (Paris, 1986); P. Lellouche, *L'Avenir de la guerre* (Paris, 1985); F. de Rose, *Contre la stratégie des Curiaces* (Paris, 1983). See also the review of Lellouche's book by D. S. Yost, 'Radical change in French defence policy?', *Survival*, 28, no. 1 (Jan./Feb. 1986); and the review of de Rose's book by a West German Defence Ministry official, Lothar Ruehl: 'NATO's French Connection', *Strategic Review*, Summer 1985.

46 In addition to the references in n. 2, the following recent titles also cover French defence policy and defence decision making: A. N. Sabrosky, 'The defense policy of France', in D. J. Murray and P. R. Viotti (eds), *The Defense Policies of Nations* (Baltimore and London, 1982); J. P. Marichy, 'The central organization of defense in France', in M. Edwards (ed.), *Central Organizations of Defense* (Boulder, CO, 1985); 'France', in S. McLean (ed.), *How Nuclear Weapons Decisions are Made* (1985); L. Hamon, 'Politique française de défense: données et tendances', in P. Boniface (ed.), *L'Année stratégique* (Paris, 1985); R. F. Laird, *France, the Soviet Union, and the Nuclear Weapons Issue* (Boulder, CO, 1985); *idem* (ed.), *French Security Policy: From Independence to Interdependence* (Boulder, CO, 1986).

Index

Adenauer, Konrad, *see* Federal
   Chancellors
Africa, 20, 148–9, 163–4, 165
African affairs secretariat (France),
   155
Afghanistan, 84, 105, 112
Algerian War, 148–9
Andropov, Yuri, 90, 94, 96, 97, 98,
   114
ANT, tactical nuclear weapons, 162
Argentina, 30–5
Armed Forces (France)
   Armaments Delegate General
      (DGA) 155–6, 157–8
   Armed Forces Chief of Staff
      (CEMA) 155, 157, 160, 161
   Chief of Staff of the Armies
      (CEMA), 157
   Chief of the General Staff of the
      Armies (CEMA), 157
   French First Army, 160, 161
   Presidential Military Staff, 154;
   Chief of (CEMP), 154–5
   Rapid Action Force (FAR),
      160, 164, 166
   Service Chiefs, 155
   Secretariat General for
      Administration, 157
Armed Forces (UK)
   Army, 16, 24
   Royal Navy, 16, 17, 29, 31, 35
   Royal Air Force, 16, 17, 25, 29

Armed Forces (USA), 62–9
   Army, 58–9, 64–6, 68
   Navy, 58–9, 64–5, 66–8
   Air Force, 58–9, 62, 64, 65–7
   Joint Chiefs of Staff (JCS) 58–
      61, 78, 80
Armed Forces (USSR)
   Chief of Staff of the Armed
      Services, 91, 98
   Main Political Administration,
      93, 103 (of the Soviet Army
      and Navy)
Armed Forces, Western Germany
   Bundeswehr (Federal Armed
      Forces), 122, 133, 134, 136,
      138–9
   Inspector General, 134–138
Asia, 20, 21, 84–5, 115–16, 148; *see
   also* China, Japan
ASMP, 160–167
Atlantic Alliance, *see* NATO
Atomic Energy Commissariat (CEA)
   (France), 156, 157, 158, 167

Ball, George, 76
Belize, 21
Brezhnev, L.I., 90, 95, 97, 98, 108,
   114
Britain, 3, 5, 6, 7, 49–51, 86, 120,
   139, 149, 150, 159
Brittan, Leon, 47
Brussels, *see* NATO

171

Brzezinski, Zbigniew, 58

Cabinet (UK), 16, 29, 46, 47
   Cabinet Committee, 29
   Cabinet Office, 17, 47
   Defence and Overseas Policy
     Committee, 16, 33, 47
   War Cabinet, 31, 34
Campaign for Nuclear Disarmament
   (CND), 12
Carrington, Lord, 33
Carter, Jimmy, 29, 58, 62, 67, 68,
   70, 75, 77
Chernenko, 90, 97, 98, 114
Chernobyl, 95, 127
Chevaline, 25, 28, 30
China, 84, 85, 113, 115
Christian Democrats (CDU) (West
   Germany), 126, 127, 128, 130,
   131
Christian Social Union (CSU), 130
Civil War (Russian), 86, 87, 93
Cold War, 54, 78, 88
Committee for State Security
   (KGB), 90, 96, 98, 100, 101–2,
   111
Commonwealth of Nations, 21, 37
Communist Party (France), 164
Communist Party of the Soviet
   Union (CPSU), 88, 89–90, 97,
   111, 112, 113, 114–15
   Central Committee, 89, 91–
     2, 93, 97, 109, 110
   Congress, 89, 90–1, 94, 101,
     110, 111, 113
   General Secretary, 90, 92, 94,
     95, 97, 98; *see also* Andropov,
     Brezhnev, Chernenko,
     Gorbachev, Kruschev,
     Malenkov, Stalin
   Politburo, 89, 90, 91, 92, 93,
     94–6, 99, 100, 103, 105, 107,
     108, 109, 115
   Secretariat, 89, 91, 92–4
Communist Party (West Germany),
   127

Council of Ministers (USSR), 90,
   92, 98, 99–101, 103; Minister, 90
Congress (USA), 61, 66, 68, 69,
   71–4, 77
Cuba, 76, 78, 149
Czechoslovakia, 104

Defence (France)
   Council of Ministers, 154–6
   Defence Council, 155–6, 157
   Defence Minister, 155, 167;
     Michel Debré, 161
   Defence Ministry, 156–8, 159
   ET (Emerging Technologies),
     166
   Foundation for the Study of
     National Defence (FEDN), 159
   Institute for Higher Studies in
     National Defence (IHEDN),
     159
   Secretariat General for National
     Defence (SADN), 155, 156,
     158
   Strategic Planning and Studies
     Group (GROUP.ES) 157,
     161; Armaments Engineer, 157
Defence (UK)
   Chief of Defence Staff
     (CDS), 37, 38–9, 40–1
   Defence Council, 38–9, 40–1
   Defence White Paper, 14–16,
     17–18, 21, 24, 27, 29, 42
   First Chief of Defence Staff,
     Lord Louis Mountbatten, 36
   Ministry of Defence, 14, 15,
     16–18, 33, 35–40, 41–7, 48
   Office of Management &
     Budget (OMB), 38–9, 41–42,
     70
   Procurement Executive, 38–9,
     43–5
   Secretary of State for Defence,
     (UK), 15, 16, 36, 38–9, 41,
     46, 47; Heseltine, Michael,
     36, 41, 47; Nott, John, 30, 31;
     Pym, Francis, 28, 30

Defence (USA)
  Defense Intelligence Agency
    (DIA), 61
  Department of Defense
    (DOD), (USA), 54, 59–60;
    Under-Secretary of Defense
    for Acquisition, 79;
    Goldwater-Nichols DOD
    Reorganization Act, 79–80
  Secretary of Defense (USA),
    56, 58, 73, 77; Forrestal,
    James, 59–60, 64;
    Weinberger, Caspar, 70–1,
    77–8
Defence (USSR)
  Academic Institutions
    (USSR), 101–2
  Central Committee: Secretary
    for the Defence Industries, 96
  Defence Council (USSR), 96,
    98–9, 105
  Department of Administrative
    Organs, 93
  Department of Defence
    Industries, 93, 96, 98, 100
  Department of Machine
    Construction, 93
  Ministry of Defence (USSR),
    93, 96, 103–6; Minister, 90,
    91, 96, 98, 103–4, 107, 109,
    110; *see also* Sokolov
  State Defence Committee,
    (USSR), 88
Defence, (West Germany)
  Ministry of Defence, (West
    Germany), 121, 133, 134–8,
    140; Minister, Strauss, Franz-
    Josef, 139
De Gaulle, General Charles, 147,
  148–9, 150, 151, 155, 157, 161,
  165

East–West relations, 4, 12, 19, 22,
  23, 26, 29, 54–7, 61, 67–8, 76,
  78, 83–4, 87, 105, 112–113, 123,
  126–9, 131–2, 134, 138, 141–2,

149–51, 162, 163, 165–6
European Defence Community
  (EDC), 149
Economy and Finances Minister
  (France), 155
Falin, Valentin, 94, 96, 99
Falkland Islands Conflict, 9, 18,
  30, 31–5
Federal Chancellors (West
  Germany), 133, 138
  Adenauer, Konrad, 124,
    125, 139
  Kohl, Helmut, 128, 131
  Schmidt, Helmut, 29, 130
  Chancellor's Office, 134–5
Fifth Republic (France), 147, 151,
  152, 154, 167
Finland, 87, 108, 142
Flexible Response Strategy, 21,
  25–6, 56, 131, 150, 166, 167
FOFA (Follow-On Forces Attack),
  166; *see also* NATO
Foreign Affairs Minister (France),
  155, 158
Foreign and Commonwealth Office
  (FCO) (UK), 17, 33, 34, 46
Foreign Affairs Minister (USSR),
  90, 96, 98
Foreign Office (West Germany),
  121, 133–4, 138, 140–1
Foreign Secretary (UK), 33, 47
Forrestal, James, *see* Defense
  Secretary (USA)
Fourth Republic, (France), 148–9,
  151
France, 3, 5, 6, 7, 35, 48, 86, 120,
  139, 147–167
French Institute for International
  Relations (IFRI), 159

German reunification, 119, 123,
  127, 151
Germany (pre–1945), 19, 87, 122,
  148
Giscard d'Estaing, President Valéry,
  152–4

Gorbachev, Mikhail, 83, 90–1, 92, 95, 96, 97, 98, 102, 103, 108, 109–10, 111, 113, 114–15
Great Patriotic War, *see* Second World War
Green Party (West Germany), 127, 128, 129–30
Grenada, 68, 77, 79
Gromyko, Andrei, 96, 97

Hadès, 160, 167
Healey, Denis, 27
Heseltine, Michael, Defence (UK), Secretary of State
House of Commons, 15, 30, 32
    Defence Committee, 15, 16, 45
    Expenditure Committee, 29
    Public Accounts Committee, 45
House of Lords, 16

Intercontinental Ballistic Missiles
    USA, 65–6, 70
    USSR, 107
Interior Minister (France) 155
Intermediate Range Ballistic Missiles, 66
Intermediate Nuclear Force (INF) 115, 126, 129, 133
Iran, 68, 77

Japan, 19, 35, 86, 87, 88, 115
Joint Intelligence Committee (JIC), 33

KGB, *see* Committee for State Security
Kissinger, Henry, 76
Kohl, Chancellor, Helmut, *see* Federal Chancellors
Korean War, 57, 65, 75, 77
Kruschev, Nikita, 76, 90, 92, 96, 106, 108, 110

Lebanon, 76, 77, 79
Lenin, V.I., 86, 92, 94

McFarlane, Bud, *see* National Security Advisers
McNamara, Robert, 6, 56, 61, 66, 69, 150
M-4, 60
Malenkov, G.M., 90
Medium Range Ballistic Missiles (MRBMS) (USSR), 107
MIRV technology, 160, 167
Multilateral (Nuclear) Force (MLF), 148

National Assembly (France) 152
    National Defence Commission, 152
    Finance Commission, 152
    see also Parliament (France)
National Audit Office (UK), 45
National Institute for Public Policy, (USA), 62
National Security Advisers (USA) 58, 76, 78
National Security Council, 58, 80
NATO, 2, 6, 17, 21, 23, 24, 25, 26, 42, 44–5, 46, 47–50, 57, 83, 113, 119, 120–6, 127, 129–30, 132, 134, 139–8, 141–2, 149–51, 157, 158, 160, 161, 162–4
    Commander-in-Chief Channel (CINCHAN), 48
    Headquarters (Brussels), 6, 20, 22, 48
    Northern Army Group (NORTHAG), 25
    Supreme Allied Command Atlantic (SACLANT), 24, 48
    Supreme Allied Command Europe (SACEUR), 24, 48, 122
Nitze, Paul, 56–7
Northhag, *see* NATO
Northern Ireland, 12
Nott, John, *see* Defence (UK), Secretary of State for
NSC-68, 56–7
Nuclear Strategy, 48, 66–7, 70–2,

112–13, 115, 125, 128–9, 131–2, 159, 166–7

Nuclear Weapons, 28–31, 56, 65–6, 67, 73, 88–9, 100, 112–13, 115, 123, 125–6, 128, 129, 140, 148–51, 152, 159–60, 161–3, 166–7; *see also* under individual names

Ogarkov, Marshal, N.V., 106, 109, 111, 114

Ostpolitik, 123, 127, 129, 132

Pacific, 84, 115–16, 163–4, 165

Packard Commission, 79–80

Parliament (France) 152–3
    Parliamentary Commissions, 154, 158
    Programming law, 152–4, 160

Parliament (UK), 15, 17, 29, 45, 46

Pentagon, 4, 29, 61, 71, 79–80

perestroika (restructuring), 91

Poindexter, Admiral, 78

Polaris, 25, 28, 29, 30

Political parties, (France), 157

Presidents (France) 153–5, 160, 161; *see also* de Gaulle, Charles

Presidents (USA)
    Eisenhower, Dwight D., 58, 75, 76
    Johnson, Lyndon, 76, 77
    Kennedy, John F., 75, 76
    Nixon, Richard, 76, 77
    Truman, Harry S., 56–7, 75
    see also Carter, Jimmy, and Reagan, Ronald

Prime Minister (France), 155, 156, 166

Prime Ministers (UK)
    Callaghan, James, 30, 34
    Heath, Edward, 29
    Wilson, Harold, 30
    see also Thatcher, Margaret

Pym, Francis, *see* Defence (UK), Secretary of State

RAND Corporation, 62

Reagan Administration, 62, 72, 73

Reagan, Ronald, 30, 70–1, 75, 77, 79, 128, 141

Red Square incident, 104, 107, 110

Russian Revolution, (1917), 84, 86, 112

Rust, Mathias, *see* Red Square incident

Ryzhkov, Nikolai, 95

SACEUR *see* NATO

SACLANT *see* NATO

SALT (Strategic Arms Limitation Talks) 115, 133

Sandys, Duncan, 27

Second World War, 19, 78, 83, 86, 88, 112, 114, 139, 148, 151

Secretary General of the Presidency (France) 155

Senate (France) 152
    Foreign Affairs and Defence Commission, 152
    Finance Commission, 152
    see also Parliament (France)

Shevardnadze, Eduard, 95, 96

Social Democrats (SPD) (West Germany), 126, 127–8, 129–30

Sokolov, S. L., 91, 96, 104, 107, 109, 110

South Atlantic, 20, 21, 33; *see also* Falkland Islands conflict

Soviet Union, 3, 5, 6, 7, 19, 20, 26, 83–117, 119, 123, 124, 126, 127, 128, 129, 130, 131, 132, 150, 151, 162, 166

Sputnik, 149

Stalin, Joseph, 86–7, 88, 90, 92, 94, 110

Starfighter aircraft, 139–40

START (Strategic Arms Reduction Talks), 133

State Department (USA), 56
    Policy Planning Staff, 56
    Secretary of State, 58; Dulles, John Foster, 76; Marshall, George, 64; Shultz, George,

77; Vance, Cyrus, 58

Strategic Defense Initiative, (SDI) 55, 70–2, 125, 128–9, 131–2, 141, 157, 166

Suez crisis, 21, 149

Supreme Soviet, 91, 92, 96, 97–8, 99, 103, 110

Thatcher, Margaret, 30, 31, 32, 33, 34, 95

Thorneycroft proposals, 36

Tornado, 17, 23, 140

Trade and Industry Department (UK) 17, 46, 47

Treasury (UK), 17, 42, 46

Trident, 25, 29, 30–1

United Nations, 21, 133

United States, 3, 5, 6, 7, 9, 17, 19, 20, 22, 29, 30, 31, 35, 44, 46, 50, 53–82, 86, 88, 111, 113, 120, 121, 122, 123, 124, 125, 126, 127, 128, 130–1, 137, 138, 140, 151, 166

Ustinov, Marshal D.F., 103–4, 108, 109

Vance, Cyrus, 58

Vietnam, 76–7, 78

Warsaw Pact, 23, 26, 91, 95, 104–5, 124, 126, 129, 131, 163

Weinberger, Caspar, *see* Defense Secretary (USA)

West Germany, 3, 5, 6, 7, 20, 24, 25, 35, 119–46, 149, 151, 156, 157, 160, 161, 163, 164, 165–6

Westpolitik, 125, 129, 140

Western Europe, 6, 20, 21, 22, 55, 56–7, 86, 120, 121, 128, 132, 135, 141, 142, 164, 165

Western European Union, 157, 166

Yazov, D. T., Army General, 96, 104, 109

DIL

Defence policy meter